Innovative Teaching and Learning in Primary Schools

SAGE was founded in 1965 by Sara Miller McCune to support the dissemination of usable knowledge by publishing innovative and high-quality research and teaching content. Today, we publish more than 750 journals, including those of more than 300 learned societies, more than 800 new books per year, and a growing range of library products including archives, data, case studies, reports, conference highlights, and video. SAGE remains majority-owned by our founder, and after Sara's lifetime will become owned by a charitable trust that secures our continued independence.

Los Angeles | London | Washington DC | New Delhi | Singapore

Innovative
Teaching and Learning
in Primary Schools

Des Hewitt and Susan Tarrant

Los Angeles | London | New Delhi
Singapore | Washington DC

Los Angeles | London | New Delhi
Singapore | Washington DC

SAGE Publications Ltd
1 Oliver's Yard
55 City Road
London EC1Y 1SP

SAGE Publications Inc.
2455 Teller Road
Thousand Oaks, California 91320

SAGE Publications India Pvt Ltd
B 1/I 1 Mohan Cooperative Industrial Area
Mathura Road
New Delhi 110 044

SAGE Publications Asia-Pacific Pte Ltd
3 Church Street
#10-04 Samsung Hub
Singapore 049483

Editor: James Clark
Assistant editor: Rachael Plant
Production editor: Nicola Marshall
Copyeditor: Rose James
Proofreader: Jill Birch
Indexer: Martin Hargreaves
Marketing executive: Dilhara Attygalle
Cover design: Naomi Robinson
Typeset by: C&M Digitals (P) Ltd, Chennai, India
Printed and bound by CPI Group (UK) Ltd,
Croydon, CR0 4YY

Library of Congress Control Number: 2014942332

British Library Cataloguing in Publication data

A catalogue record for this book is available from
the British Library

MIX
Paper from
responsible sources
FSC
www.fsc.org   FSC® C013604

ISBN 978-1-4462-6668-7
ISBN 978-1-4462-6669-4 (pbk)

TABLE OF CONTENTS

ABOUT THE AUTHORS

Des Hewitt

Professor Des Hewitt is Head of Primary Teacher Education at the University of Warwick. He works extensively in teacher education at a national and international level, developing novel ways to train the next generation of teachers, while always working for the good of children in school. He has a particular interest in the development of language and learning in the primary years. Having worked in education for the last 25 years he has taught from 5-year-olds to 50-year-olds, from early years to Ph.D. Universities in Finland, Hungary and Germany have been working with him on a range of research projects: teacher memories, learning spaces, and working with football community sports coaches in schools to name a few. More recently, he has been involved in an international project on 'Academic Integrity', focusing on the moral aims of education. Des started his working life in commerce. The spirit of academic enterprise still pervades his work.

Susan Tarrant

Susan Tarrant has worked for several years as a primary teacher during which time she was able to develop her passion for the effective use of ICT in learning and teaching in schools. While mentoring student teachers from the University of Derby, Susan worked on projects using innovative ways of ICT to support learning. Now, as a university teacher in primary education, she leads ICT (now computing) across the B.Ed. and PGCE programmes at the University of Derby.

ACKNOWLEDGEMENTS

We would like to thank our families for their patient support, during the writing of this book. Thank you especially also to our editorial team of James Clark and Rachael Plant who have helped us complete our writing.

SAGE would like to thank the following reviewers whose comments on the initial proposal helped to shape this book:

Rita Headington, University of Greenwich

Gianna Knowles, London South Bank University

Fiona Patrick, University of Glasgow

Anne Robertson, Institute of Education, University of London

Sarah Trussler, Leeds Trinity University

Chris Wilkins, University of Leicester

CHAPTER 1

WHAT IS EDUCATION FOR?

Chapter guide

In this chapter you will learn about:

- Aims of education
- Historical and contemporary views of education
- Innovation in education
- Creativity in education
- Education for the twenty-first century

'What is education for?' You may feel that this question is irrelevant to you as a teacher. Aren't teachers told what to do? Do teachers really have a choice as to what they teach and why? There are probably many teachers who feel like this. But think carefully about why you wanted to become a teacher. Do you see yourself as blindly following the orders of educational technocrats? Are schools merely factories for learning, following a teaching manual established by people in government?

Reflection point

Remember when you qualified as a teacher.

- Why did you want to become a teacher?
- What do you think education is for?
- Have your views changed?

As Alexander (2010) suggests, there are no simple answers. It may be that different teachers have different views in the same school. Different schools probably have different views; this distinguishes one school from another. Different types of schools and schools for different ages of learners certainly aim at different outcomes and ways of working with children: compare early years' education (3–5 years) with secondary education (11–18 years). In one educational setting, socialisation and the development of cognitive, social and emotional skills through child-led play (Edwards and Mercer 1987), predominates. In another school, preparation for the world of work and further study through work experience and preparation for public examinations is more important. What differs in this example is the age of the learner and the particular purpose attributed to learning.

We might agree therefore, that education is for different purposes according to the age of the child. At an earlier stage, there is a focus on the intrinsic value and the developmental purposes of education. Education is important in itself, because it helps children to develop as individuals. Whereas in secondary schools, the extrinsic purpose is also important. Education enables young people to be prepared for adult life. Should education be to empower our children with the skills that allow them to develop their imaginations and creativity, to be critical thinkers? Or is education to equip them with the skills that will enable them to get a job? If education is about helping people to live happy, successful lives then schooling needs to also be about future job skills as well as their emotional future.

Of course, even this view can be queried. Reading and writing in an early years' setting, enables children to enter a wider world of imagination and provide a means for self-expression. Reading and writing, along with many other skills, are also important in the world of work. So the early focus on literacy skills fulfils a dual purpose: supporting individual development and personal growth; as well as a longer-term preparation for the future. This is a long-standing, but not mutually exclusive, dichotomy. Education is for the development of the individual learner as well as preparation of the individual for living in the wider society as a child and later as an adult. Bruner (1972) placed this into a theoretical framework in his paper on 'immaturity'. While development has a physical genetic aspect, in a complex and rapidly changing society, socialisation of the individual into the means of living, thinking and acting in and through culture, provides a flexible way to adapt to life as it is and as it will become. Bruner calls these 'tools' for learning and thinking in the 'cultural pool'. He sees education as a way for children to learn, acquire and develop the use of 'cultural tools'. 'Cultural tools' are, for example, ways of thinking, communicating and responding to the world – learning how to hold conversations in both formal and informal situations to get things done or learning how to use new technologies. Anyone who was born before 1990 will recognise the impact of different ways of communicating through technology: for example, texting and social networking through mobile technology has completely changed how adults and many children interact on a day-to-day basis.

 ## Classroom case study

Using a classroom visualiser

Objective: to learn about the life cycle of a frog and collect evidence by making observations. To record the progress and create a mini film with text and music.

A classroom visualiser offers many opportunities for creative learning and teaching. Evidence in the classroom has shown that it can have a positive effect on the children where many want their work to be displayed and discussed on the visualiser. Children can take control of their own learning by using it to problem-solve, peer-assess, share findings in science which in turn promotes language development as children begin to explain what they see.

In this example, the visualiser was used to support learning in science where the children had to investigate, watch and record the changes made from frogspawn to tadpole. The frogspawn was kept in a tank with a transparent bottom and no lid. It was placed directly onto the visualiser and lit either from the top down or from the bottom upwards. Using the digital zoom facility the children were able to magnify the frogspawn and project it onto the interactive whiteboard. It provided an excellent visual focus for the learners and opportunities for whole class discussion. Using the video facility, the children were able to capture high-quality video clips of each stage of development. Over the next few weeks the children watched the frogspawn hatch into tadpoles and were able to capture every part of the life cycle in detail. Being able to project the live images of the tadpoles onto such a large screen was a very exciting experience for the children and

(Continued)

(Continued)

provided a good stimulus for talk for writing. The children worked together in small groups to share what they had seen and produced a much higher quality of writing with accurate diagrams. To challenge the more technologically able learners, some children were able to import the video clips into Windows Moviemaker Live and create a short film where they added text and music, appropriate to the genre of film.

In his analysis of the aims of primary education, Alexander (2010) plots the influence of pervasive views on the aims of education. One of those is about the importance of the 'basics' as a preparation for adult life. The Newcastle report of 1861 stated: 'The duty of state in public education ... is to obtain the greatest possible quantity of reading, writing and arithmetic for the greatest number' (Alexander 2010: 175).

While this view of education is often considered to be a view of the English establishment, it is pervasive. On the other hand, there is evidence of a parallel view of education for a broader experience of the world: for instance, including an appreciation of the liberal arts and the broader curriculum. This is indicated in the Haddow report of 1931 and the Plowden report of 1967 (Alexander 2010), where education for the development of self and wider experiences was seen as important. We believe that these two views of education are entirely compatible. In fact the teaching of basic skills in both literacy and numeracy is futile if it remains decontextualised from the wider curriculum. The wider curriculum remains a foreign land where the skills are too weak to access and understand the language of this new world of learning.

The world of psychology has certainly influenced our views of what is important in education: Haddow (1931) was influenced by John Dewey (the American psychologist famous for his views on reflection) in the emphasis on engaging with 'general culture', Plowden (1967) was heavily influenced by the constructivist theories of Jean Piaget in his depiction of the importance of an education for childhood in itself. From the 1970s political and economic factors became even more important. Likewise many countries have been in the grip of an economic crisis in the early part of the twenty-first century. At these times, the role of schools and education come into question. What is education for and what contribution do schools make to society? What skills do young people need when they leave school in order to find a job? The question increasingly being asked is 'what skills do young people need for the jobs which don't yet exist?'

Difficulties in the first part of the twenty-first century are not the first economic crisis of the last fifty years. For instance, in the 1970s there was an oil crisis associated with the supply of oil from the Middle East. When there are many problems in society, it is not surprising that governments look to education for solutions, but also in some cases that schools become scapegoats for society's ills. In the 1970s, governments began to question the role of education and schools. In England, Prime Minister James Callaghan made a speech at Ruskin College, Oxford, entering the debate about the purpose of education: 'The goals of our education, from nursery school through to adult education, are clear enough. They are to equip children to the best of their ability for a lively, constructive, place in society, and also to fit them to do a job of work' Callaghan (1976).

In the nineteenth century, the view of education was somewhat different. Dickens' novel *Hard Times* was a reflection of the values in educational institutions at that time. One of the central characters, Mr Gradgrind, the notorious headteacher, who forbade the use of imagination, play, creativity, even thinking, was only concerned with cold facts and numbers:

> Now what I want is Facts. Teach these boys and girls nothing but Facts. Facts alone are wanted in life. Plant nothing else, and root out everything else. You can only form the minds of reasoning animals upon Facts. Nothing else will ever be of service to them. (Dickens 2003: ch 1)

More recently, the influence of approaches to education in the United States can be seen to have influenced those in Europe. For instance Hirsch's theories of 'cultural literacy' are referred to directly by Gove (2011) who in a recent official statement on the aims of education in England explained his view that education is a good in itself. By instilling in children important knowledge, this will bind society together. He says therefore, that education and society are inextricably linked. In his view democracy is stronger when individual citizens have a stock of knowledge on which to draw which allows them to stand out against tides of opinion which are driven by passing fashions and populist rages.

 Reflection point

Try to summarise your view of the many influences on the aims of education: for instance

- Your understanding of how children learn.
- Your view of the place of education in the economy and government.
- Your school's stated and unstated view of education.
- Your own personal experiences of education.

One conclusion that you might come to is that education is indeed important for children, but trying to come to an overarching idea as to the aims of education is virtually impossible. Official curricula of the last fifty years provide some evidence of overlap. While the balance may be different we have educational aims centred around:

- Development of language, literacy and mathematical skills;
- Acquisition of knowledge, though the focus is very much contested;
- Religious and moral development;
- Preparation for adult life and the wider world.

Robin Alexander (2010) reported on the widest review of primary education in England since the Plowden report (1967). The 'Primary review' took 'soundings' from a range of stakeholders (children, teachers, parents and academics) to identify a curriculum and an approach to primary education fit for the twenty-first century. The 'Primary review' reminds us of some of these enduring aims of education, but there are others:

The three R's (reading, writing and arithmetic) and beyond;

The whole child;

Faith and spirituality;

Balancing individual and societal needs;

Community and citizenship;

Addressing disadvantage;

Global awareness and concern about the future.

Alexander (2010: 184)

We highlight some aims of education which demonstrate a political and economic sensitivity. For instance, the need to balance individual and societal needs seems to recognise the tension between the child's needs and that which is important for the society. This seems counter to the more child-centred approach of Plowden. Critically, we can see the influence of economic reality in the focus on 'global awareness'. Surely, no one can doubt the importance of global awareness given the economic crisis which ensued from the sub-prime loan defaults in the US and the consequent domino effect in the leading world economies. What Alexander points out is that we need an education for the twenty-first century: not one devised and constructed in the image of the nineteenth century. Edwards and Mercer (1987) contrast a factory model of education with a model based on the family. Society has changed: the old industrial models will not suffice. Hargreaves (2003) explains the new challenges for education today: 'We live in a knowledge economy, a knowledge society. Knowledge economies are stimulated and driven by creativity and ingenuity. Knowledge-society schools have to create these qualities; otherwise their people and their nations will be left behind' (Hargreaves 2003: 1).

The important point here is that to be a successful economy and a successful society, knowledge and learning are important. Traditional approaches to change in industry, whereby large corporate bodies develop products in a top-down way, have been challenged by a need for entrepreneurs who can design and produce electronic materials from their PC.

Take for instance the market for news, traditionally the province of the newspaper barons, but now open to anyone who has a laptop and an Internet connection. The consumer is as much the producer in some cases: individuals creating a new way of working or a new product out of need (Wright 2012). Set ways of acting, prescribed ways of thinking, and static forms of knowledge will not be good enough! To be adaptable needs flexibility; to be dynamic means to be swift of thinking and responsive; and to cope with uncertainty requires resilience. Overall, a knowledge society must be a learning society. A principal theme of this book is that to be a knowledge society innovation needs must be fostered. Hargreaves (2003) highlights the kind of learning and teaching which a 'knowledge society' needs:

- Deep cognitive learning;
- Learning in ways which teachers were not taught;
- Commitment to professional development;
- Working and learning in collegial teams;
- Treat parents as partners in learning;
- Developing and drawing on collective intelligence;
- Building a capacity for change and risk;
- Fostering trust in processes.

In a report to UNESCO by the International Commission on Education for the Twenty-first Century (Delors 1996), they reflect on the challenges facing education in the future:

> School should impart both the desire for, and pleasure in, learning, the ability to learn how to learn, and intellectual curiosity. One might even imagine a society in which each individual would be in turn both teacher and learner. There is no substitute for the teacher–pupil relationship, which is underpinned by authority and developed through dialogue .... It is the responsibility of the teacher to impart to the pupil the knowledge that humankind has acquired about itself and about nature and everything of importance that it has created and invented. (Delors 1996)

These could be seen as the aims for education and learning in the knowledge society. We have introduced two new concepts here: the knowledge society and 'innovation'.

Innovation

Innovation, like creativity, is a term which means many things to many people. Before we explore some of these meanings in education and the wider community, it is worth returning to the origins of this word. The word innovation derives from the Latin word *innovatus*, which is the noun form of *innovare* 'to renew or change', stemming from *in–* 'into' + *novus–* 'new'. So there is a sense that 'innovation' means doing things differently. This is very relevant to the previous section on the knowledge society. Open up any self-help book on 'innovation' (for example Wright 2012) and you will see quotes and prescriptions for becoming more 'innovative'. These dimensions are summarised below:

Innovation involves invention: this means doing something differently in the classroom. There is the implication of novelty, or new ways of approaches to old problems. However, coming up with something new is worthless if there is not a way to implement the approach.

Innovation often involves incremental change: subtle changes over a longer period of time can produce innovation, sometimes more effectively than waiting for the grand-gesture change.

Innovation should not be confused with the latest trend: more likely to be the latest fashion than a genuinely different way of doing things. Be especially wary in education of so-called innovative forms of teaching, which promise to parachute in and make a difference, with very little effort from the teachers in school.

Innovation can be confused with marketing hype: this can often be a problem in schools where the pressure to make progress in learner outcomes means that schools are constantly bombarded with information about the latest approach to teaching or the latest equipment which will inspire children. Remember these companies make a living from selling things: as a teacher you need to judge for yourself, with the facts and think about how this approach or this resource could be used in your particular school.

Innovation often results from subversion: those in control in an organisation can see change as a threat and therefore respond to new ideas with defensive strategies. Faced with a headteacher in school who says 'In my school you do it this way' may well induce passivity in their staff or a subversive desire to do things 'the right way'.

Innovation is focused on improvement: change for change's sake is pointless. However, the great discussion is around the actual focus for change and importantly how we might measure this. Innovation in education, therefore, implies a change to something (an object, a process or procedure, a person, their role) and some means of recognising that a change has actually taken place.

 Reflection point

Consider your own experience in school. Using the following table of prompts, think about your own understanding of the term 'innovation' in education:

Table 1.1 Reflection on innovation

Reflect on examples of innovation in education	What makes this innovative?
An approach to teaching	
A resource	
Organisation of the school or classroom	

 Classroom case study

One in..., one out..., one inside out

One example of 'innovation' in education comes from a colleague. In considering the children's experience of the curriculum in a primary school, one teacher recognised the importance of a more active form of learning. Inviting a visitor to the classroom, or sometimes taking the children on a walk to visit a place near to the school improved the children's engagement, and their general enjoyment of learning. The teacher and school wanted a way to encourage more teachers in the school to adopt this approach, calculating that this would improve learning and teaching across the whole school. She came up with the following phrase to help her colleagues change their practice. For every longer project or topic, the teachers followed the above phrase:

(Continued)

(Continued)

One in: the topic would involve at least one visitor to the classroom;
One out: the class would go on one visit, near to the school, to reinforce learning in the topic;
One inside out: the teacher would change one learning experience from previously teaching the topic. So an aspect which was previously taught in class, would be taught this time outside the classroom
This approach had the benefit of great simplicity; but it was also improvement and action. Importantly, this approach encouraged individual teachers to make changes without waiting to be told what to do – it encouraged initiative.

We now bring the ideas of innovation and education together to examine why innovation is an important factor in addressing national and international concerns today.

Innovation and education

In the first part of this chapter, we explained how many Western countries have moved from an industrial approach to society and the economy towards a 'knowledge society'. In the 'knowledge society' the distribution of knowledge and information is more important than the production and distribution of things (Drucker 1993). Different educationalists have argued quite entertainingly that school systems are still modelled on an industrial design, in which children are classified by age and treated as one homogeneous group with little consideration of what best suits their learning needs in today's world (Robinson 2010). Others have argued that the knowledge economy needs creativity, innovation and ingenuity. Edwards and Mercer (1987) gave the metaphor of education as a 'family' as an alternative to the industrial model. Istance (2008) argues that survival in the knowledge society requires all the skills of family and community: cooperation, analysis, resilience, enterprise, analysis and innovation.

The Centre for Education Research and Innovation (CERI) is an important meeting place for developments in educational innovation in the Organisation for Economic Cooperation and Development (OECD). David Istance is currently Head of CERI and here we consider the reasons provided by his organisation for the need for innovation in learning, education and schools. Periodically, the OECD publishes the results of a transnational comparison of tests taken by millions of children around the world, which are summarised in the PISA international league tables, which compare the progress made by 15-year-olds around the world in reading, mathematics and scientific literacy. As Istance (2008) explains the PISA tests focus on the ability to process information and solve problems in different areas. In common with the 'knowledge society' PISA tests emphasise skills in real-world practical settings.

Claxton (2007) says 'every time we learn something, we learn something about learning'. Of course, learning from an educational exam that learning is fixed, not negotiated and subject to a high-stakes performance in a stressful experience on one particular occasion, gives a very particular view of learning. We argue that this does not privilege the development of innovation in schools, teachers or individual learners. In the following section, we examine those approaches to learning and teaching which are likely to have most impact on learning; and how this develops our understanding of innovation.

We could argue about the concepts of 'impact' and 'learning'. By impact, we could identify short-, medium- and long-term differences in learning over time. In some cases, these differences may not be enduring: in fact short-term gains may be cancelled in the long term by an enduring decreasing effect on learning. By learning, we could distinguish cognitive, emotional, social and moral developments: arguably a distinction between academic progress and development of the 'whole child' (Edwards and Mercer 1987). Then the measurement of learning progress can change our views of impact and progress: performance in standardised formal tests may privilege a certain objectivist and positivist view of impact and progress; whereas autobiographical and self-reported progress may provide a subjective view of how learners see themselves. Depending on your view of the world, you may believe that one of these views is more important than the other. Hattie (2012) particularly focuses on the evidence from over 50,000 articles discussing research that involved over 240 million students. His 'meta analyses' compare and contrast research into the impact of different approaches to teaching and learning and the impact on achievement. Hattie (2012) explains that achievement is wider than just school examinations: it includes critical evaluation skills and the ability to take part in society as a 'good citizen'. It involves the development of character, motivation and positive dispositions to learning.

There are significant implications for school leaders and teacher educators. As Hattie (2012) says, if we expect children and young people to achieve in this wider view of education, then they must also demonstrate through their values and their practice a commitment to developing critical evaluation in the knowledge society. We argue that critical evaluation skills not only involve a commitment to innovation, risk and adaptation, but that education through innovation is most likely to develop critical evaluation skills. The two concepts go hand in hand.

The findings were that the children retained much more information. This may have been due to the different learning style and also the excitement of talking to other children from a different school. They were more enthusiastic about what they were learning and much more willing to write, which, incidentally, included more adjectives! Further lessons using video links to improve literacy were also successful, such as using the live link for interviews between the 'big bad wolf' and the 'three little pigs' which involved literacy skills as well as ICT skills.

An important concept presented by Hattie (2012) is 'visible learning'. This is the learning seen explicitly by the teacher and learner. He argues that 'powerful, passionate and accomplished teachers':

- Focus on students' cognitive engagement with the content of what is being taught;
- Focus on problem-solving and teaching strategies relating to the content of learning;
- Focus on new knowledge and then how fluency and appreciation of this knowledge develops;
- Focus on feedback which helps learners achieve goals;
- Seek feedback on the progress and proficiency of all learners;
- Understand learning;
- Focus on learning from the point of the learner, appreciating that learning is not always linear.

Many teachers will read this list and recognise these characteristics in their own teaching or that of colleagues who are seen to be good teachers. There is nothing magical about the items on the list: isn't it just good practice? We should also say that 'visible teaching' is not an easy option; it is not a 'silver bullet' to fire at the class to make everything come right in the face of educational challenges. However, we do believe that visible learning is a useful concept because it encapsulates and summarises much of what is good practice in learning and teaching (see for example, Alexander 2010; Pollard 2008; TLRP 2004). It seems to us that 'visible learning' is not a menu of teaching tips but a set of teaching practices, attitudes and motivations which characterise teachers who are able to best help their students to achieve through their classes. As Hattie (2012) says, ultimately, the best way for any teacher to improve their practice is to focus on learning and teaching from the learner's point of view.

Much has been said about the importance of creativity in the classroom. Hargreaves (2003) considers this to be important in the development of the knowledge society. 'Creativity' is often used interchangeably with the term 'innovation'.

What do we mean by creativity?

'Creativity' is a much-debated topic and it has been challenged and defined over decades. What may have changed is our perceptions of what it means today.

Tony Blair stated in the *All Our Futures* Report by the National Advisory Committee on Creative and Cultural Education: 'Our aim must be to create a nation where the creative talents of all the people are used to build a true enterprise economy for the twenty first century where we compete on brains, not brawn' (NACCCE 1999).

What constitutes creativity? Is it someone who exhibits creative genius, someone who shows originality or something more spontaneous? Is it someone who utilises their creativity for good and moral causes? Is it, as Tony Blair hopes, someone who uses their creative talents to help their country to succeed? Do we even know what creativity looks like or, as a teacher, what we need to be looking for? In school, we hear the word 'creative' used regularly, usually referring to story-writing, art or music. Are children being creative when we ask them to recount a familiar story, but with their own twist? Many theorists view 'creativity' in terms of the product, the final outcome, that has been created as a result of this creative action. Mumford (2003) suggests: 'Over the course of the last decade ... we seem to have reached a general agreement that creativity involves the production of novel, useful products.'

All Our Futures (NACCCE 1999) may be a good starting point for a definition of creativity. NACCCE and Mumford (2003) approach it in terms of creativity for learning and define creativity as 'imaginative activity so as to produce outcomes that are both original and of value' and go on to break the term down into four characteristics:

- thinking or behaving imaginatively;
- the activity has a purpose that is directed to achieving an objective;
- these processes generate something original;
- the final outcome must be of value in relation to the objective.

They believe creativity is possible 'in all areas of human activity and that everyone has creative capacities' (NACCCE 1999). Benson (2004) agrees with this and goes on to say that these four features 'if taught well should provide children with opportunities to show and develop their creativity.' Creativity needs opportunity. Benson (2004) states that in the 'curriculum', we need to offer opportunities in all areas to develop, explore, investigate, question and take risks so that children acquire important skills and knowledge that will help to develop their creativity.

Morris (2003) also makes explicit reference in his writing to aims of the National Curriculum (Qualifications and Curriculum Authority 1999), and agrees that: 'the curriculum should enable pupils to think creatively and critically, to solve problems and to make a difference for the better'. However, Kaufman and Beghetto (2009) express concern that in some classrooms, students have the opportunity to forge their creative potential into creative talent; in others, students experience limited (if any) encouragement for their creative ideation and expression. So for some students a less 'creative classroom' means that learners have less opportunity to develop their own ideas and express themselves in an articulate and challenging way.

Starko (2010) says there are two major criteria for creativity: 'novelty' and 'appropriateness'. He believes that to be creative, an idea or product must be new, unique. Karkockiene (2005) says there is no universal agreement on what creativity actually is. As stated earlier by NACCCE, many authors have shown that the common link to the definitions of creativity is the ability to produce work that is both novel and appropriate (Sternberg 2006) but that it must also add value in the world. The question arises through Cohen (2012) whether this definition can only be applied to creativity in adults because children are unlikely to produce something truly new or something valued by people other than their family or peer group.

The cultural context (the country, civilisation and the time) are also of great importance in any consideration of creativity. All of these have a significant impact on the different perspectives on what it means to be creative. For example, during his lifetime Van Gogh was never famous as a painter and struggled to make a living as an artist, possibly rejected by contemporary audiences. However, Van Gogh's artwork today is considered to be amongst the greatest. Van Gogh created his paintings because he had something to communicate, and something to share with the world: 'I want you to know that if you see something worthwhile in what I am doing, it is not by accident but because of real intention and purpose' (Vincent van Gogh cited in Ghiselin 1985).

Where does creativity come from?

Albert Einstein said that the secret to creativity is knowing how to hide your sources. Everything comes from somewhere. Einstein was very honest when he said this. He implies that you can build on someone else's existing idea or knowledge, change it, improve it or use it in a way that nobody has done before so that it becomes a new and original idea whereby the original sources become less important. Adair (2007) tells us about a visitor to Henry Ford's factory. The tour was extensive and Ford's achievements very impressive. On asking Mr Ford how he managed to accomplish all that he did having started with very little, Ford replied: 'Every man starts with all there is. Everything is here – the essence and substance of all there is' (Adair 2007).

Ford meant that we cannot make something from nothing. We need somewhere or something to start from and are surrounded by materials and resources that can be used. Our subconscious 'borrows' ideas or characteristics of things that we already know or have seen, and uses those as a foundation or a building block. We rarely form new ideas out of nothing, but use our experiences either consciously or subconsciously to 'seed' something new. This is the essence of creativity, when the mind makes connections and transforms what is available into something not only new but of value and with purpose.

Steve Jobs, co-founder, chairman, and chief executive officer of Apple Inc. summed this up when he said:

> Creativity is just connecting things. When you ask creative people how they did something, they feel a little guilty because they didn't really do it, they just saw something. It seemed obvious to them after a while. That's because they were able to connect experiences they've had and synthesise new things. (Jobs 1996)

Your task as a creative thinker is to combine ideas or elements that already exist. If the result is an unlikely but valuable combination of ideas or things ... then you will be seen as a creative thinker.

Creativity in education

As we have already established there are several definitions of 'creativity' and Loveless (2001) agrees that the NACCCE Report (1999) framework:

> presents a definition which is a useful framework for educators ... Creativity in education can encompass learning to be creative in order to produce work that has originality and value to individuals, peers and society, as well as learning to be creative in order to support 'possibility thinking' in making choices in everyday life.

 Classroom case study

Children were testing different materials to find out which one was waterproof. They used a range of materials, looked at them under a microscope and made the connection that those materials with holes allowed water to flow through and that the bigger the hole the faster the water flowed through the material. While most children accepted that some fabrics were waterproof and some others were not, one child, silent for a while, obviously pondering on the different aspects of the activity, suddenly exclaimed, 'We need to fill the holes to make it waterproof, if we crayoned over the fabric the wax would go into the holes.' (Information provided by the Association for Science Education)

NACCCE (1999: 36)

This illustrates how creative thinking by the child enables them to make connections and in doing so, move their own learning forward demonstrating a real understanding of the key idea. In terms of teaching should we be teaching *creatively* or teaching *for* creativity? Is it possible to do both? What is the difference? Teaching creatively might be described as teachers using highly imaginative approaches to make the pupil's learning more interesting, engaging, exciting and effective, for example, the use of technology in the classroom such as video conferencing. Teaching for creativity might best be described as using different methods of teaching to develop the pupil's own creative thinking. If teachers are supposedly the role model, then surely we should be striving to teach creatively ourselves so that we develop the creative abilities of our pupils.

Starko (2010) reflects on a lesson he observed and participated in where the children had to follow specific, choreographed moves using a parachute to create various forms and shapes. The teacher narrated, the class followed step-by-step. The results were visually spectacular. The author asks:

> Who was being creative? ... as a participant, my thoughts were not on communication or originality, but on counting my steps and remembering when to duck ... A teaching activity that produces an enjoyable, or even creative, outcome does not necessarily enhance creativity unless the students have the opportunity for creative thinking. The parachute activity might be considered creative teaching because the teacher exercised considerable creativity in developing and presenting the exercise. However, creative teaching ... is not the same as teaching to develop creativity. (Starko 2010)

Are all children creative?

Kaufman and Beghetto (2009) believe that if we were to follow the 'Four C Model of Creativity' then every child *is* potentially creative. In terms of 'big-C' and 'little-c' creativity, little-c incorporates the kind of everyday creativity that you would expect to see in the classroom regularly as part of the children's development, such as problem-solving or adapting to change. Big-C creativity, however, is considered by the authors to be a much rarer occurrence when you see a much more extreme form of creativity that is original, unique, or one that is 'reserved for the great'. Simonton (Kersting 2003), sums it up when he says, 'at the little-c level, creativity implies basic functionality, and at the big-C level, it's something that we give Pulitzer and Nobel Prizes for'.

It most definitely would be a bleak world without 'creativity'. Starko (2010: 10) suggests that 'without creativity we have no art, no literature, no science, no innovation, no problem solving, no progress'. He goes on to say:

It is, perhaps, less obvious that creativity has an equally essential role in schools. The processes of creativity parallel those of learning ... Students who use content in creative ways learn the content well. They also learn strategies for identifying problems, making decisions, and finding solutions both in and out of school.

Wolk (2008) believes that as educators, we must 'Allow students to create original work, and show off that work. Give students and teachers time to tinker.'

Morris (2003) states: 'Creative teaching may be defined in two ways: firstly, teaching creatively and secondly, teaching for creativity.' Many teachers see creative teaching in terms of the first. Teachers *can* be creative in their pedagogy but can also promote the creative thinking and behaviour of their pupils. Whether they can actually teach children to *be* creative is open to debate. Does this also mean that teachers have to develop *their* own creativity in order to teach creatively because, as mentioned earlier, creative processes draw from knowledge and practical skills?

Creativity requires the ability to solve problems progressively over time, applying previous knowledge to new situations and ultimately using these skills to identify new problems. Those learners who question and apply these skills and knowledge, and across different contexts, begin a journey of learning, discovery and innovation.

Innovation and creativity

What does 'innovation' really mean and how does it differ from creativity? Literature reviews indicate that the relationship between creativity and innovation can be quite different though the words are often used synonymously. Firestien (1996) says 'creativity is getting the idea, and innovation is doing something about it', and Levitt (1925–2006) defines creativity and innovation as: 'Creativity is thinking up new things'.

Both believed that creativity was not just coming up with ideas, but what you actually did with them. Innovation is about taking the idea and making it useful or of value. However, the words creativity and innovation are often used interchangeably and McGuiness and Nisbet (1990) believes they mean two very different things, 'because while creativity implies coming up with ideas, it's the bringing ideas to life ... that makes innovation the distinct undertaking it is'. Vehar (2008) also agrees that perhaps the two words should not be used synonymously: 'Creativity is required for innovation, but is not the same thing, since the innovation goes beyond the phenomenon of the creative product to its introduction, launch, commercialisation or exploitation.' Vehar admits that there is an overlap between the two definitions, but cannot give them equal weighting: 'Although you can't have the latter without the former, you can have the creativity without innovation.' We have to agree that they are very closely linked and it may be considered ambitious to attempt to separate the two terms.

The process of innovation is lengthy and complex. Innovations can take several centuries to evolve into their modern-day forms and are rarely the achievements of one person alone. Edison's electric light bulb is a prime example. It was in fact, the product of a whole team of engineers who took existing ideas from other inventors and developed them further. So it wasn't a new idea, it was the advancement of existing ideas.

Thomas Edison, Henry Ford and Leonardo da Vinci are all deemed to be great innovators, but what defines them as this? Is it because they introduced new ideas or methods, or produced something of great value to others? Unfortunately in da Vinci's, case he was not recognised for his achievements until at least 300 years after his death! Henry Ford did not invent the car. He took an idea that was already there (Karl Benz is generally acknowledged as the inventor of the first *modern* automobile in 1886) and changed it into something *new*, which was a simple and reliable car that most Americans could afford (the Model T). So if this is being creative, why was Ford an innovator? Through passion, resilience and sheer determination, Ford also came up with the idea of the assembly line to mass produce the cars. This revolutionised factory production. Assembly-line methods were faster, much more efficient and a cheaper way to build products. The impact of this was immense and changed factory production for ever. Therefore, by Levitt's definition, Ford is considered an innovator.

On a final note, innovative practice is often linked to the use of different technologies in the classroom. There is evidence that using multimedia to teach in the classroom can both create a more multisensory interactive way of learning for children and convey information in a more memorable way for some. Can the use of technology be considered as innovative teaching or creative teaching? Payton and Williamson (2009) in their research into curriculum and teaching innovation ask what you would expect to see from an innovative teacher in their classroom.

 Classroom case study

A junior school in Slough set up a link with a school in Delhi to reflect the fact that 90 per cent of its students were of South Asian origin. Through this link, children were able to stay in touch with their cultural routes and develop relationships via e-mail with students in India. The link has been useful in several areas across the curriculum for projects such as exploring global differences in weather and examining some moral issues in Personal, Social and Health Education.
Payton and Williamson (2009)

What better way to address diversity and other global issues by linking directly with those countries involved? The learning will be memorable. The teachers have used technology that already exists in a useful and valuable way to promote learning and build links.

Chapter summary

- Education is for the development of the individual learner as well as preparation of the individual for living in the wider society as a child and later as an adult.
- A knowledge society must be a learning society. Innovation in education is important in order to encourage a knowledge society.
- 'Innovation' means doing things differently; but this should not be confused with the latest shallow fad, for innovation implies improvement and adding value.
- Visible learning (Hattie 2012) includes all those characteristics which when made explicit by the teacher and learner result in an increase in a learner's achievement.
- The single most important aspect of 'visible learning' is for the teacher to focus on learning from the point of view of the learner.
- Creativity involves elements of originality, novelty and adding to value. For this reason, it is a concept closely associated with innovation.
- Innovation in general often takes an existing idea or approach and transforms it into something new. For this reason, innovation always builds on what came before.

Further reading and research

Hargreaves, A. (2003). *Teaching in the Knowledge Society*. New York: Teachers' College Press.

Lortie, D. (1975). *Schoolteacher: A Sociological Study*. Chicago: University of Chicago Press.

Simon, B. (1985). *Does Education Matter?* London: Lawrence and Wishart, pp. 13–31.

Tarde, G. (1903). *The Laws of Imitation*, translated by E. Clews Parsons. New York: H. Holt & Co.

Watt, D. (2002) *How Innovation Occurs in High Schools Within the Network of Innovative Schools: The Four Pillars of Innovation Research Project*. Alberta: The Conference Board of Canada. Retrieved 20 March 2002 from http://www.schoolnet.ca/nisrei/e/research/pillars/index.asp

CHAPTER 2

TEACHING AND LEARNING IN SCHOOLS

Chapter guide

In this chapter you will learn about:

- Freedom, responsibility and agency in learning
- Families and the impact of attachment on learning
- The creative curriculum: purposeful learning in authentic contexts
- Enquiry-based learning

Introduction

How we learn is as important as the objective of our education and matters at all stages of learning. This is especially important for children in the early years of learning. A barren and boring experience of learning, no matter the content, is very likely to demotivate the learner and sow the seeds of disaffection for the long term. For instance, in English it is argued that a high-quality interaction with a low-quality text is to be preferred to a low-quality interaction with a high-quality text. Of course, the two are not mutually exclusive. We should aim for a high-quality learning experience in all classrooms, in a relevant and purposeful area of knowledge which also develops key skills for future life. We must also recognise that learning is its own reward. Learning should be an end in itself. Developing curiosity and pleasure for learning are important ends in themselves.

In the previous chapter, we examined the important concepts of innovation and creativity: what they are and why they are important in education. In both the importance of change, novelty and adding value were seen as central. National and international perspectives suggest that creativity and innovation are both important as objectives for children's learning and the curriculum. If agreement on an exact definition of creativity and innovation is beyond most commentators, there seems to be common agreement that learners and teachers should do this in creative and innovative ways. There also seems to be a recognition that 'all that glisters is not gold'. Starko's (2010) example of children following neatly, but quite mechanically, choreographed moves by the teacher in a school concert, might suggest creativity more on the part of the teacher than the children. Likewise a flourishing classroom display might be more evidence of a teacher's, or teaching assistant's, artistic talents, than those of the children. That is not to say that we do not accept the importance of learning which is directed by the teacher, or an environment which is made exciting by a talented teacher. We echo the words of Paulo Coelho (1998: 23), when he says that 'teaching is only demonstrating that it is possible. Learning is making it possible for yourself.'

 Reflection point

- Reflect on classroom displays of children's work on the walls.
- Consider successful performances by children in school.
- Review successful creative work by children in art and stories.

In each of the above, what is the contribution of the teacher or other adults?
   What is the contribution of children?
   According to Coelho's quote, in these examples how did the teacher demonstrate possibilities for learning and how did children make learning their own?

In this chapter, we make a distinction between learning that is creative and innovative and the acts of creativity and innovation in themselves. We believe that good teaching and learning should result in a change in understanding, should involve new learning and should add value to the lives of the learner and the teacher. An important area which will be discussed is the role of freedom and responsibility in learning. To what degree do teachers and learners make choices in education? In the following section, we consider how the learner makes decisions in their learning.

Freedom, responsibility and agency in learning

As in society, the debate about the role of freedom, responsibility and control in school learning has been widely debated. Different groups (Institute for Ideas 2012; *The Independent* 2013) demonstrate diametrically opposed views.

For instance, an Institute of Ideas (2012: p.19) position paper argues that 'children develop into adults through imbibing subject knowledge' and that a focus on self-esteem, learning to learn and technology for learning is merely a fad.' The writer of this paper goes on to say that 'the technology required for teaching subjects is as simple as the pedagogy: pencil and paper, whiteboard and marker pens, good books and direct instruction' (p. 20). In this view, the teacher or a higher institution such as a government ministry chooses the focus of learning, to ensure that learners learn the facts, knowledge and important skills which are intrinsic to developing what Hirsch (1988) calls 'cultural literacy'. The argument from Hirsch is that students will never understand what they learn and especially what they read, if they do not understand an identifiable base of knowledge which is specific to the culture. These are often portrayed as facts about a society, its culture and history which the learner must learn.

A different view of learning is put forward in a letter to the Secretary of State for Education in England (*The Independent* 2013). The writers' views challenge a proposed School National Curriculum for England which many commentators would say mirrors the conception of learning promoted by the Institute of Ideas above. One hundred Professors of Education in England criticise the proposals as follows:

> Much of it demands too much too young. This will put pressure on teachers to rely on rote learning without understanding. Inappropriate demands will lead to failure and demoralisation. The learner is largely ignored. Little account is taken of children's potential interests and capacities, or that young children need to relate abstract ideas to their experience, lives and activity. (*The Independent* 2013)

At the heart of this debate is the role of freedom, responsibility and control in learning in schools. Of course, we could talk about this at the macro level: for example, the government control of a central National Curriculum. We could talk about this at a local management level: for example, a headteacher in a primary school requiring teachers to teach certain knowledge in certain ways. These are important topics; and may even explain why different types of learning are present in the classroom. For the moment, however, the focus is on the teacher, the learner and the classroom. In the following questions, who decides: What will be learned? How it will be learned? Why this aspect of learning is important? Who takes responsibility for planning, progression and assessment of learning? Where does the control lie: with the teacher or with the learner?

Gibbons (2004: 461) argues for a paradigm shift in education towards 'self-directed learning by combining freedom with responsibility, reflection with action, and challenge with opportunity'. Glennon (2008) explains in detail the nature of responsibility and freedom in a higher education context. In his classes, students negotiate learning objectives and outcomes which they see as relevant, setting their own assessment deadlines, which they review against a negotiated set of evaluation criteria. The role of the teacher is to help the learner by helping students to develop and apply self-directed learning skills. Central to the success of this approach is a learning covenant agreed between the learners and their teachers. Acting as a learning contract, this guides the teacher and learner through a particular learning sequence. Of course, the approach is more subtle than learners being left to their own devices: a range of learning projects appears to drive the development of self-directed learning. Active learning is said to develop from active engagement in the learning content and the learning process. Starting with the teacher, Glennon cites the influence of Palmer (1998) who identifies the following important principles in teaching:

- Good teaching cannot be reduced to technique;
- Good teaching comes from the identity and the integrity of the teacher;
- Community is at the heart of reality and therefore at the heart of teaching;
- Community in education is expressed through the interrelationships of teachers and learners.

Innovation comes in challenging, problematic classroom learning experiences which emphasise the independent voice of the child.

 Reflection point

Some people say that learning is as much an art as a science; and that teaching is as much about the person, and who you are, as it is about the skills of teaching.

(Continued)

(Continued)

Do you agree with this view?
If this is the case, what are the implications for your own professional development? Should you spend as much time on developing yourself as a person, as well as developing your understanding of approaches to teaching and learning in the classroom?

Glennon quotes John Dewey in identifying experience at the heart of education: the best learning takes place when the learner is given something to do rather than something to learn. 'Making the individual a sharer or partner in the associated activity so that he feels its success as his success, its failure as his failure, is the completing step' (Dewey 1966: 14). This amounts to a sharing of responsibility and freedom in the choice of learning. While it might seem easier to polarise the debate, we argue here for a sharing of responsibility, freedom and control in learning. It is a journey of self-expression culminating in the development of a personal identity. On the other hand, learning is a process by which an individual is socialised into a knowledge set and ways of acting and making meaning (Bruner 1991). This is a problematic and complex tension which is often irreconcilable in the classroom. Accountability, such as school inspection, performance management of teachers and school league tables, can dictate that control of learning rests more with the teacher. When the improvement of 'student outcomes' is seen as a priority, in an area of social and educational deprivation, control of the choice of curriculum content and approaches to learning may be held more strongly by the teacher and the school. Some would see that schools in this position have a duty to provide the basic skills and understanding which will enable underachieving children from deprived backgrounds to survive in a society which values a certain form of education. In this form of educational emancipation, so the argument goes, if you can't change society for the better, then you need to play by its rules and that means you need to learn the rules in school. Freire see education as transformational when teachers and learners are enabled to reflect critically on their roles: 'The teacher is no longer merely the-one-who-teaches, but one who is himself taught in dialogue with the students, who in turn while being taught also teach. They become jointly responsible for a process in which they all grow' Freire (1993: 67).

Freire's model of critical literacy emanated from Brazil, where hunger and poverty were important factors, and it seems far away from the state education systems of contemporary Europe, even if in England today there is a rhetoric of local decision-making with freedom for teachers to make decisions. Freedom and responsibility imply an exercise of judgement by the individual. Of course, you may see education and learning in school as an entirely passive process. But most people would agree that learning should be seen as an active process on the part of the learner. The contribution of the learner to this process implies the concept of 'agency'. Teachers, learners and their families are all actors in the community of learning in school: they exercise agency by making conscious and subconscious decisions in the classroom. If learning is seen as an active construction of knowledge, then agency in learning and the development of active participants in the learning process is important. Bruner (1996: 93) calls this the agentive mind. In this approach the learner is seen as 'proactive, problem-orientated, attentionally focused, selective, constructional and directed to ends'. Indeed in psychology, it has long been held that learning is an active process: approaches in the tradition of Bruner, Piaget, Zimmerman and Vygotsky are identified as constructivist, even though the respective emphases on language and the social dimension are different.

 Classroom case study

Hewitt (2007) identified a tension at the classroom level with simple procedures like developing a focus for learning in a lesson through explicit learning objectives. Where these objectives are articulated in language which the learner does not understand, where they are irrelevant to the life of the learner and where the purpose for the learning is out of any context, it is easy to see that a learner will be demotivated.

For instance, a learning objective 'to learn how to read and spell a split digraph in Consonant Vowel Consonant words' means little to a five-year-old child in the early years of school.

This comes back to the argument for a more rounded, more relevant and more developmentally appropriate education referred to by the letter from the one hundred education professors (*The Independent* 2013).

Ultimately, school leaders might argue that a short-term focus on a more didactic teacher-directed form of learning is justified by improvements in the basic skills of students as evidenced by school performance data. However, much like society we argue that the ends do not justify the means. An enjoyable, challenging and stimulating classroom experience in which the learner and teacher share responsibility for directing learning is an important end in itself. Over-emphasis on teacher direction, an undervaluing of the learners' contribution to decisions about learning and a lack of opportunities for children to take responsibility in the classroom are all likely to develop 'learned helplessness'.

If you spoon feed children, when you teach them, all you'll get from them is the shape of the spoon.

One interpretation of the 'problem with learning objectives' focuses is the notion of agency in learning. If humans are motivated to achieve goals then an understanding of this concept is important. Goals are stable, higher-order entities that function as abstract, organising structures and remain fairly stable over time (Austin and Vancouver 1996). They can be seen as culturally specific. For instance, Tamis-LeMonda et al. (2007) identify parents' views on individualism in children. Tamis-LeMonda and her colleagues explain that this is motivated by different Western views of the young learner:

- Personal choice ('That's why I'll let them decide what they want to do. If I like something but they don't, they won't have to do it');
- Intrinsic forms of motivation and persistence ('You know, no matter what happens, just kind of have that positive, you know optimism');
- Self-esteem ('That's the way you learn ... Love what you are'); and
- Self-maximisation ('I don't want him to think that he can't have or he can't do or he can't accomplish').

(Tamis-LeMonda et al. 2007)

Families and the impact of attachment on learning

Parents and the community are important agents themselves in the development of children's learning. Parents are an important influence on their children's learning. It is said that in the West, a traditional Anglo-Saxon and European goal for children's early learning is to develop the self: for example, self-esteem and self-maximisation as in the above analysis. Whilst the Western focus on individualism may be contrasted by a focus on collectivism in some Eastern cultures, it could equally be said that there are differences between families and communities within a culture.

There is an important connection between child-rearing, early child relationships and approaches to learning. This is explained by attachment theory and theorises how individual children approach learning themselves. Ainsworth et al. (1978) explained that caregivers' responses to children in early social interactions lead to the development of patterns of attachment. These patterns, for example, lead to secure relationships with children. As with many aspects of learning, these experiences lead to internal working models which will guide the individual's perceptions, emotions, thoughts and expectations in later relationships. Importantly, these working models affect how learners respond to the challenge of learning later in life. Of course, this is not the only factor which influences children's responses in the classroom, but 'security of attachment' is an important factor in how a child responds to a new task which is challenging and involves taking a risk. The child who has a secure attachment will learn from a socially and emotionally secure base, whereas the child who has a more disorganised pattern of attachments due to more fragmented early experiences may be task-avoidant. 'Task-avoidant' learners may prefer to avoid risk and expect a more directed experience of learning, in which they choose to adopt a more passive or even resistant approach to learning. However, that is not to characterise task avoidance as a learning style. In fact it demonstrates that early emotional and social development in children can have a long-term, but not irretrievable, impact on the ability and desire of a child to take responsibility for their learning and to engage with innovation. An associated concept in learning is 'resilience'. Psychologists would say that resilience in learning is an individual's ability to cope with stress and setbacks. This functions at a cognitive, emotional and social level.

The American Psychological Association (2014) suggests ways to develop resilience:

1. Maintaining good relationships with close family members, friends and others: secure relationships provide a strong base for learning and life.
2. Avoid seeing crises or stressful events as unbearable problems: this emphasises learner agency. Things do not have to stay as they are.
3. Accept circumstances that cannot be changed: change what you can change within your sphere of influence.
4. Develop realistic goals and move towards them: learners can take control of their learning.
5. Take decisive actions in adverse situations: taking control requires personal agency.
6. Look for opportunities of self-discovery after a struggle with loss: every time you learn something, you learn something about learning.
7. Developing self-confidence: recognition of one's own abilities and be positive about what you can do as a learner.
8. Keep a long-term perspective and consider the stressful event in a broader context: difficulties in learning may not be immediately resolved in the short term.
9. Maintain a hopeful outlook, expecting good things and visualising what is wished: a positive approach attitude to learning not only makes learners more solution-focused, it can facilitate the relationships with others, which in itself can facilitate learning.
10. Take care of one's mind and body, exercising regularly, paying attention to one's own needs and feelings: it is possible to improve resilience for learning as it is to improve resilience more generally in life.

Other theorists consider resilience in learning, but call it something different. For instance, Jenny Moon (2009) calls this 'academic assertiveness': skills and approaches to learning which facilitate the overcoming of challenges. While Moon's work is predominantly focused on university learning, it is useful to consider what she sees as assertive behaviours in learning:

- the finding of an appropriate 'voice' or form of expression through which to engage in critical thinking or debate;
- the willingness to challenge, to disagree and to seek or accept a challenge;
- the ability to cope with the reality or the likelihood of not being 'right' sometimes, making an error or failing; effective recovery from these situations;
- the willingness to change one's mind if necessary; the openness to feedback on one's performance (academic or otherwise);
- willingness to listen and take account of the viewpoint of others, awareness that others can make mistakes and reasonable tolerance of their failings;
- autonomy – a willingness to be proactive; to make and justify independent judgements and to act on them;
- an appropriate level of academic self-esteem.

(Moon 2009)

 Classroom case study

In primary schools the language might be different, but many people would agree with the above. For instance, developing the voice of the learner was a focus for Devon County Council. They did this through pupil voice conferences. The aim of these events was to collect the views of Devon children and young people on aspects of their education to inform future developments at a local and county level. They hoped to establish a culture of ongoing meaningful consultation with young people at a school and learning community level (Devon County Council 2013). In the 'pupil voice' conferences students made suggestions about teaching and learning, but how much schools were able to respond is debateable: pupils made suggestions like 'employ more teaching assistants, swap schools for a day'. In Moon's conception of academic assertiveness the willingness to challenge, to disagree and to seek and accept a challenge may actually be seen as a threat by some schools and teachers.

As Glennon (2008) states, promoting freedom, responsibility and learning in class almost always creates more work for the teacher and learner. More constrained, more controlled learning may be easier for the teacher and the learner, though the quality of learning may be much less effective. One response to the development of freedom and responsibility is the so called 'creative curriculum'.

A 'creative curriculum'

> The touch stone of an excellent curriculum is that it instils a love of learning for its own sake.This means that primary children must not only learn what to study, they must also learn how to study and thus become confident, self disciplined individuals capable of engaging in a lifelong process of learning. (Rose 2006)

To have an understanding of what a curriculum sets out to do is to understand its purpose and aims. Most countries have some form of curriculum, but it is worth noting that in England, it only applies to maintained schools, not to independent schools or to home-educated children. Academies however are 'obliged to offer a broad and balanced curriculum' but are 'only required to follow the National Curriculum for the subjects of English, mathematics, science' (Rose 2006). In terms of the National Curriculum for England the prevailing view, as Male (2012) states, is that its aim is about children's entitlement to 'a common set of learning', a minimum entitlement for every child. The curriculum 'sets out the body of knowledge, skills and understanding that a society wishes to pass on to its children and young people' structured around 'aims and values, subject content and skills' (Rose 2006). Each school can respond to and create their own curriculum plan from this, taking into account their own local context and unique features.

In May 2003, the Secretary of State, Charles Clarke, launched 'Excellence and Enjoyment', a strategy for primary schools that would build on achievements and aim to create a richer, more varied and exciting curriculum in which learners would strive to achieve higher standards (DfES 2004). Clarke claimed, 'I believe that what makes good primary education great is the fusion of excellence and enjoyment.' Consequently, 'Excellence and Enjoyment' was introduced for schools around 2003 to enable and empower schools to have both the freedom and challenge to be innovative in their curriculum design and how they teach, while taking into account the individual characteristics of their school (DfES 2004).

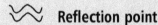 **Reflection point**

Reflect on how a school might consider their local context and unique features as part of their curriculum.

- Are there creative approaches to teaching?
- Does the curriculum develop creativity in the children?
- What are the implications for children and teachers?

'Creative curriculum', very much a twenty-first century term, is used frequently amongst schools, but what does it mean? Craft (2005, cited in Male 2012: 141) agrees that a 'creative curriculum is not about doing things differently just for the sake of being different'. Creativity needs a purpose and it could be argued that the purpose is to improve and enhance the quality of learning, which might be by providing stimulating and inspiring experiences.

In the past, school curricula have sometimes been described as 'plodding' (Male 2012), relatively prescriptive (Rose 2006), somewhat linear and often planned over several years of a child's journey through school. However, the fundamental mistake here is assuming that the way children learn is purely linear and that they all take a similar path. On the contrary, as children learn, they continually make connections between different experiences in a much more non-linear way, building on what they have already learned. Consequently, developing the kind of curriculum that is actually required can be a daunting challenge. Children need a curriculum that is relevant to them right now in their lives and doesn't take them away from what they need to learn. It needs to provide sufficient challenge but also allow them to take risks and make mistakes; to work and learn from one another collaboratively, to question, analyse and solve problems and to provide opportunities to make their learning self-directed. This is quite a tall order.

Reflection point

- Consider what you think a 'creative' curriculum might look like.
- Reflect on your own learning sequences.

How 'creative' are you when it comes to designing a learning experience that is both relevant to the children and will enhance their learning?

What does a creative curriculum look like in schools?

When planning for learning, the effective teacher is naturally reflective and so instinctively evaluates what has been successful or not so that they can build on this, thus improving and strengthening future planning. This is a starting point of planning for a creative curriculum.

Creative thinking is at the heart of curriculum design; learning opportunities need to be offered that develop higher order thinking to encourage higher forms of learning. It could be argued that 'flexibility' is also a key to a more creative curriculum. Flexibility and a creative use of time may enrich the curriculum. Learning experiences could range from a whole-school learning event lasting for a week, to specific days, so that timetables are more flexible and allow for the learning choices and needs of the children, also developing the voice of the learner, as mentioned earlier in the chapter. This lends itself to a more cross-curricular approach, but one whereby the links made could be to real life, meaningful experiences that will help the children to make sense of their world. This agrees with the point made earlier by Craft (2005) of the importance of finding more effective ways of enabling children to learn. Consequently, when a curriculum is enriched and provides varied learning experiences, children respond much more positively and achieve well.

 Classroom case study – examples from a creative curriculum

Example 1: International week

During this week, the whole school came off timetable to focus on a week of carefully planned learning experiences to promote diversity by focusing on different countries from around the world. The children had the opportunity to learn about different languages, stories and legends, religions, diversity, customs, heritage, music and many other aspects that linked into every area of the curriculum. This culminated in a special assembly where parents were invited to share and celebrate learning and achievements.

Each day began in 'arrivals' (the school hall). The children had their passports checked and stamped when they arrived in their country (classroom). Different countries were visited by the children in the form of 'workshops' that linked to that country and culture and were run by staff

(Continued)

(Continued)

and invited guests. The activities ranged from using Kenyan artefacts to inspire storytelling, creating music and performing it on African instruments made by the children, looking at time zones and currency, using innovative ways with ICT to create presentations linked to Scottish legends, designing and making jewellery linked to a culture.

At the end of the week, findings showed that the children were so enthusiastic and motivated about learning new knowledge and skills that they wanted to do this more often. There was a feeling of excitement throughout the school, with children working dynamically together with a shared sense of purpose. With careful planning, careful use of time and using a skills-based approach, the curriculum was enriched by a wide range of learning experiences and visitors to the school. Though this would be difficult to sustain all of the time, the real benefits in terms of learning far outweigh anything else. As well as the skills and knowledge of all staff, the curriculum during this week was further enriched by the children's own experiences, visitors with expertise and skills in areas such as: speaking Mandarin; African drumming skills; Chinese cooking skills; and English country dancing.

- What are the benefits of an event like this, in terms of learning?
- How will you ensure that all learning is relevant and meaningful?

Following this change in approach, teachers discovered that the children took ownership and control of their learning and became more involved. Their ideas were more notably developed and in some cases more creative. Feedback from the project showed that not only had their curriculum become more creative and exciting but importantly, this approach had enabled the children to remember facts and were motivated and interested in what they were learning. By offering learners the appropriate opportunities 'to develop their cognitive and creative potential', a more powerful form of learning developed.

Despite this freedom to design a more creative and innovative curriculum, a report by the European Commission that looked at the role of creativity in education, suggested that teachers did not feel the curricula actively encouraged creativity (Cachia et al. 2010). It was felt that the curricula was 'overloaded with content' and there was not enough time for flexibility, risk or even innovation. However, the report also stressed the importance of seeing creativity as a 'required skill that should be encouraged and developed in most subjects'. Proposals from the report suggest that curricula and learning objectives should provide a consistent definition of creativity which takes into account the broad nature of creativity in all subjects. Curricula should be regularly reviewed and adapted to take into account learners' needs and 'that awareness is raised of the link between teaching practices and creative outcomes, making it clear that creativity and innovation are not subject-related and can be fostered in all students' (Cachia et al. 2010).

 Classroom case study – examples from a creative curriculum

Example 2: Using local resources

During a year-long study, a school trialled a different approach to curriculum planning where each topic began with an out-of-classroom visit. Though this approach doesn't come without its own issues of organisation, the school felt strongly that there were insufficient links to the local community. By approaching learning in this way, the teachers were striving to create more exciting and memorable experiences by using the outdoors and local resources. It was to create a more 'real-life' context to their learning and to take account of what knowledge the children may or may not already have, and also what they would like to find out.

The school's approach was to block foundation subjects and science along with key learning skills in the afternoons with a strong focus on acquiring *new learning* independently and the teachers' role being more of a facilitative role. English and mathematics continued to be taught daily in the morning. In all cases, the National Curriculum programmes of study were used as a starting point.

Of course, curriculum content is one thing. The curriculum covers a multitude of skills, knowledge and especially different approaches to teaching and learning. We will return to this in Chapter 4, where we look at different ways to develop thinking in children. One approach which is often associated with the 'creative curriculum' is an 'enquiry-based' approach to learning.

Enquiry-based learning

Gandhi stated in 1976, 'To my mind, education is the spirit of enquiry.' What is enquiry? According to *Fowler's Modern English Usage* (1926) *enquiry* is the act of questioning. However, if you were to look at the other frequently used spelling of the word, *inquiry*, then we would more likely be participating in a formal inquest.

Enquiry-based learning was originally a teaching program used in America (Mohan 2007) introduced by J.R. Suchman, professor at the University of Illinois in the late 1960s, where questioning was used as a powerful tool to develop thinking and learning, driven by a process of enquiry. This approach provides children with the opportunity to engage with a scenario or problem with a context, often real life, which can be open-ended and have multiple solutions or responses. The so called Socratic method is still in evidence today through projects. The essence of this project is that classrooms are communities of enquiry and the belief that whatever is being learned will be enhanced if approached in a more philosophical and dialogical way. The project title refers to Plato's account of Socrates' dialogue with the boy Menon. In this, the boy is enabled, through Socrates' questioning, to 'discover' Pythagoras' theorem for himself.

During an enquiry process, discussion naturally encourages and generates questioning and 'a good question generates new questions' (European Commission 2008a). Concepts can be challenged and examined from differing perspectives which can ultimately progress and move learning forward, increasing knowledge and understanding. Children by nature are adept at challenging and questioning everything if allowed that freedom within the classroom, so the process of enquiry is a natural process to their way of thinking.

However, according to Lipman and Sharp (1998), to become educated, the children also have to experience 'the intellectual challenge in learning, just like Socrates encouraged Menon through that very same process to discover Pythagoras' theorem for himself. Rather than being too quick to provide the answer, it is about allowing and encouraging the children to engage actively in the process of discovery, however challenging it may be. Lipman et al. (1980: 45) observed that 'When children are encouraged to think philosophically, the classroom is converted into a community of inquiry', where children begin to listen to one another and build on each other's ideas, even challenge one another, just as Socrates encouraged his pupils to do. If children can't make sense of something, they will naturally ask questions. They will begin to compare things, observe, and gather enough information that will help them to make sense of something.

〰 Reflection point

- Consider what the benefits of enquiry-based learning are.
- Reflect on your current practice – do you promote an enquiry-based classroom?

Think about the above and consider the implications this would have on your planning. Is enquiry-based learning an approach that you might already be doing?

What are the benefits of enquiry-based learning?

There are multiple benefits to using enquiry-based learning. Hutchings (2012) regards it as a way to 'inspire students to learn for themselves, bringing a real research-orientated approach to the subject'. Another benefit noted by Hannafin et al. (1994) is that 'open-ended learning environments immerse learners in experiences that foster understanding through extended exploration, manipulation, and opportunities to find out through discovery, which is arguably at the heart of curriculum areas such as science or maths'. This view is supported by Edelson et al. (1999) who believe that it provides valuable opportunities for pupils to improve their understanding of both science content and scientific practices, as science is essentially an enquiry-based process, driven by questions and exploration.

It is essential that an open-ended task has a clear starting point, as this will provide the freedom that allows this type of enquiry and learning to take place (Kahn and O'Rourke 2005). The children are given opportunities to draw on their prior or existing knowledge and from this identify their own learning needs, therefore making the learning self-directed. They also argue that providing the opportunity for these learning experiences will stimulate their curiosity and actively encourage the children to do what comes most naturally to them, explore and investigate. It has also been noted that important skills such as listening, communication, empathy, tolerance, negotiation, patience, time management, focus (Hutchings and O'Rourke 2006) develop considerably during the enquiry-based learning process, which also seems to suggest Vygotsky's theory of learning as a social process. Children learn most effectively when they are given the opportunity to learn from one another and 'learning is frequently most effective when learners have the opportunity to think and talk together, to discuss ideas, question, analyse and solve problems, without the constant mediation of the teacher' (Education Scotland 2012).

Role of the teacher in enquiry-based learning

Hattie (2003) argues that the role of the teacher is an essential one. The teacher in successful enquiry-based learning has much more of a facilitator role, providing encouragement, support, motivation and opportunities throughout the process. Edelson et al. (1999) state the importance of creating accessible tasks, prior knowledge, the ability to manage an enquiry and also resource constraints. No longer should it be that the teacher is 'the one who knows' and imparts knowledge and that the student is 'the one who learns' (Camhy 2007). Dialogue between teacher and children changes and becomes 'the sealing together of the teacher and students in the joint act of knowing and re-knowing the object of study ... Instead of transferring the knowledge statically as a fixed possession of the teacher, dialogue demands a dynamic approximation towards the object' (European Commission 2008a). Learning is therefore not wholly led by teacher instruction but more by teacher *and* student enquiry and 'it should not involve one person acting *on* another, but rather people working with each other' (Paulo Freire, cited in Smith 1997, 2002).

The teacher's role can give a context and meaning to the experience (Eric 2005; Kahn and O'Rourke 2005). The word 'pedagogy' is used frequently within teaching and means 'leading children'. Sutcliffe (2011) reminds us that teachers can lead or guide children to develop enquiry skills. Enquiry-based learning places the responsibility for the learning process on the children themselves and is very much about working collaboratively and cooperatively.

 Classroom case study – example of enquiry-based learning

Science with a class of five- and six-year-olds

A more constructivist approach to learning was taken during this project, similar to 'The 5 Es' (Enhancing Education 2002) which consists of five distinct stages of learning: Engage, Explore, Explain, Elaborate, and Evaluate. The objective was for the children to use enquiry as a process and to build on new ideas by drawing on prior knowledge, understanding and skills, while linking learning to a real-life context.

There had to be a clear sequence of lessons that would take into account not only the content the children required to learn, such as where electricity comes from, the function of different elements to a circuit, but also the processes, such as enquiry, i.e. how to make a bulb light up and working together collaboratively. Most importantly, the children needed to be allowed the time and freedom to explore and investigate this task in a real-life context and apply prior or new knowledge. The real-life context was to apply the circuit to the design of a fully functioning lighthouse such as the one in the Grace Darling story.

The role of the teacher in this case was one of facilitator, in which they had to guide, observe, monitor and assess understanding and provide resources including books and laptops with a selection of websites to assist research. It was important to keep the task simple to understand so the children could understand the purpose of the task and apply their knowledge. Otherwise there is the danger of trying to learn new processes and new content at the same time, frustration levels potentially increasing and consequently becoming a barrier to learning. The children were carefully grouped and input was provided, being careful not to 'give away' any possible solutions. Importantly, they were given the freedom to approach the task in their own ways.

The potential concern with enquiry-based learning is that children might not be able to find a solution to a given question. However, this was unfounded in the example above. After research was carried out by the groups with enough time for exploration of the materials and solutions, the groups were able to build a circuit. Once the children were at the stage of applying their knowledge of circuits to a real-life context, for example, building the light-house, the children were secure in their knowledge and understood the concept of circuits. Some learners developed their learning further by enquiring 'how can we turn the light off?' which led to more complex circuits. Ultimately, the learners made the choice to pursue an enquiry. They made it possible for themselves.

Chapter summary

- Teaching is only demonstrating that it is possible. Learning is making it possible for yourself.
- An enjoyable, challenging and stimulating classroom experience in which the learner and teacher share responsibility for directing learning is an important end in itself.
- Good teaching cannot be reduced to technique; it comes from the identity and the integrity of the teacher.
- Community is at the heart of reality and therefore at the heart of teaching.
- Community in education is expressed through the interrelationships of teachers and learners.
- Teachers, learners and their families are all actors in the community of learning in school: they exercise agency by making conscious and subconscious decisions in the classroom.
- An enjoyable, challenging and stimulating classroom experience in which the learner and teacher share responsibility for directing learning is an important end in itself. Over-emphasis on teacher direction, an undervaluing of the learner's contribution to decisions about learning and a lack of opportunities for children to take responsibility in the classroom are all likely to develop 'learned helplessness'.
- Early emotional and social development in children can have a long-term but not irretrievable impact on the ability and desire of a child to take responsibility for their learning and to engage with innovation. 'Security of attachment' is an important factor in how a child responds to a new task which is challenging and involves taking a risk.
- Creative thinking is at the heart of curriculum design. It is not just about the content but about offering learning opportunities to 'allow ambition and challenge through higher order thinking'. 'The creative curriculum' will only

be deemed a success if it can evidence that children's learning and their ability to learn has been enriched and that standards have risen.
- Enquiry-based learning provides children with the opportunity to engage with a scenario or problem with a context, often real life, which can be open-ended and have multiple solutions or responses.

Further reading and research

Ainsworth, M.D.S., Blehar, M.C., Waters, E. and Wall, S. (1978). *Patterns of Attachment: A Psychological Study of the Strange Situation*. Hillsdale, NJ: Erlbaum.

CHAPTER 3

HOW DO CHILDREN LEARN IN THE EARLY YEARS? LINKS TO THEORY AND INNOVATION

Chapter guide

In this chapter you will learn about:

- How young children learn
- The meaning of play
- What free play looks like in an early years setting
- The value of the outdoor environment

Introduction

> Young children are natural learners. They are like explorers or research scientists busily gathering information and making meaning out of the world. Most of this learning is not the result of teaching, but rather a constant and universal learning activity as natural as breathing. (Meighan 1997)

Meighan's quote could quite easily be referring to how young children use play to learn. There have been many debates about the value of learning through play, but the fact remains the same: children are motivated by play and learn best through experiences linked with this. It is interesting to note that research within neuroscience has shown that the cognitive structures of a child's brain are continuously shaped by experience acquired by the child. Early research by Isaacs (1929) found that through engaging in play, 'the child's mind grows' and more recent findings indicate that play 'stimulates novel neural and chemical reactions and interactions that enhance brain plasticity' (Sutton-Smith 1997: 20), suggesting that play does in fact shape the brain. Goswami and Bryant (2007: 20) found that learning depends on the 'development of multi-sensory networks of neurons distributed across the entire brain'. Nothing has been pre-programmed genetically and so the brain is therefore receptive and sensitive to certain kinds of information. For example, 'a concept in science may depend on neurons being simultaneously active in visual, spatial, memory, deductive and kinaesthetic regions, in both brain hemispheres' (Goswami and Bryant 2007: 20).

By understanding the complexities of the brain and the interrelationship between play, the environment and the brain, we can begin to have a deeper understanding of how play contributes to the physical and emotional aspect of a child's development (Lester and Russell 2008). These findings both justify and strengthen the argument for a play-based curriculum.

As children develop and attempt to make sense of the world around them, they actively work to construct 'causal frameworks' to help explain why or how things happen as they do (Legare 2008). Goswami and Bryant (2007) believe that the knowledge gained through any teaching or experiences, such as imaginative play, language and imagination, are all crucial to the development of such frameworks. They also point out the importance of teachers' understanding and recognising that while children attempt to construct a 'theory' of why something has occurred, this also reflects a general human tendency to seek information that appears to confirm one's theories (Goswami and Bryant 2007). Therefore, to help children to construct their own understanding of the world it is important that they are given the opportunity to experience carefully planned and facilitated play-based activities that build on knowledge and understanding and that enable children to move further in their development and learning.

The historical development of play

Throughout history and across different cultures, there is evidence of play amongst children from as early as the Neolithic period, for example, small clay and stone balls were found in a village in China, believed to be toys from the Yangshao Culture. Evidence from Ancient Greek and Roman times showed that children's play reflected the society and culture in which they lived, and that physical activities in particular usually took place alongside adults (Lester and Russell 2008).

The philosopher Plato (427–347 BCE) clearly linked learning to play in his work *The Republic* (Plato 1955). Here, he discusses the use of a learning approach with young children, which clearly shows his understanding of them and the value of learning thorough play: 'Enforced learning will not stay in the mind. So avoid compulsion and let your children's lessons take the form of play' (Santer et al. 2007: 1), which for its time, was a somewhat controversial view. The eighteenth-century philosopher Jean-Jacques Rousseau agrees with this: 'a child must not be constrained to keep still when he wishes to move, nor to move when he wishes to remain quiet … They must jump, and run, and scream, whenever they have a mind to do so' (Rousseau 1763: 47).

Plato further justifies the use of play in education through his dialogues, *Laws* and *The Republic* and believes if children were to become builders, they should *play* at building houses, and the role of the teacher is purely to guide the children through play towards their goals. However, some may argue that this may be seen as a way of controlling children (Theories of Play), while others may argue this has similarities to adult-led activities seen today in early years settings. His work also argues that 'play could be used as a method in education by noting that in Egypt, arithmetical games had been invented for the use of children so they found learning a pleasure and an amusement' (Plato 360 BCE). We see play-based learning as very much a recent form of education, however, it seems that philosophers from as early as Plato had already considered the impact this has on children's learning! Were the Ancient Greeks using innovative ways of learning over 2000 years ago?

Despite advanced thinking in Ancient Greece, it is only in relatively recent years that we have started to truly consider the value of play as a possible natural process for learning.

Research has shown that if you simply 'tell' someone a piece of information, that person will only retain 5 per cent of what you tell them. By actively 'doing' something, this helps us to understand and make sense of it. Children make sense of their world by doing things, and their 'doing' is 'play' which, according to Heseltine (2013: 4), is a developmental process that 'takes place most effectively when we are young'. He believes that this only takes place with young children and not adults who can often misunderstand what 'play' is, mistaking the physical process of an activity for play. For example, Heseltine explains that if a child is building a sandcastle, it could be argued that they are playing. However, the activity is the 'tool which allows the internal conscious and unconscious process, "play", to take place. Therefore there is a fundamental difference between the activity (building the sandcastle) and the process (play). During this, the developing child internalises and processes what they are learning through the activity (Heseltine 2013: 4).

Heseltine's argument is that if an adult were to build a sandcastle with the child, then the processes are slightly different and there are 'clear physical and mental developmental differences between play and recreation' (Heseltine 2013: 4), and unfortunately, this belief of 'adult recreation' being play has resulted in this 'play' being viewed as a frivolous activity. If this is the case, then as an early years educator, it is essential to be able to differentiate clearly between the two.

Gilbert (2013) however, claims that adults *do* need 'play'. Cited in Gilbert's research, play experts Patrick Bateson and Paul Martin suggest there is a strong need for play in the adult workplace and stress the benefits, such as physical and social skills or improved problem-solving abilities. Interestingly, they also point out that 'activities are more likely to be perceived as play (and therefore attractive) rather than work (and therefore unattractive) if they are entered into voluntarily' (Gilbert 2013: 186).

How young children learn

For some considerable time, it was believed that very young children were unable to form complex ideas (Bransford et al. 2004), some held the 'empiricist' view that children are like a blank canvas or 'tabula rasa', a Latin term meaning blank slate, 'on which the record of experience is gradually impressed' (Bransford et al. 2004: 79). This belief was held by many such as Aristotle and the seventeeth-century philosopher John Locke, who said, 'Let us suppose the mind to be, as we say, white paper, void of all characters, without any ideas: How comes it to be furnished? … whence has it all the materials of reason and knowledge? … from experience' (Darling-Hammond et al. 2001: 4). Locke believed that children's minds were ready to be shaped by an accumulation of experiences and perceptions which combine to develop more complex ideas and that education should be the structure for such experiences (Darling-Hammond et al. 2001). Locke, however, was 'no advocate of play, which he considered to be silly and trivial' (Lester and Russell 2008). A later, more controversial view was that of Rousseau in the eighteenth century who believed that it was actually *education* that should be shaped around the child and we should celebrate 'the concept of childhood' and allow children to develop naturally (Darling-Hammond et al. 2001).

Rousseau believed that play was not just liberating, but the right of the child. In his book *Émile, or on education* he discusses the early physical and emotional development of Émile, from infancy through to adulthood. What is of particular interest is his second 'book' which covers the phase of development from age five to twelve. Rousseau firmly believes that during these years education should be derived not so much from books but from the child's interaction with the world. He understood the importance of play which he saw as an 'instrument' for the development of the senses: 'let all the lessons of young children take the form of doing rather than talking, let them learn nothing from books that they can learn from experience' (Rousseau 1763: 101).

It is interesting to note that as Rousseau concludes this chapter, it is evident that as a result of the child's education they use inference and understanding of their physical world to engage with and accomplish a task. It could be argued then that this approach is the precursor of the Montessori method, whereby rather than just 'feeding' young children with information, they learn by doing and engaging in meaningful and purposeful activity.

There have been many other theories of how children learn which have found their way into mainstream educational theory, such as the concepts of constructivism. In terms of play, Jean Piaget believed that children constructed knowledge through play by interacting with objects such as toys and to help them make sense of their world. Piaget believed that play had a strong influence on development, therefore playing an essential role in education. In terms of 'play', Lev Vygotsky developed Piaget's theory further, but placed emphasis on the importance of social interaction and how 'others', such as adults or peers, interacted through play with the child.

The meaning of play

Though we have established the importance of play in learning, there seems 'to be no coherent understanding of "play" within social policy' or a definitive definition within education (Lester and Russell 2008: 2). Andrews (2012) believes that it is the child's approach that defines 'play' and the underlying processes, not the observer's assumptions about the activity.' However, Bruce and Meggitt (1999) believe it can have many different connotations used in different contexts, and, in terms of early years practice 'there is an urgent need to clarify what it means'.

Take the typical dictionary definition of the verb, 'to play', and it is defined as engaging 'in activity for enjoyment and recreation rather than a serious or practical purpose' (Oxford Dictionaries 2013). The verb can also be used with 'at', which in turn, subtly shifts the meaning to become one of more imaginative play, for example if playing at something, this is to 'amuse oneself by engaging in imaginative pretence' such as 'playing at soldiers'. It could be argued then that play is doing what you *want* to do, rather than what you *have* to do and is therefore considered to be the opposite to work, suggesting activities of a more recreational nature rather than educational (Heseletine 2013). Therefore, this has led to much debate as to whether play-based learning should be advocated in the classroom.

Smith and Pellegrini (2008) define 'play' as an activity which is done for its own sake and characterised by means rather than ends. They suggest the *process* holds more importance than the actual goal and the activity is performed for its own sake, not for any external reward. Smith and Pellegrini break play down into different types, each having potential benefits for the child, for example, social play, rough-and-tumble play, object play, pretend play, language play and loco motor play. When using 'pretend play', this allows children to engage with their emotions as they act out and freely express uncertainties and anxieties with objects such as dolls. This helps them to deal with and work towards resolving significant issues, such as divorce, birth and death, in the familiar and secure context of play. Bruce (2011) agrees that during pretend play, many emotions such as a sense of loss and rejection, pride and anger are explored through play, helping children to deal with these anxieties. The benefits of 'loco motor play' which takes place during playtime for example, is also seen to be beneficial, as Smith and Pellegrini suggest young children are much more able to engage in more sedentary tasks following a period of physical activity. This type of play is also a great motivator. Take for example, the New Zealand All Blacks rugby team. Before every match they perform the formidable haka war dance and we can see for ourselves the impact this has on their motivation for playing. The players use both bodies and voices in this 'dance' to prepare and ready their brains for action (Gilbert 2013). Gilbert suggests that by thinking of the brain as a muscle, like any other muscle, it needs to be warmed up before activity. In this case the activity is learning and Gilbert believes that this will ultimately make for effective learning.

Free play in early years

A 2006 report provided information about the value of free play in early years education (Santer et al. 2007). At the heart of the findings are the individual child and the concept of choice and opportunity to make their own decisions. The child is free to use their 'ideas, feelings and relationships that have been experienced, and to apply these to what they know and understand with control, mastery and competence' (Bruce and Meggitt 1999: 241). Play is child-initiated, where the child takes the lead and chooses what, when and how they want to do something, with adults responding to cues from the child. 'Free play has no external goals set by adults and has no adult imposed curriculum' (Santer et al. 2007: xi).).

Children are by nature spontaneous, inquisitive and imaginative explorers that enjoy investigating through a process that comes naturally to them. It is Roussou's (2004) belief that if the environment is enjoyable, varied and challenging, learning is more likely to take place. However, she points out that learning must also be taken seriously through meaningful and challenging tasks and raises concerns about the potential disadvantages of learning through play. Roussou suggests that if learning is seen to be too much fun then children may not take it seriously. For example, if looking at technology-based games, Alan Kay, the pioneering American computer scientist, recognises there is a difference between 'soft fun' such as a computer game where the game does most things for you, and 'hard fun' where the child learns to play a musical instrument 'rather than just listening to it', which in turn, encourages the child 'to stretch and grow' (1998, cited in Roussou 2004). Therefore, it could be argued that computer-based learning may have its flaws. However, Malone and Lepper (1987, cited in Roussou 2004) disagree and suggest there *is* opportunity for learning through these types of games in terms of motivation, engagement and interactivity, and 'consider games as providers of intrinsic motivations for learning'. In the words of DeVries et al. (cited in Shipley 2013: 14), 'we need to develop a way of thinking that helps us distinguish what is of educational benefit to children and what is not'.

In terms of learning, the familiarity of play provides the opportunity and freedom to practise in a safe and unpressurised environment where children can begin to put into practice what they already know. Children are expected and 'allowed' to 'repeat, rehearse and refine skills, displaying what they do know and practising what they are beginning to understand' (Tucker 2010), these are all characteristics of child-initiated play. Play helps children to 'function at their highest level' while also performing an essential role in helping children to build relationships with others by teaching them how to take turns, to listen, to empathise, and so become more aware of others and their feelings, (DCSF 2009: 14). Play is described as a 'coordinating network of developmental and learning strategies' where 12 features of play are identified (see below). When all or most of these features are present and are coordinated, this develops more of a free flow character to become 'free-flow play' (Bruce 1999, cited in Forbes 2004).

Twelve features of play

1 In play, children use first-hand experiences that they have in life.
2 Children make up rules as they play and so keep control of their play.
3 Children make play props
4 Children choose to play – they cannot be made to play.
5 Children rehearse the future in their role play.
6 Children pretend when they play.

(Continued)

(Continued)

 7 Children sometimes play alone.
 8 Children and/or adults play together, in parallel, associatively, or cooperatively in pairs or groups.
 9 Each player has a personal play agenda, though they may not be aware of this.
10 Children playing will be deeply involved and difficult to distract from their deep learning. Children at play wallow in their learning.
11 Children try out their most recent learning, skills and competences when they play. They seem to celebrate what they know.
12 Children at play coordinate their ideas, feelings and make sense of relationships with their families, friends and culture.

(Developed from Bruce 2011)

For this play process to be effective, Bruce stresses that it is essential for play to be well coordinated. Adequate time needs to be provided and free choice of activity so that their play is self-motivated and voluntary. By allowing this, play begins to flow and the complexity of learning will grow as they begin to explore, experiment and interact with others. These activities are intended to provide experiences to help the child begin to understand the world around them. According to Bruce, 'when the process of play is rich, it can lead children into creating rich products in their stories, paintings, dances, music making, drawings, sculptures and constructions, or in the solving of scientific and mathematical problems' (Bruce 2001, cited in QCA 2008: 46).

〰️ Reflection point

- During free play, what strategies have you used to develop and deepen meaningful play to ensure higher levels of thinking?
- What experiences have you provided for the children to apply what they have been learning?

The importance of learning through play

Brunton and Thornton (2010) look at the benefits of using play as a developmental tool with young children. For young children, play is their work which engages their minds and develops knowledge, skills and understanding. During play, children take control of their own learning by making choices, exploring and taking risks, which in turn builds confidence in their abilities and belief in themselves as learners. They are more willing to 'have a go' and put into practice skills learned, transferring the learning acquired in one play context to another. 'Where learning is secure it is likely that children often initiate the use of that learning' (Standards and Testing Agency 2012: 10).

In 2011, it was recommended by the Tickell enquiry into early years education that 'playing and exploring, active learning, and creating and thinking critically, are highlighted ... as three characteristics of effective teaching and learning, describing how children learn across a wide range of activities' (p. 27). These characteristics of effective learning are seen to play a central role in learning and feature across early years through to the first year of primary school, underpinning all seven areas of learning and development in the Early Years Foundation stage. The report states that a play-based approach 'combined with instructional yet playful teaching' (p. 28) clearly helps children to develop the skills to become good learners, such as being flexible and adaptive. Areas of learning are to be 'delivered through planned, purposeful play' adopting a flexible approach that takes into account the individual developmental needs of every child (Tickell 2011: 28). Learning through play is seen to be a balance between child-initiated learning and adult-led learning, but what exactly does that mean?

Shipley (2013: 14) warns that a potential barrier to using play may be 'the tendency of early childhood educators to rely on abstract notions of play to justify and describe their play-oriented curriculum [which] ... include vague, general statements to justify the play-oriented curriculum and vague characterisations to describe play in early childhood education'.

Child-initiated learning

A self initiated activity is an activity wholly decided on by the child and is the result of an intrinsic motivation to explore a project, or express an idea. In doing this the child may make use of a variety of resources and demonstrate a complex range of knowledge, skills and understanding. (Qualifications and Curriculum Authority 2008: 9)

Children are much more likely to be motivated to join in an activity if it is something that they themselves have chosen to do and are more likely to persevere, even when faced with failure. It encourages them to develop thinking skills and they are more likely to learn if allowed to make their own mistakes. If and when they do succeed, there is a real sense of achievement. As part of child-initiated learning, children plan what to do, review and share ideas with others. Discussing how to solve problems helps them to see mistakes and difficulties as challenges not failures.

The role of the adult

'You can discover more about a person in an hour of play than in a year of conversation.' (D'Angour 2013 p.293)

Though writing hundreds of years ago, Plato was accurate when he made this point, and observation by an adult is very much a key part of the structure of an early years setting today.

Vygotsky recognised the important role that both adults and peers play when helping children to develop new ideas and skills with his concept of the 'zone of proximal development'. He suggests that children will learn subjects more effectively just beyond their range of existing experience and knowledge if they are supported by another adult or peer. This will then bridge that distance from what they know or can do independently and what they can do or know with assistance (Schunk 2012). In an early years setting, adults and children are very much considered as 'critical partners who work together and support the child's learning process' (Jaeckle 2008).

Adults work alongside the children to extend the children's thinking and understanding by listening to the language they use, then carefully introducing new vocabulary as part of the play; observing the children at play and intervening if either invited by the child to do so, or to prevent play becoming repetitive or superficial during free-flow activities. They also model being a learner themselves by talking out loud. Adults are then able to plan and provide suitable learning environments and resources for play to facilitate the children's experiences (Lester and Russell 2008). This supports and extends learning by building on the children's ideas, observed during play, and also by using what the children already know.

Some adult-led sessions may be needed to introduce materials, objects or skills in a real-life experience, such as gardening, so that children can then use these experiences in their own play. While this approach of learning through play is recognised as useful, it is also important that there is a balance of both adult-directed activities and child-initiated activities that can be guided by adults. As (Tickell 2011: 29) states in her report, 'when working with young children, the exchange between adults and children should be fluid, moving interchangeably between activities initiated by children and adult responses helps build the child's learning and understanding', so that the child is still able to make their own choices and decisions.

The role of the adult is clearly still an essential one, whether it be to guide, model or engage in talk about a new skill or discovery, during and after play, or to carefully plan the learning environment and resources.

 Classroom case study

Scenario 1

Some five-year-old children are playing with a tap and rusty old bucket outside. They are throwing in mud, dead leaves and some sand from the outdoor area. A teacher sees them and tells them to stop making a mess, to tidy things up and come back to the table activity they were given.

 Reflection point

- Reflect on a similar situation that you have observed in your school.
- Consider how you could have approached this differently.
- What could the learning outcomes have been instead?

The outdoor environment

Let him be taken out daily into the open meadow. There, let him run and frolic and fall down a hundred times a day; so much the better, for by this means he will learn the sooner to pick himself up. (Rousseau 1763: 43–44)

 Classroom case study

Scenario 2

Some five-year-old children are playing with a tap and rusty old bucket outside. They are throwing in mud, dead leaves and some sand from the outdoor area. A teacher sees them and tells them to stop making a mess, to tidy things up and come back to the table activity they were given.

(Continued)

(Continued)

However, the teaching assistant has been thinking about how she could develop the children's talk and understanding of story. Rather than stopping them in their tracks she decides to dress up as an old witch and bring a big spoon outside with her.

'Hubble, bubble, toil and trouble.' She stirs the magic soup the children have made.

She 'tastes' the soup and turns into a Giant who can see beyond the moon. One by one the children 'taste' the soup. One turns into a terrifying dragon, another becomes a lonely swan, another a monster who eats computers ... and so on. Each time the teaching assistant takes a photo with an iPad. In a following lesson, the teacher helps the children to produce a short story with a beginning, a middle and an end based on their 'magic soup' character.

Research and evidence has shown that the use of the outdoor environment plays a key role in children's development and learning. Friedrich Froebel, who was heavily influenced by the work of Rousseau, compares the use of the outdoor environment as venturing into a new and different world (Santer et al. 2007). He saw play as one of the highest forms of learning and in particular, recognised that outdoor play should be valued and not seen as a risk (Tovey 2012). Froebel recognised that it offered numerous opportunities for challenge and adventure and the unpredictable and changing nature of an outdoor environment, due to weather and seasons, this would encourage and develop children's natural curiosity (Lilley 1967).

Children become more deeply engaged in their learning and play when they have the freedom to explore and experiment in a controlled and safe environment (Jaeckle 2008). It is stated very clearly in England's Early Years Curriculum that careful planning should ensure, where possible, indoor and outdoor environments are linked so that children are able to move freely between the two (DfE 2012). In the Reggio Emilia approach, founded by Loris Malaguzzi, educators believe the child 'is eager to interact with and contribute to the world' (Learning and Teaching Scotland 2006: 7), and therefore, the environment is often referred to as the third teacher in their approach (Jaeckle 2008). For the benefit of both the children's development and learning, it is crucial then that the educator provides environments where children are allowed to explore.

We all remember the excitement of going outdoors for a lesson at school, but how often did this realistically happen? Most schools have somewhere that could be used for learning outside, even if it is just the playground, so why are they not used more often? Is it the fear of children hurting themselves, the weather, behaviour? Or is it because we live in fear of health and safety regulations or risk assessment? Shouldn't we be allowing children to take a risk, to be allowed to explore and test their own boundaries? Froebel sums up why we should let children take those risks: 'it is the boy who does not know his strength and the demands made on it who is likely to venture beyond his experience and run into unsuspected danger' (Lilley 1967: 126). Claxton (2007) agrees and believes that taking risks is all part of a tool kit to become effective learners and allows children to try new and different ways of doing things, rather than keeping with the same, safe way of doing something. We know that children like to test and push their own limits, particularly when they have the freedom and joy of outdoors, climbing that little bit higher, running that bit faster, willing to take more of a risk. So we need to ask how we can transfer this 'willingness to take a risk' indoors, into other activities such as writing or maths. If we could recreate such an environment indoors that is challenging, adventurous and children recognise that they *can* take risks, would children achieve better results?

Look at the two examples below.

Example 1

A two-year-old sets off into the garden with a bundle of clothes pegs. Finding some tall plant stems he sets about trying to fix the clothes pegs to each stem. On finding a thistle he recoils his hand in surprise at the sharp prickles but immediately touches it again, fascinated and joyous at the new experience.

Example 2

A mixed age group of children in a workplace nursery enjoyed playing on a rope swing. They soon discovered that if they twisted the rope round and then let go, the swing, with a child inside, rotated at great speed.

(Tovey 2012)

Reflection point

Research has shown that if you overly protect children from risk, they are not as well equipped to deal with situations. Children are active and proficient learners who should not be treated as passive or helpless. We need to be able to trust them, not underestimate them (Tovey 2012).

(Continued)

(Continued)

- Are you overly protective with your learners?
- How could you use the outdoor environment in a similar way to the above examples?

It is clear that an element of innovation is required to skilfully and carefully plan environments and materials that can be combined creatively, to not only provide children with appropriate opportunities for challenge for their individual stage of development, but to also allow them to safely take risks so that they learn. Claxton (2007) said earlier that risk-taking is part of the 'learner's toolkit', so as educators, we need to see taking risks as a 'pathway to learning as children learn effectively from discovering what works well and what does not' (Education Scotland 2009).

To finish, and for a moment of reflection, consider this quote from 1967 with reference to the nineteenth-century philosopher, Froebel:

A well-planned outdoor area has pathways, hiding areas, tunnels, concealed entrances and exits which invite exploration and a sense of adventure. A rich outdoor area offers infinite possibilities for challenge and adventure, and the chance to discover or create what Froebel referred to as 'new worlds'. (Lilley 1967: 126)

Chapter summary

- Play-based learning is a complex and well-debated subject and findings both justify and strengthen the argument for a play-based curriculum.
- Characteristics of effective learning are seen as playing and exploring; active learning; and creating and thinking critically. These play a fundamental role in learning.
- Children's brains are not pre-programmed genetically and can be shaped through play by a process of developing multisensory networks of neurons that enable learning.
- The benefits of play are recognised from as early as the Ancient Greek philosophers who understood the benefits and impact of play-based learning.
- The meaning of 'play' is widely debated amongst philosophers, educators and researchers. There is no one defining answer.

- The value of free play in the early years setting has been recognised to be of immense benefit to the individual learner. However, it requires careful and thoughtful planning so that learners are immersed in rich experiences.
- When learning is secure, children will transfer new skills and knowledge from one play context into another.
- Children are much more likely to be motivated to learn, persevere, show resilience when faced with failure and develop problem-solving skills if they are involved in the planning and choice of activity.
- The role of the adult should be to move interchangeably between activities initiated by children and adult responses to develop the child's learning.
- The use of the outdoor environment plays a key role in children's development and learning. Children become more deeply engaged in their learning and play when they have the freedom to explore and experiment in a safe environment.

Further reading and research

Bruce, T. (2011). *Learning through Play: Babies, Toddlers and the Foundation Years*, 2nd edn. London: Hodder Education.

Chilvers, D. (2012). *Playing to Learn: A Guide to Child-led Play and its Importance for Thinking and Learning*. London: ATL, the education union.

Lindon, J. (2010). *Understanding Child Development – Linking Theory and Practice*, 2nd edn. London: Hodder Education.

CHAPTER 4

THE DEVELOPMENT OF CHILDREN'S THINKING SKILLS – LINKS TO THEORY AND INNOVATION

Chapter guide

In this chapter you will learn about:

- Key concepts in the development of thinking
- Learning through problem-solving
- Thinking and talk
- Thinking and reading

Introduction

It is often agreed that 'man's search for meaning is the primary motivation in his life' (Frankl 1959: 105), but the current obsession with school accountability and testing in many countries does nothing to sustain the child and teacher striving together for meaning. For instance, tests and league tables are unlikely in themselves to sustain an education for creativity and higher order thinking. This chapter will explain what we mean by the development of higher-order thinking: in particular, there will be a discussion of problem-solving and how to develop effective forms of thinking which will enable children to improve their learning in all areas of the curriculum.

There are many excellent primers on children's cognition and the various stages of development such as Smith et al. (2003); and it would be beyond the scope of this book to present a generalised introduction to the development of thinking and cognition in children. However, there are some important aspects of thinking in innovative teaching and learning which will be covered in this chapter:

- Developing thinking and problem-solving is an active process in the child, whereby new experiences and information can lead to a change in the organisation of information in the learner. This reconstruction of knowledge has led to this approach to learning being called 'constructivism'. Various versions have ensued: for example, social constructivism (Bruner) and sociocognitivism (Zimmerman).
- Learning is essentially a social process emphasised in theoretical models such as those of Bruner and Vygotsky.
- Motivation and confidence in the classroom underpins effective learning: anxiety can significantly impair interpretation and decision-making.
- Teachers can influence the child in being more effective in solving problems and in applying their thinking in different aspects of the curriculum: classroom behaviour can also be seen as a social aspect of problem-solving.
- Being explicit about decisions in problem-solving is an important skill for teachers, to enable children to build their understanding of otherwise obscure aspects of thinking.
- Memory works at the short- and long-term level, but in the classroom working memory is very important. For example, working memory allows the holding of information in the mind, to be processed for reasoning and comprehension especially. In reading comprehension and mathematical problems this is very important.

Memory and decision-making are all bound up in the organisation and operation of a child's thinking. This can be more or less organised. Richard Bowman (2011) illustrates this with John Steinbeck's book *Cannery Row*. Steinbeck (1945: 34) wrote of the reluctance of one of his characters to try to think about things: 'it meant casting around in his mind for an answer and casting about in Hazel's mind was like wandering alone in a deserted museum. Hazel's mind was choked with uncatalogued exhibits. He never forgot anything but he never bothered to arrange his memories.'

Reflection point

Do you have any children in class who appear to have disorganised thinking like Hazel in *Cannery Row*?
What does it mean for a child to have organised thinking?

Wang and Peverley (1987) explain that organising the information in your thinking means that new information is integrated with previous learning and that the original information can be retrieved at will and used in a range of different contexts. Organisation is therefore a very important step in the learning process. As children develop in the early years and primary school, the knowledge they learn goes through a number of transformations. How this thinking develops will be explained next.

Key concepts in the development of children's thinking

There has always been a debate about the role of nature and nurture in the development of children's thinking. Children are born, their brains develop and as they develop most children's thinking also develops. While understanding of the role of the brain in thinking has improved in recent years (Yilmaz 2011), models of the relationship between thinking and the role of the brain are still speculative. For instance, Yilmaz (2011) identifies common understanding of the role of the front part of the brain in reasoning. Blanchette and Richards (2010) suggest that anxiety in learners is associated with activity in the section of the brain known as the amygdala, which is involved in memory activities. Emotion interacts with four types of processes: basic attentional effects; priming of concepts and knowledge structures; computational capacity; and reflective processes.

The brain is therefore a connected and complex whole. Activity in one part of the brain can have an impact on another part of the brain. So, for example, anxiety can have a limiting effect on memory. Anxiety leads to more threatening interpretations in a learning task. According to Blanchette and Richards (2010) anxiety increases perceptions that there will be future negative events, and risk aversion in decision-making. This paints a portrait of anxiety as a state where information processing is focused on identifying potential threats and minimising potential negative outcomes. Research on fear content and reasoning strategies is consistent with this pattern (Blanchette and Richards 2010). The effects of sadness appear to be rather different. Here it would be interesting to compare our understanding of sadness and depression. They suggest that sadness does seem to induce more careful and systematic processing, which is sometimes beneficial and sometimes not.

When it comes to learning, cognition and emotion are inextricably linked. Likewise the brain is wired to respond to the social dimensions of learning. Rock (2010) gives a rather strong representation of the brain as a 'social organ', in which physiological and neurological reactions are profoundly shaped by social interaction in the classroom'. Students, who are harshly reprimanded, for example, experience it as a 'neural response, as powerful and painful as a blow to the head'. This is very important for young children. In Chapter 3, attachment theory was introduced to explain how early social bonds, the patterns of relationship building between young children and their caregivers, impact on the learner's approach to new activities later in life. According to Buber (1958) 'it is relationship which educates'. A sense of relatedness is central to sustaining a healthy, productive classroom environment. Rock (2010) explains that 'group punishments, for instance such as unexpectedly denying a class the opportunity to engage in social interaction on the playground, predictably arouse a threat response in the brain, activating the same neurochemicals that flood the system when one is subjected to physical pain' (Rock 2010: 95). On a more positive alternative, story has a powerful impact on the listener. A funny story from the teacher can raise the morale of the class, which can result in the brain secreting the hormone oxytocin, which disarms threat responses. Reducing levels of threat enables the areas of the brain associated with memory to work more effectively. Working memory is an important aspect of the learning process; hence the importance of developing positive relationships in class, from a purely cognitive point of view. Miller (2011) explains how recent research into cognition and memory has important implications for the teacher.

Short-term memory allows an individual, for example, to store information heard (numbers in a calculation) or seen (letters on the page). The information which can be stored is quite limited unless stored in a different way. Typically, that is why most countries have phone numbers with less than six numbers and that any additional codes or combination of numbers are learned as a separate group. However, short-term memory plays a limited role in most real-world memory tasks and should therefore not be a major concern when planning for learning.

Working memory is important in holding information from different sources, so that the brain can use it for the purposes of understanding. For instance, holding phonological information from the decoding of individual letters to eventually read words is the process we call 'decoding' in phonics. Especially for young learners, as for everyone, even asking someone to juggle two things simultaneously may be pushing the limits of cognitive capacity.

Attention is central to learning and memory. Relevance and purpose of the learning activities will affect the attention paid by the learner. For example, a young child may be fascinated by the opportunity to explore the different qualities of water in the natural environment, while an older child may be fascinated to sit for an hour reading the latest Harry Potter book. Without attention, there is no memory. Varying the type and sensory modality of learning activities may be helpful, not as a way of matching student learning styles but rather as a way of promoting attention and engagement across learners in general.

Piaget (1952) talked about the important stage of egocentrism in early childhood. There is a qualitative difference in children's thinking compared with adults' thinking. At an early age, Piaget believed that children see the world from their own subjective point of view. Their understanding of the world is purely subjective because they cannot see the world from another person's perspective. Donaldson (1978) challenged this view, saying that the nature of experiments to investigate egocentrism are framed in quite formal, 'disembedded' contexts apart from the real world of the child. By locating activities in a context more familiar to the child, they are able to demonstrate much more sophisticated forms of thinking than were originally suggested by Piaget's 'stages of development'. Fascinatingly, the early years practitioner Dunn (2004) explains that very young children and babies are capable of empathy, friendship and even a sense of humour! An alternative explanation in Baron-Cohen et al. (1985) suggested that most children develop a theory of their own mind and other minds, such that they are able to understand the intentions of others. Typically, in children diagnosed with autism, the child's theory of mind can be absent or at least so focused on themselves that they are unable to interpret the world from another's point of view. This is such a central psychological mechanism, that its absence can severely impact on learning and day-to-day living. Interpretation of the world around is very difficult, where only literal information can be processed. The nuances of facial expression and the intention behind those expressions all weigh heavily in autism. For all children interpretation is an important part of thinking.

Learning through problem-solving

Problem-solving is a real-world application of thinking, reasoning, judgement, and decision-making in all learners. This can be in subject, formal and school-type situations: with a problem presented to a child. For instance, a worded mathematical problem might involve interpretation of words, identification of the numerical problem and computation of the mathematical solution. More informal problems are encountered in everyday life although there is certainly something qualitatively different about them. A young person wants to go and see a football match; and they want their parents to take them as there is no bus to the city, and in any case it would take too much effort; so they need to work out if there is enough time on a Friday night after school to get there. While the first mathematical problem appears to rest more squarely on formal cognitive problem-solving, the second example involves a combination of cognitive, social and emotional problems. Arguably the second is a more realistic problem because it depends more on the individual's purpose. While the first is a 'presented' problem the second is a 'discovered' problem.

Sternberg (2006) explains the steps in problem-solving:

1. Recognise or identify the problem
2. Define and represent the problem mentally
3. Develop a solution strategy
4. Organise his or her knowledge about the problem
5. Allocate mental or physical resources to solve the problem
6. Monitor progress towards the goal
7. Evaluate the solution for accuracy

The problem with many school-based problems is that they are 'school problems': presented by the teacher, chosen by the teacher, relevant to the teacher, assessed and evaluated by the teacher. A real-life discovered problem is more difficult because it requires the learner to identify the problem; but in doing so this is likely to be a problem more relevant to the learner. If a child has experienced failure in problem-solving, there may be little desire to take the first steps in identifying the problem to be solved. This reflects an issue of agency, as explained in Chapter 2. Boud et al. (1985) explain that in approaching a problem a pupil is likely to think about possible demands that will be made on them by the forthcoming activity. Knowledge about the activity is social, emotional and cognitive in the structure suggested by Sternberg. Finally, evaluating a solution for the problem, the learner will remember the costs and benefits at a social, emotional and affective level that will serve as a pool for future problem-solving.

Powell and Makin (1994) explain that this requires a different way of looking at problem-solving. Essentially the teacher tried to get pupils to relearn a view of problem-solving situations in which they became the significant actors and the task became the context within which they operated. So, for example, the teacher needed to stress what the pupil had done and draw attention to what that pupil had achieved and learnt, e.g. 'So you learnt some of the advantages of using string to measure and some of the disadvantages ... you learned from the things that went wrong didn't you?'

Reflection

What words would you use to encourage children to take control of problem-solving?

How will you model the steps in problem-solving?

How do you feel about children taking greater control of the problem-solving task?

Some examples of how to do this are outlined below:

1   Face-to-face. Place yourself between children and get on their eye level. Speak calmly and respond in a gentle manner.
2   Recognition. 'You look very angry.'
3   Inquire. 'I want each of you to tell me what happened.'
4   Echo. 'John, you are saying that Chris took the tricycle away from you.' 'Chris, you are saying that John doesn't want to share the trike with you.'
5   Negotiate. 'John wants to let you ride the tricycle for 10 minutes, and then he can ride it for 10 minutes.'
6   Down time. 'Great! You solved the problem.' Follow up to make sure the problem has been solved.

Lamm et al. (2010)

Powell and Jordan (1993) describe a pupil's inability to take a next step in a particular sequence and suggest that what he lacked was a sense of trust in his own judgement of what to do next rather than a lack of knowledge or skill. Similarly, in one episode during their study one child stopped work entirely when she came to what she interpreted as an 'end point', whereas two others carried on beyond what they fully understood on the basis of a cooperatively made decision. Involving children in their own learning is a powerful motivating factor. While many school characteristics affect learners' performance, a significant one is the extent to which pupils feel that they have control over their own learning. We reiterate here the importance of social and emotional factors in thinking.

Successful problem-solving involves ensuring a match between the nature of the problem, how it is presented, or discovered, and the tools by which it may be solved. Csikszentmihalyi states that 'people are most highly energized about their work when their mix of skills closely matches their individual and team-work challenges' (Katzenbach 2006: 62). Csikszentmihalyi called that balanced state of interaction as 'flow'. This is 'a highly energized state of intense concentration coupled with a seemingly intoxicating sense of personal causation'.

Bowman (1982: 16) illustrates this in an analysis of students' personal video games. He says that both academically engaging classrooms and video game systems exhibit a common, unmistakable ethos or ambiance (flow in action).

Bowman (1982) explains that an inspiring activity for problem-solving, like a child's experience of playing video games, involves:

- clarity of task;
- clear awareness of participant roles and responsibilities;
- choice in the selection and execution of problem-solving strategies;
- potentially balanced systems of skills and challenges;
- a progressive hierarchy of challenges to sustain interest.

Moreover, each reflects:

- unambiguous feedback;
- affirmation of the instructiveness of error;
- seemingly infinite opportunities for self-improvement;
- provision for active involvement in tasks which are rooted in the high probability of success;
- freedom from fear of reprisal, ridicule, or rejection;
- an overarching recognition of the need for learners to enjoy what they experience in the classrooms of life.

 Reflection point

Analyse an activity you have recently undertaken with a group of children in school. How does it match the above criteria?

Plan an activity with children, to be led by children and following the characteristics set out above.

What were the benefits and challenges of this approach from your point of view and from the children's point of view?

Schools in most countries exist in a state of tension caused by competing priorities. There is the need to develop basic skills in children so that they perform well in public examinations and tests; while also engaging children in interesting, motivating activities in the classroom. Simply, the reality in many schools is keeping both the authorities happy and children happy. The classroom reality is that Csikszentmihalyi's concept of flow may not be that evident in many lessons. Some would argue that schools are never going to be the best place for children to be inspired to learn in such an all-consuming way. So what does this mean for classroom teachers? What have we learned about problem-solving that teachers can put into practice to further engage children in more stimulating and purposeful learning? One approach builds on the notion of problem-solving in the classroom.

'Problem-based learning' is commonly used in professional learning in universities: for instance, in medicine to develop active learning which is relevant to learners in an authentic context. It emphasises the active participation of learners often organised in groups. The role of the teacher is quite different. On the one hand they move away from being an expert with the learner as novice, to being a facilitator of learning. Where the solution is unknown, the teacher can actually become part of the problem-solving group, so long as they do not stray back into their usual teaching role. The sequence typically involves identifying the problem, checking for what the learners already know about the problem, and establishing what they need to know to resolve the problem. In schools teachers will be aware of KWL grids which can be used for examining any topic:

K – what do you know about a topic?;
W – what do you want to learn about the topic?;
L – what have you learned about the topic at the end of the activity?

In order to accomplish the problem-based learning activity, students are divided into groups. Of course, if groups are to be more than just a collection of individuals, then the roles which individuals take on in the group must be discussed and shared out appropriately. Choosing a problem is an important step. If we are to avoid the issue of presented problems which lack authenticity, then it is important that learners feel that they have some control in the choice of the problem. Identifying what is known, what information is needed, and what strategies or next steps should be taken is an important point at which the teacher should be involved. Sweller (1988) argues that the domain-specific knowledge required to complete many problem-based learning activities is too high for learners to be successful. He suggests that the strategies for completing a task (often referred to as 'schema') or ways of thinking around problem-solving are often quite dependent on the context. What sets the expert apart from the novice is that they have a wealth of experience of different contexts and the schemas relating to different problems. Modelling of possible solutions, tools and strategies for solving a particular problem can help to avoid some of the criticisms of problem-based learning. Modelling can involve a range of cognitive, social and emotional tools:

Reflection point

In what way can teachers successfully model aspects of the problem-based learning?

- By establishing a classroom environment which facilitates problem-solving: for instance, classroom displays which model new vocabulary in the topic and 'what next?' suggestions for dealing with barriers to completing the activity.
- By modelling language appropriate for the task: for instance, language to explore, suggest and hypothesise.
- By modelling with other adults important roles within the problem-based learning context: for instance, a reader, a writer, a negotiator, a researcher for new information.

This list is not exhaustive but it should set you thinking about the way you can address the challenges of problem-based learning through explicit modelling.

As can be seen from the above, the classroom itself is a useful resource in facilitating learning in solving problems. At a certain level, problem-based learning starts with unstructured play at home, and is then developed through child-initiated activities for learning in school in the early years. Only then does the more formal problem-based learning become evident. However, it is clear that control and direction are principal factors. There are similar, more child-focused, approaches to learning which will be explained in the following sections. At each stage, the classroom environment can facilitate problem-based learning with authentic role-play settings, displays of relevant vocabulary which might be used in tasks, access to the Internet so that children can use the available resources when they need to. Wi-fi-enabled tablet computers are an excellent tool for doing this. The important thing is that children should have a range of resources available so that they can make choices for what they want to use and when. Language is a very important resource for thinking. Indeed Vygotsky (1978) sees this as being central to the development of thinking. Along with more recent theorists, such as Robin Alexander, the role of language in the classroom, and in particular its use by both children and teachers, has come under the spotlight as an important resource for developing thinking. Alexander suggests that different ways of using talk in class are central if children are to develop 'cognitive power' through talk and reading.

In the remainder of this chapter we will explore how talk and reading are important ways to develop thinking. The challenge for us as teachers and adults is to examine our role in the development of thinking in the self-regulating learner. Creativity and innovation are again central themes.

Thinking and talk

Alexander (2006) argues that talk in the form of dialogue builds 'cognitive power'. This echoes the social nature of thinking. As Vygotsky (1978) explained, psychological processes first develop through sociological processes. We develop thinking of the world through our interactions with others. In that sense, all thinking is rooted in a dialogue with the world. Even when we experience the world seemingly alone, it is the cultural patterns of thinking and ways of experiencing the world that shape the process. How teachers and adults achieve this in class is the focus of research by Wegerif (2005). Like Alexander (2006) and Mercer (1987), Wegerif (2005) attaches great importance to talk as the vehicle for developing thinking and learning in the classroom. Talk can be classified into different types:

- **Playful talk** supports relationships that are an important part of achieving the task. Yonge and Stables (1998) question the idea that it is 'off-task' talk, arguing that it has an important social, emotional and communicative function.
- **Cumulative talk** is focused on group identity, with sharing and a desire to understand each other but without any critical challenges.
- **Disputational talk** is focused on individualised identity so that argument is seen as a competition which each seeks to win.
- **Exploratory talk** goes beyond group or individual identity towards the process of shared inquiry, allowing critical challenges and explicit reasoning within a cooperative framework.

Talk of itself is useful, serving a range of purposes, all of which support the learning process. Wegerif (2005) focuses on a particular aspect of talk for learning, known as exploratory talk. This is the talk which Alexander (2004: 32) considers to be important in developing 'cognitive power'. The teacher's role is considered to be central. Their role is to structure questions which provoke thoughtful answers. The teacher is not asking questions just to elicit a closed set of responses which conform to a prescribed body of knowledge. In dialogic teaching answers provoke further questions and are seen as the building blocks of dialogue rather than its terminal point. If the development of thinking is a social process of guided construction, effective individual teacher–pupil and pupil–pupil exchanges are chained into coherent lines of enquiry rather than left stranded and disconnected. The point Alexander (2004) makes is often made by early years educationalists and drama theorists such as Dorothy Heathcote (Wagner 1999). A teacher's questioning can stifle children's thinking even when this is through open-questioning if it does not build on the child's perspective: when intent is clearly on children being led to a perceived teacher view on a topic or an answer (Phillips 2013). This per- haps mirrors other work on the teacher's role in developing motivation. Bowman (2011: 118) suggests that the 'Question has moved from how to motivate students' to 'how can educators be deterred from diminishing – even destroying – intrinsic student motivation and classroom morale through unpro- ductive policies and practices?' In this perspective, learning is seen as a natural faculty, perhaps subject to certain classroom pedagogies which effect redistri- bution of the control of learning in such a way as to diminish the role of the learner in the construction of knowledge.

Mercer and Sams (2006) talk about the role of the teacher in guiding (but not controlling) the child in constructing their knowledge of a particular area through talk. A good teacher explores a topic with the children through oppor- tunities afforded in the lesson through discussion. Is a statement true, unclear or even wrong? Experiences in, and beyond, the classroom are starting points for discussions. The teacher's role in developing thinking through talk there- fore is centred on:

- Providing children with guidance and practice in using language for reasoning that will enable them to use language more effectively as a tool for working on problems together;
- Improving the quality of children's use of language for reasoning together, which will improve their individual learning and understanding of a topic;
- The teacher as an important model and guide for pupils' use of language for reasoning.

While the work of Mercer and his colleagues frequently focused on children's learning in science and mathematics, their work is relevant to all aspects of learning. In practical terms, teaching children to think for themselves is a subtle process. Ultimately, the teacher can open up thinking through dialogue or close it down through protracted teacher-dominated questioning. Many dif- ferent thinking routines have been developed which target different types of thinking. Examples include:

- 'Think–Pair–Share' (reasoning and explanation);
- 'See–Think–Wonder' (exploring interesting things);
- 'What makes you say that?' (interpretation with justification).

In the following example, we explore in more detail a practical approach which aids children in accessing their prior knowledge: making their prior knowledge visible through talk.

 Classroom case study

Making thinking visible

Inspired by the Buzan (1993) quote: 'The only barrier to the expression and application of all our mental applications is our knowledge of how to access them' (p. 35), I began my journey with the analogy of the 'filing cabinet' with the aim of developing a powerful tool for the transference of skills from one year level to the next. Documents/information stored in a filing cabinet is labelled for quick retrieval. By using this analogy with the children, I help them to visualise where our learning for each day goes and to understand that knowledge is never lost, but rather that it is always retrievable because it has just been 'filed away'. Indeed, I have also created a cartoon depiction of a filing cabinet in our brains and display this, on one of the classroom walls, as a visual prompt for the children. I then discuss the process of reusing information (prior knowledge) at different stages of the day to allow for retention of information or skills. So children understand that when we learn something, we need to file it away in the Filing Cabinet in our brains for future use, perhaps in the next year level and maybe beyond; they also understand they can keep adding to a file by retrieving the information already stored and building upon it, making the file larger and more detailed (Colcott et al. 2009).

In the last example, the teacher used a metaphor of the filing cabinet to aid children's understanding of the role of memory in learning. This act of visualisation is made possible by the teacher's explanation of the metaphor. In this case the metaphor is explained through the teacher talk, but older children often enter the social and cultural knowledge landscape through reading. While it is not the objective of this book to explore the processes by which reading develops, it is suggested that reading itself provides a powerful contribution to the development of thinking.

Thinking and reading

There is much discussion around the process by which children are taught to read (Flynn and Stainthorp 2006). Typically there is much research for or against ways to promote a particular approach to decoding text: for instance, systematic synthetic phonics has been in vogue in many schools in recent years. Less clear is the approach to developing reading comprehension in many schools. Yeh and Lai (2012) suggest that students who demonstrate accuracy and fluency (as measured by speed) with reading but struggle with comprehension are often able to navigate undetected through schools by, as Tovani (2000) states, 'fake reading'. Fake readers rely on class discussions and lectures to glean information. However, this frequently invisible group of students is not actually gaining the long-term skills needed for success in life.

 Reflection point: beyond decoding, readers as thinkers

Consider your own experiences of teaching children who appear to be good readers.
   Focus on one child. How good is the child at:

- decoding the text?
- understanding the text?
- understanding a range of vocabulary?
- applying their knowledge of the world to infer the meaning in the text?

There is considerable pressure to measure children's reading performance based on their ability to read a book accurately. Decoding however often develops in advance of understanding, so it is even more important that the teacher plans for the teaching of reading comprehension.

Reading comprehension is important for developing thinking and draws on many of the processes inherent in language comprehension. Reading for meaning involves mastery of a range of vocabulary, inference and verbal reasoning. For example, comprehension involves literal and inferential understanding: inferential understanding involves understanding meaning beyond the words of the immediate text. This involves understanding the words, and then by drawing on understanding of the world around us through a process of verbal reasoning skills to make an informed analysis of what has not been said by the writer. Written language is often more sophisticated in grammatical structure, purpose, vocabulary, compared with the oral language in the learning of younger and less able children. This is important because the ability to access more sophisticated texts allows the reader to access more sophisticated language. More sophisticated language allows the writer to express more sophisticated ideas either more efficiently or in different ways. Reading involves the application of skills in different contexts, for example, in relation to different genres of texts. This may be important as a cultural tool (Bruner 1996). Reading is not only a powerful tool to access new forms of knowledge; it also allows culture to mould thinking in a culturally mediated way. In a very specific way, as Wittgenstein (1953) suggests meaning is use. By accessing the written language of books, the reader is guided or channelled to an understanding by the writer, through a dialogue with the text. Of course, reading a book is just as much an act of great pleasure as it is an induction into new and existing worlds. Parks (2011) explains that the intense pleasure associated with reading involves the weaving of a spell of 'enchantment': from the Latin, *incantare*, to sing or to chant. The opening sentences to a novel are an invitation to enter a separate world of rhythm and sound, mental activity and social positioning (Parks 2011: 67).

Reading therefore has a social, emotional and cognitive function, similar to that of talk. While words in spoken and written form may of themselves appear to form a separate act, Darnton (2009) makes a case that they are much closer. He says that in the nineteenth century groups of artisans, especially cigar makers and tailors, took turns reading or hired a reader to keep themselves entertained while they worked. Even today many people get their news by being read to by a news reader. Television may be less of a break with the past than is generally assumed. In any case, for most people throughout most of history, books had audiences rather than readers. They were better heard than seen (Darnton 2009: 168). The processes of reading and talk then are closer than we might think. Contemporary forms of reading may provide a form of social, emotional and intellectual activity more or less equivalent to that offered historically by storytelling.

Brown and Palinscar (1984) recognised that by making the processes of thinking visible through discussion, children could be encouraged to become better readers. This is fundamental to an approach to teaching reading comprehension called 'reciprocal reading'.

 Classroom case study

Reciprocal reading

Brown and Palinscar (1984) identify four main strategies in reciprocal teaching (summarising, questioning, predicting, clarifying). This might look like the following in practice (adapted from http://www.readingrockets.org/strategies/reciprocal_teaching):

1 Group the children: 4–5 is an ideal number: you can choose either mixed-ability or organise by ability.
2 Each member of the group should be given one of the four reciprocal reading roles:

- Summariser
- Questioner
- Clarifier
- Predictor.

3 The readers should then read a part of the text from the point of view of their particular role. They will then respond in role, according to the given reciprocal reading strategy.

- One person will summarise the text to that point.
- One will pose questions about the text: asking about confusing vocabulary, sentences, sections and ideas.
- Another will then offer some interpretations, suggesting clarifications of the text.
- Finally, the predictor looks forward and makes suggestions about the next steps in the story.

4 Readers can carry on in these roles over the lesson, and change later in the week. Once children become more confident, roles can change within a lesson.
5 Throughout, the teacher's role is to support students' ability to apply the four strategies. The teacher hands over control for reading and most importantly the application of the reciprocal reading model to the readers, as they become more confident and are able to apply strategies with less support.

The power of reciprocal reading lies in the provision of reading roles which are shared, first by the teacher through modelling, and then through the peer group in the form of peer-supported group work. As Vygotsky would have explained, the reciprocal reading strategies themselves become internalised as routines which children can then draw on to support active reading comprehension. Jeffrey and Craft (2004) explain that learners model themselves on their teacher's approach, find themselves in situations where they are able to take ownership and control and are more likely to be innovative, even if the teacher was not overtly planning to teach for creativity. Thus the learner goes on to successfully master the suite of reciprocal reading strategies.

Chapter summary

- Problem-solving is a real-world application of thinking, reasoning, judgement, and decision-making in all learners.
- Developing thinking and problem-solving is an active process in the child. Learning is essentially a social process.

- Motivation and confidence in the classroom underpin effectiveness: especially important is the role of anxiety in impairing interpretation and decision-making.
- Teachers can influence the child in being more effective in solving problems and in applying their thinking in different aspects of the curriculum.
- Successful problem-solving involves ensuring a match between the nature of the problem, how it is presented/discovered and the tools by which it may be solved.
- Classroom behaviour can also be seen as a social aspect of problem-solving;
- Being explicit about decisions in problem-solving is an important skill for teachers, to enable children to build their understanding of otherwise obscure aspects of thinking.
- Exploratory talk involves a shared inquiry with critical challenges and explicit reasoning within a cooperative framework.
- Reading for meaning involves mastery of a range of vocabulary, inference and verbal reasoning.

Further reading and research

Alexander, R.J. (2006). *Towards Dialogic Teaching: Rethinking Classroom Talk*, 4th edn. Oxford: Blackwell.

Edwards, D. and Mercer, N. (1987). *Common Knowledge: The Development of Understanding in the Classroom*. Abingdon: Routledge Revivals.

Jeffrey, B. and Craft, A. (2004). Teaching creatively and teaching for creativity: distinctions and relationships. *Educational Studies*, 30(1): 77–87.

Mercer, N. and Sams, C. (2006). Teaching children how to use language to solve maths problems. *Language and Education*, 20(6): 507–28.

Wegerif, R. (2005): Reason and creativity in classroom dialogues. *Language and Education*, 19(3): 223–37.

CHAPTER 5

WHERE DO CHILDREN LEARN?

Chapter guide

In this chapter you will learn about:

- The classroom environment
- The impact of the use of space
- The new and emerging 'virtual' space for learning

The classroom environment

A learning environment is what the child makes of it (Strong-Wilson and Ellis 2007), and children have the creativity and ability to create their own worlds, finding uses for objects and spaces that adults could never begin to imagine. Rasmussen (2004) makes a clear distinction between 'places for children' and 'children's places', the difference being that 'places for children' are structured places created by adults for children whereas the places where children invest imaginative energy are 'children's places'. This is a significant difference. The learning environment created in a school is only one of a number of environments the learner might occupy, and possibly the only one where teachers may have any direct influence. 'While teachers and practitioners may not be able to influence the wider environments of family, community and society, research shows that the learning environment has a powerful influence on children's achievements' (DfES, 2004).

Where children learn is complex, individual and even idiosyncratic in some cases. With circumstances and opportunities individual to each learner, children develop and learn in the context of their own unique environment in terms of school, local community, home, cultural influences and of course, their own personal needs and relationships. This is recognised as a key characteristic of effective learning throughout the Early Years Foundation Stages (EYFS) and is clearly referred to as 'enabling environments' (Department for Education 2012). These environments are defined as ones which value both people and learning, are rich in resources relevant to a child's culture and community, provide opportunities and support children to take risks and explore. If children feel valued as individuals and welcomed into classrooms which take into account their various cultures, languages, and needs, then surely this is an environment in which they will want to learn.

An approach that continues to underpin the work in the EYFS in mainstream schools is the Montessori educational approach. Developed by the Italian physician and educator Maria Montessori, it is practised in many dedicated schools worldwide (Al et al. 2012) as well as in some mainstream EYFS settings. The belief that the environment is crucial for learning is fundamental to the philosophy of the Montessori approach. Montessori believed that education takes place through the child's own unique interaction with their environment (D'Emidio-Caston and Crocker 1987) and that a child relies on the environment, processing everything through their senses, to help them to understand their world. In order to grow and meet potential, she believed the solution was to prepare a 'suitable environment for the child where he may manifest his higher tendencies' (Montessori 1966: 86), therefore, adapting the environment was seen to be essential for child development.

In Montessori schools spaces are created to allow children to be independent of adults and have the freedom to explore and choose. These spaces, referred to as the 'prepared environment' (Montessori 1966), have been carefully prepared to stimulate and support learning. Cupboards are made to be child-sized and shelves set at heights that allow children to find, use and replace materials easily, in order to encourage and further develop independence (Al et al. 2012; Montessori 1966). Resources and materials are carefully chosen to facilitate the child's learning and designed so that 'if children make mistakes, they can see and correct them without close teacher supervision or intervention' (Lillard 2013: 159). It is evident that this approach has clearly been adopted in many early years settings today. However, what is not common practice in mainstream settings is the use of neutral colours. The physical environment in a Montessori environment is calm and harmonious with walls painted in neutral colours to encourage children to both relax and learn at the same time. Shelves are uncluttered, displaying only a few objects so as not to over-stimulate or distract children and provide a much calmer environment where they can learn at their own pace. By contrast, when entering a typical primary school classroom in a mainstream setting, you can be assured of being greeted by a profusion of brightly coloured displays proudly showing children's work and an abundance of different texts and aids to support the children in their learning. Is this environment suitable for learning or is it overly stimulating or cluttered? Consider how many times you have had to remind your children to look at the 'word wall' or the other displays to aid them in their writing? If your answer is 'often', why might this be? Is it because the information is difficult to see, or has been displayed for some considerable time, so that the children no longer 'see' it? Have you ever stopped to consider the environment from the perspective of a child and imagine what it would feel like to learn in your classroom?

Tarr (2004: 1) studied the primary classroom environment and considered the impact of wall displays: 'From a small chair in a corner, I counted 19 different, decorated, scalloped borders segmenting portions of the bulletin boards lining the walls. The boards were filled with words: a word wall, class rules, a calendar, alphabets, numbers, shapes and colours, and a plethora of cartoon people and animals.' When considering the impact and value of such wall displays on children Tarr (2004) questions whether the children would actually find it difficult to concentrate or focus on their work. She concludes that whereas some classroom displays are colourful and have children's work displayed, further guidelines may also be needed to help teachers to consider the actual purpose of the displays and classroom aesthetics. The reflection point below offers some advice for the classroom.

The Reggio Emilia approach to education proposes the classroom environment as the third educator (Strong-Wilson and Ellis 2007). Like the Montessori approach, it regards the aesthetics of the environment as critical for learning, taking into account its valuable contribution to children's learning. Teachers are encouraged to critically examine their environments and determine whether or not they actually contribute to children's learning and bring into question the 'usefulness' of displays. The classroom is very much a reflection of the kind of teacher you are: however, it is fundamentally important that the environment is also conducive to learning, not disruptive to learning and this should be taken into consideration for a more inclusive learning environment.

Reflection point: de-cluttering your classroom

Critically evaluate your classroom environment and determine whether it contributes to the children's learning:

- Consider placing emphasis on important or new material so that the children can easily identify it.
- Ask the children which displays are helpful and remove any unnecessary displays.
- Consider a colour theme instead of several different colours.
- Be consistent with your use of fonts – are they child-friendly to read?
- Are your displays at a child's-eye level?

 Classroom case study

Using the Year 2 classroom environment to inspire

In line with the school improvement plan which required the improvement of writing across all key stages, a different approach was needed to inspire the children to write more creatively. Rather than use the classroom learning environment in the traditional way, it was decided that something more inspiring was needed.

Following several lessons planning 'creepy' stories and input into the use of settings, adjectives and story structure, the class were due to write after morning break when the mood may have been a little 'flat'. To create an atmosphere all curtains and blinds were closed, including the sticking of black paper over any glass panels on the doors so the room was dark apart from the glow that was emitted from the IWB, similar to being in a cinema. The lack of light was an initial concern as it was unclear whether this would upset some children and also hinder their writing; therefore, some small lanterns were strategically placed in areas of the room to emulate candles. A slide show of different images of settings and characters to inspire was looped to play continuously on the IWB. At the same time, some carefully selected sound effects were played such as footsteps on gravel, thunder and lightning, howling wind, and sea waves crashing.

As soon as the children came through the doorway, they were totally immersed in the environment of sounds and imagery and the sense of awe and wonder was palpable. Each and every child knew what was expected of them and after watching and listening and some quiet discussions amongst themselves, the children became very quiet and completely absorbed in their story and began to write.

Any concerns and fears about the impact on behaviour were completely unfounded and not an issue. In fact the use of such a learning environment had a positive impact on those learners who usually became distracted and disengaged, encouraging those children to want to write instead. Though initially concerned about the reduction of light in the classroom the children confirmed that they were quite able to see and write, and believed that it actually helped them to concentrate much more as their surroundings no longer distracted them, including their peers.

The total immersion of the children in the imagery and sounds proved to have a significant impact not only on the quality of ideas and description evident in the writing, but the 'believability' of their stories and the structure. Though it was a risk to create a learning environment such as this, the outcomes for the children far outweighed it.

Space makes a difference

Despite evidence from research that the use of space and movement within a classroom may significantly impact learners and their potential to learn, fitting growing class numbers into a relatively small area is still an issue. Organising classrooms to maximise learning potential and to address complex issues of peer relationships is a challenge for most teachers and can occur several times in the school year. When observing how children react and behave if working in close proximity to one another in small, enclosed spaces, it becomes apparent that this can have a negative impact on some learners. Conversely, others find large, open areas such as the playground space equally intimidating (Hirst and Cooper 2008). Considerable time and angst is spent analysing where to position pupils both in terms of space in the classroom and also grouping for both differentiation and relationships. The consequences of how we group or separate our pupils can potentially have a significant impact on learning.

Some research studies have used the metaphor of 'dance' to help understand and analyse the complexities of classroom spaces and classroom relationships, suggesting that a teacher is the 'choreographer' and children the 'dancers' (Hirst and Cooper 2008; Gordon et al. 2000). The practices within school are described as not dissimilar to a complicated dance (Gordon et al. 2000) where the classroom becomes the space for children to try out and initiate new steps and improvise the 'dance', taking into account diversity and different styles, creating new hybrid dances and spaces to suit specific purposes.

'The diversity of the dances, the groups within the groups, the fragmentation and the conflicting spaces remind us of the ever-changing, complex and dynamic places that classrooms are for students and teachers' (Hirst and Cooper 2008: 443). The use of space is never static and is always in the process of evolving (McGregor 2003).

 Classroom case study

Year 4 science lesson

Pupils in a Year 4 class were building on their knowledge of how temperature is a measure of how hot or cold objects are. Their next stage of learning was to investigate how thermal insulators help to keep things either warm or cool.

Unlike the numeracy and literacy lessons, pupils were given the choice of who they would like to work with for the main task. A friendship group of differing abilities chose to sit together at a table, in the furthest corner from the teacher. During the task the noise levels increased and the group started to disrupt others, and the teacher became frustrated at what seemed to be a lack of engagement in the task.

Due to the noisiness of the group, for the following science lesson the teacher chose to split the group and position them away from each other. As a result the pupils became disengaged from their learning and consequently began to disrupt others in their new groups and so did not learn or achieve their goal. However, when marking their books, the teacher found that the pupils had in fact completed their task with great success. The pupils had been immersed in meaningful dialogue which was constructive, creative and innovative. The 'noise' was the process of the transfer of knowledge which supported their learning, and on reflection, the teacher realised that splitting the group for subsequent lessons had not been the most effective solution.

This group had worked particularly well together and learned collaboratively in a group environment, the stronger ones supporting the weaker ones. In terms of a learning space, it was not the spatial position that helped them to learn, but the dynamics of that group environment where the children were able to work collaboratively. Though they may appear to be noisy and, in some teachers' eyes, disruptive, children can learn in groups where communication and collaboration play a key role in the learning experience and the process of the transfer of knowledge (Miller 2009).

When 'choreographing' practices in the classroom, it is important that teachers consider the significant impact of how space, location and positioning are controlled and the consequences this may have for the dynamics of learning (Hirst and Cooper 2008). The use of space and where children learn is not just the *physical* environment but the *social* space: 'Schools are not static self-contained entities but institutions continually being produced by inter-connecting relationships and practices which extend in space and time' (McGregor 2003: 353).

Therefore how we manage the space, location and positioning in which learning takes place should be carefully considered, as these provide specific experiences that 'stimulate the senses, encourage the exchange of information, and offer opportunities for rehearsal, feedback and application' (Chism 2006: 24), all integral components which support learning. From the moment a child enters the room the learning process begins and so careful planning and facilitation and an effective arrangement of space and resources will enhance that process for the learners (Legutke and Thomas 1991). There is a risk of taking spatial arrangements for granted in the classroom layout, and consequently 'we often fail to notice the ways in which space constrains or enhances what we intend to accomplish' (Chism 2006: 23). For example, consider the common assumption that a classroom always has a 'front' to it, predominantly where the interactive whiteboard is placed, and reflect on how often the board is used. Is this where all the learning takes place in the classroom? Could your input be elsewhere?

Important questions have been raised about the design and function of the traditional learning environment and the growing need for an alternative that supports new and different opportunities. We need to support this transition from traditional teaching and learning to new approaches which requires the overall learning space to respond in new and more flexible ways (Bransford et al. 2004; Miller 2009). Classrooms, though bound by the space they have, need areas that are suitable for interaction between pupils. They must not feel so big that this may lead to a lack of interaction, or so small that the space potentially begins to create conflict between children (Radunovich and Kochert 2011). The way in which tables and chairs are laid out impacts upon actual space to move, so consideration needs to be given as to whether each lesson needs the same configuration. Could the layout be regularly changed to benefit learning? Subject to budget, there is of course a myriad of different solutions to create the optimal learning space, such as investing in mobile furniture and interactive whiteboards which can provide great capacity to change and adapt the learning environment to support the pedagogical and collaborative needs of both the learners and practitioners, potentially enhancing that learning process (Miller 2009). Of course using the classroom is not the only learning space and greater consideration could be given to the use of the outdoors.

Reflection point

Critically evaluate your classroom and consider whether it is 'fit for learning'.

- Could you reposition the tables and chairs to create a more effective learning environment or different learning spaces?
- Ask your children which classroom configuration they prefer.
- What elements of your environment promote learning and support all children? This could also include displays, resources for learning and deployment of ICT equipment.
- What are the most successful elements?

Learning outdoors

In recent years there has been a noticeable decline in children's access to, and a lack of engagement with, the natural world. There is a growing risk of what has been termed 'nature deficit disorder' (Louv 2005; Moss 2012: 2). Symptoms are described as: 'diminished use of the senses, attention difficulties, and higher rates of physical and emotional illnesses'. It would be very easy and convenient to blame the rapid development of technology and the lure of screen-based games for this demise, but we must not fail to forget the benefits that technology also brings to children in terms of their learning, as we will discuss in Chapter 7. Louv (2011: 34–7) believes the main reason why children rarely go outdoors is more likely to be a symptom of 'well-meaning, protective house arrest'.

Using the outdoors as a learning environment is not a new concept by any means and is well-researched. Montessori was a great advocator of using the outdoors, and believed that nature should be used to inspire children who should be taken out into nature, rather than being kept confined in the classroom. The Forest School movement began several decades ago in Scandinavia and following research undertaken, some schools in the UK are beginning to embrace this concept. Some have embedded the use of outdoors as part of their curriculum, providing invaluable life experiences for children, and some are adapting their outdoor areas to be used to their maximum potential if there are little or no woodlands nearby.

A study that looked at the positive impact of learning outdoors found that initially some teachers experienced anxiety and concern about taking their class outside. Their reasons included fear of potential behavioural issues, losing control and teaching outside of their 'comfort zone' (Boyd and Colquhoun 2013).

However, findings indicate that children were in fact much better behaved than when indoors and teachers agreed that greater levels of learning had taken place due to greater involvement, risk-taking and engagement with the outdoor learning activities. As Jones (2012: 6) points out: 'If we never took a risk our children would not learn to walk, climb stairs, ride a bicycle or swim; business would not develop innovative new products … scientists would not experiment and discover, we would not have great art, literature, music and architecture.'

Other benefits found were that children's recall of their activities was much greater than when indoors, and in terms of relationships, it was agreed that pupil–teacher relationships were strengthened, and that everyone learnt something new about each other (Slade et al. 2013). Sigman (2007) found that children exposed to nature did much better in areas such as reading, writing, maths and science as a result of learning outdoors. Their concentration, self-discipline and behaviour were greatly improved as was their ability to work in teams. However, it was not just a consequence of learning outdoors, it was found that children learn in very different ways and can experience improvements in four specific ways:

- cognitive impacts (greater knowledge and understanding)
- affective impacts (attitudes, values, beliefs and self-perceptions)
- interpersonal and social impacts (communication skills, leadership and teamwork)
- physical and behavioural impacts (fitness, personal behaviours and social actions). (Sigman 2007: 9)

It is worth noting that when thinking back to our schooling, the days that most of us remember are those when the teacher was brave enough to take the class outside for learning.

Virtual learning environments – the new learning environment?

To be able to appreciate the significant changes in educational learning environments some historical context is necessary. Four hundred years ago, only the privileged few had access to a limited number of books and few could read. During the mid-seventeenth century the educational landscape and learning environment was incomparable to what we know today and for the lucky minority, there was limited opportunity to learn from a very small number of printed books, orally delivered lectures or to learn from their natural environment (Matijević 2012). It was not until more than two centuries later that textbooks for students were introduced and some children began to attend school, though most poor children still worked.

As a result of a great technological revolution during the Victorian era, other forms of communication such as the electric telegraph, the forerunner of today's Internet, and the telephone emerged, paving the way for the technologies we know today. Such innovations have allowed personal communication, on a previously inconceivable scale, to became commonplace in our workplaces, homes and schools. We now live in a world which relies heavily on complex structures of domestic and worldwide communications, a far cry from what our predecessors had access to. This new, rapidly developing learning environment has made it necessary to review and find new, creative pedagogies to take advantage of, and use effectively the technologies we have for learning so that 'the way we handle them on a daily basis actually fits our expectations and needs' (Coplin 2013: 2).

The Internet, social networks and multimedia resources provide an exciting and stimulating learning environment that offers both children and teachers opportunities that were not around fifty years ago to use a more informal learning environment, as a strong alternative to formal learning (Matijević 2011). Whether this is a better environment is questionable, but as technology already plays such a significant role in our learners' lives at home and in their communities, educators need to consider how they can synthesise technology into the educational learning environment. In his study on 3D virtual worlds, Merchant (2010) looks at the potential of gaming and virtual world play in education, but also questions the notion of how transformative practice can be achieved with the use of such new technologies, suggesting that 'changes in teacher preparation, continuing professional development as well as wider educational reform may be needed'.

As well as challenging pedagogical practice, the use of conventional spaces in which our children learn is being equally challenged. While school building structures remain the same, our infrastructures have significantly changed so that children no longer need to be constrained to the physical classroom and can become mobile in their interactions with learning environments, learning in places previously considered as impossible. The challenge now is for teachers and schools to create an environment in which creativity and innovation can flourish, without being bound by the conventional building structures and infrastructure.

'Collaboration is a central tenet of the new Social Web' (Pifarré and Kleine Staarman 2011: 188) and tools such as the wiki, characterised by its powerful information-sharing and collaboration features, bring with them the potential for exciting opportunities in a virtual learning environment. Wikis allow the learner to actively participate by adding new content or editing content to a series of webpages collaboratively, with the added advantage of being anywhere globally. Findings have indicated that by using this virtual learning environment, it can support collaborative and constructivist learning approaches and knowledge-construction processes (Luo 2010; Parker and Chao 2007).

 Case study

Using wiki software to improve geographical and historical skills in Year 6

In a bid to improve knowledge of their local town both geographically and historically, the class were asked to work in groups to create a wiki that would reflect their local area. They were divided into mixed-ability groups to support the less confident users of the technology. Discrete lessons had been previously undertaken in the creation and use of wikis so that the technology was not a barrier to learning. Careful consideration was also given to rules and etiquette when using the wiki as members of the group would be able to delete content.

Over a period of half a term, the groups worked on their wikis during the allotted lesson time in school so that the teacher could guide and offer help, the rest of the time was managed by each of the groups, virtually, in their own time.

The value of using wiki software meant that the children could work on their project wherever they were and in their own time, as long as there was an Internet connection. The technology enabled them to create a dialogic virtual space whereby the users could write at the same time in their virtual environment and collaboratively edit their writing, creating content using hyperlinks to link to other information and photographs. Being able to work at home provided children with extra opportunity and time to reflect on what others had written and added on the pages before having to respond themselves. The challenge faced by the groups was deciding what content was suitable to be included and so teamwork and collaborative thinking was essential. As the project developed, a group leader naturally emerged and guided the group towards their end goals. Wider links were also made with others in the local community and included within the wiki pages using hyperlinks to video interviews and photographs.

Working in a virtual environment such as this had many benefits for the learners. The children became not just users of the tool but creators of knowledge, held discussions, challenged and developed their own ideas

(Continued)

(Continued)

providing a platform for local debate on issues such as recycling and river pollution, and ultimately problem-solving. As the project developed, it was interesting to note that so did the quality of language used, though it is important to point out that the project was not assessed on literacy, but on geographical and historical knowledge, understanding and skills. Added benefits of using wiki software were that the history of all revisions was kept and could be referred back to if necessary, by the users, enabling the group and teacher to reflect on changes made. Increased communication amongst the wider local community locally was also a benefit and brought with it the possibility of global links for the future.

In terms of pedagogy, for the teacher this was a risk as it was unclear whether the technology would become a barrier and whether the learners would follow the rules and etiquette laid down. However, through careful planning the end result was hugely successful and all learners achieved their goals. The wiki was made available to the school community, including parents, so that their work could be shared and celebrated. There was a great sense of personal achievement and pride. Confidence had grown immensely by the end of the project, all children felt that they would be able to create and use a wiki in other areas of the curriculum and agreed that working in a virtual environment helped them to learn as they could engage in the task when they felt like it. Further work was scheduled to look at the design and layout of the pages created as it was felt that a common template or 'style' was needed.

Chapter summary

- Organising classrooms to maximise learning potential and to address complex issues of peer relationships is a challenge and careful consideration has to be given to the available space in a classroom and the most effective layout for learners to achieve.
- There is a need to support the transition from traditional teaching and learning to new approaches which require the overall learning space to respond in new and more flexible ways.
- Research indicates that there is a new and emerging learning environment: the virtual space.
- The challenge is for teachers and schools to create an environment in which creativity and innovation can flourish, and not be bound by the conventional building structures and infrastructure.
- There has been a decline in children's access to and lack of engagement with the natural world, despite evidence to show that using the outdoor environment to learn can help children to improve across the curriculum and socially.

Further reading and research

Bransford, J.D., Brown, A.L. and Cocking, R.R. (eds) (2004). *How People Learn: Brain, Mind, Experience, and School*. Washington, DC: National Academies Press, 1999. Available at: http://www.nap.edu/html/howpeople1/

Hirst, E. and Cooper, M. (2008). Keeping them in line: choreographing classroom spaces. *Teachers and Teaching: Theory and Practice*, 14(5–6): 431–45.

Merchant, G. (2007). Writing the future in the digital age. *Literacy*, 41(3): 118–28.

Rasmussen, K. (2004). Places for children – children's places. *Childhood*, 11: 155–73.

Reh, R., Rabenstein, K. and Fritzsche, B. (2011). Learning spaces without boundaries? Territories, power and how schools regulate learning. *Social & Cultural Geography*, 12(1): 83–98.

Strong-Wilson, T. and Ellis, J. (2007). Children and place: Reggio Emilia's environment as third teacher. *Theory into Practice*, 46(1): 40–47.

Svinicki, M.D. (2004). *Learning and Motivation in the Postsecondary Classroom*. Boston, MA: Anker Publishing.

A CURRICULUM FOR INNOVATION

This chapter discusses the need for a less defined and prescriptive curriculum in which teachers and learners work in ways that are more responsive to children's needs. Personalising teaching according to the needs of the learners is seen as an important aim for innovative education, and this requires more precise and accurate forms of assessment, led by teachers and learners. On the other hand, challenging and inspiring learning should not set out with predefined ideas of what the children should achieve. Performance and instrumental forms of learning are illustrated which ultimately demotivate and disempower both learners and teachers. Maria Roldau maintained in *Schooling for Tomorrow*, a volume reflecting on 1990s Portuguese developments, that doing 'good experimental things' means predominantly something interesting and innovative (OECD 2003).

Introduction: what is the curriculum?

In previous chapters, we have discussed some approaches to the knowledge, skills and values which should be taught, and how they could be taught in primary schools. Approaches like enquiry-based learning also suggest how students can be taught. In recent years, schools have become interested in what many call a 'creative curriculum', which we discussed in Chapter 2 with respect to the development of creativity. In this chapter, we focus on the contribution of the curriculum to innovation and how innovation might drive the curriculum itself. But we start first with some of the big ideas in the curriculum.

The first fundamental question for the curriculum is: what knowledge, skills and values should be included and why? McNeil (1977) identifies five approaches to the curriculum:

- **Humanistic**: focuses on personally satisfying experiences, such as the growth and personal integrity of each individual.
- **Social reconstruction**: puts larger social needs over individual ones.
- **Technologist**: sees the curriculum as a technological process for efficiently producing ends demanded by policy makers.
- **Academic**: emphasises the curriculum as a means to introduce learners to subject-matter disciplines and organised fields of study.
- **Cognitive process**: seeks to develop a set of cognitive skills applicable to learning almost anything.

If the curriculum is seen as being a polarised and singular domain, it would be very convenient to say that the above positions are exclusive. We argue that these are dimensions to the curriculum which should be promoted together. So for instance, innovation should promote individual as well as collective growth, recognising the contribution of new technologies to what we learn and how we learn. Learners' personal and collective development forms part of the academic traditions of subject disciplines. Intellectual discipline is itself an important quality for resilient learners and forms part of the cultural heritage which binds us together in society.

There are always practical considerations to consider when organising the curriculum. Broadly the values, context and ways of working for both teachers and learners are part of the framework. Leithwood (1981) proposes nine specific dimensions to be considered. In the following list we question some of the assumptions made in respect of curriculum organisation in a primary school:

- **Platform**: beliefs and assumptions behind curriculum decisions such as positions, orientations or principles to the curriculum. The values and beliefs of central government do not always match those of the school or teachers. The values and beliefs of a school management team do not always match those of the teachers. The values and beliefs of the teacher do not always match those of the children and their families. This context can therefore be problematic for curriculum development.
- **Objectives**: the intended outcomes from broad aims to standards of student performance. In many countries of the world, especially in England, teaching and learning objectives have become something of a tyranny resulting in a closed form of learning. This issue will be discussed in more detail below.
- **Learner entry behaviours**: competency requirements for a particular programme. Schools rarely have a choice to select children based on required competencies before entry to a primary school. In any case, primary schools are often community-based and therefore both morally and legally often have a commitment to teach children of all backgrounds, abilities and dispositions. Where there are significant learning difficulties, school must be prepared to provide the mainstream and specialist support these children need.
- **Assessment tools and procedures**: tests form part of the summative assessment in school, but the formative aspect of assessment and teaching is important for progress. Both formative and summative assessment is often linked to accountability measures of a school. Teachers and the school are judged at inspection and through league tables, based on the progress in learning and the achievements at key points in the school. There is much debate that this measure of accountability can become dominant and progress and outcomes in learning are focused more on adults than children. Schooling becomes a bureaucratic exercise rather than a landscape for children's personal and academic growth.
- **Instructional material**: includes written, visual, audio or other material. In many countries, textbooks and their electronic equivalent are a mainstay for managing the curriculum content and approaches to teaching. Should these be produced centrally or in school? Flexibility in the use of materials is more likely to offer opportunities for locally agreed arrangements which encourage innovation in content and pedagogy.
- **Learner experiences**: different learner profile descriptions are likely given the cultural, economic and social contexts of children and the communities from which they come. Parental education is one important factor influencing children's learning.
- **Teaching strategies**: patterns of teacher behaviour can be managed as inflexible institutional menus of pedagogy. However, the ability to adapt to

new situations, new frameworks and new children requires the capacity to think and act as an autonomous professional.

- **Content**: comprises facts, concepts, principles or generalisations and thought systems. Attitudes to learning and the ability to collaborate with other people go beyond learning knowledge. There is often a distinction made between declarative knowledge ('knowing that') and procedural knowledge ('knowing how'). While declarative knowledge is often open to conscious questioning, procedural knowledge often means that skills are applied automatically and without conscious attention. Teachers make the point that children can deploy skills discretely but often have trouble in applying these fluently in combination.

- **Time**: indicates preferred patterns of emphasis regarding the other curriculum dimensions. Attribution of time to different areas of the curriculum timetable is important; but the availability of time for teachers during the school week to collaborate, develop their ideas and consider the challenges of teaching and learning is vital in the implementation of the curriculum.

Neither pure centralisation nor decentralisation works for curriculum decision-making and related innovations. Very prescriptive centrally led curriculum guidance may not allow teachers to bridge children's experiences and learning goals, as it can lack ownership and commitment to change. At the same time, widespread and sustainable change cannot automatically rely only on schools, which are assumed to be motivated without a central level of support and leadership. Curriculum standards and frameworks can provide general goals and a vision for innovation, to be eventually dovetailed in schools according to the local context (Fullan 2007). The relationship between centrally led and school-led curricula can often be that of mutual adaptation or 're-invention' (Darling-Hammond 1998). To promote innovation in education 'the trade-off between freedom to experiment and general coordination needs to be properly managed'.

A curriculum which seeks to inspire innovation in learners, must first inspire innovation in teachers. Logically it is possible that any curricula can lead to inspiring teaching and learning; but here we argue for an innovative curriculum.

Curriculum for innovation and innovative curriculum

In previous chapters we noted important characteristics of innovation: improvement through incremental change, subversion and invention. For individuals to make real change in learning, teaching and assessment in the classroom, innovation can only come with the freedom for individuals to make choices at a local level, sensitive to the context. Freedom is therefore an important feature of curriculum development. Teachers must be able to innovate when they: make decisions about changes in content, consider broad aims for learning and develop an assessment approach focused on learning rather than accountability. Freedom facilitates experimentation and risk-taking in the choice of topics and approaches to teaching in the classroom. Personal and professional freedom comes with responsibility and requires a commitment to personal and academic integrity. Of course, league tables and oppressive school inspection regimes have a natural impact on school. A reduction of freedom and an over-emphasis on performance can lead to 'gaming' by teachers to focus only on those characteristics rewarded by the league tables and inspection regimes. Schools can become 'learning factories'. This moves teaching away from the needs of learners for administrative and bureaucratic reasons alone. Ultimately, league tables are focused on the development of political capital rather than educational success.

A curriculum for innovation should encourage risk taking and experimentation through enquiry-based learning. As we argue throughout this chapter, a curriculum for innovation should move away from fixed learning objectives towards more open learning aims. There is no reason why some skills, for instance in relation to the teaching of mathematics and English, should not still be taught in a discrete way, in order to give children the 'tools for the job' in speaking, reading, writing and numbers. It is critical however, that learners have meaningful activities in meaningful contexts, within which they can apply such skills. The focus here is on what children learn and how they learn. Fundamentally, a curriculum for innovation highlights learners' contribution to society in terms of their new thinking, experiences and social engagement.

An innovative curriculum encourages teachers to experiment with new forms of knowledge, taking different approaches to knowledge and school learning. Innovative teachers take risks, they experiment with different teaching strategies which engage learners. We do not advocate risk-taking and experimentation for the sake of it. However, if learners are preparing for a changing society in which they must adapt to new forms of knowledge, and technology, then these first experiences should come in school. In social constructivist cognitive theories (Zimmerman 1995) there is evidence that a problem-solving approach to learning encourages the adaptation of children's thinking in ways which are more likely to develop learning. We would argue that children do not need lessons in how to become resilient in school; however, by taking a challenging, problem-solving approach to learning, particularly where they have to cooperate and collaborate with peers to develop understanding, then resilience will develop. Resilience is a characteristic of successful learners who have overcome challenges, facing setbacks and eventually overcoming the many barriers. This is the case for both children and teachers as learners. As David Hargreaves has suggested (2010), when we move to a period of less prescription from the centre and more innovation from the front line, it means the centre has to do more than simply monitor; it has to look for intelligence. We need an intelligence system that identifies the best examples of innovation with rigour.

The curriculum can be seen as facts and knowledge and as activities and experience. While the Haddow report (1931) implies that activities and experience are more powerful than facts and knowledge in the statement of the curriculum, we argue that such a polarised position is unhelpful. Polarisation in this area has often been the result of over-politicisation. The curriculum will always be political, but when particular pressure groups and those in government seek to impose ideologically, centrally driven curricula, the pedagogical rationale is lost and the role of the teacher as professional is undermined.

Subjects, cross-curricular teaching, skills and teaching to the test

Fixed notions of subjects and ideologically driven pedagogical dogma do nothing to sustain curriculum coherence in the classroom (Kelly 2009). As one contributor suggested in evidence submitted to the House of Commons review of the National Curriculum in 2009, the National Curriculum is very appealing if you like to control what happens in school, because you can always make a new announcement every week that this and that is going to be added. Politically motivated, centrally driven changes, even when made with the best of intentions, have tended to keep adding to the curriculum, adding to the content and adding to the accountability of teachers at a local level.

The role of subjects in the curriculum and the balance of needs of the individual and society in the school curriculum, have long been discussed in debate on the curriculum. Subject pressure groups have long attempted to influence national policy with respect to their specific interests within the primary (5–11 years) and secondary curriculum (11–16 years). In primary education there have been times when schools have been overburdened with too much content and too many subjects. For instance, the first National Curriculum for England and Wales (DfE 1989) was underpinned by two aims, echoing the 1944 Education Act: to promote the spiritual, moral, cultural, mental and physical development of pupils, and to prepare pupils for the opportunities, responsibilities and experiences of adult life. It was structured around 'key stages' and a subject-based curriculum, covering the 'core' subjects of English, mathematics and science, and the 'foundation' subjects of art, geography, history, music, physical education and technology, with all subjects studied from age 5 up to age 16, modern foreign languages from age 11. Schools would also be required to teach religious education and areas such as personal, social and health education, though these subjects sat outside the National Curriculum. A number of non-statutory 'cross-curricular' themes and generic, or life, skills were added to this basic framework in the course of its implementation. In 1993, a curriculum review was instituted as a response to teachers' complaints that the National Curriculum and its testing arrangements were simply too unwieldy and, indeed, could have led to proposed teacher boycotts of the key stage tests.

In 2006 there was a government-instigated 'root and branch' review of the primary curriculum in England led by Sir Jim Rose, which took place at the same time, some would say in competition with, an independent review led by Professor Robin Alexander and a team at the University of Cambridge. Both came to the conclusion that the curriculum should be slimmed down. Rose suggested that the choice between knowledge and skills was a false dichotomy. However, while the Cambridge Primary Review contained extensive analysis of the problems the government view was that it said too little about what might be done in practice to address them. At the chalk face there was a common view that much of the changes amounted to tinkering with subjects, and that suggestions for curriculum development amounted to the 'same wine in different boxes'. The Education Select Committee indicated that the National Curriculum should be a basic entitlement for literacy and numeracy and offering general guidelines on breadth and balance to be interpreted by schools and teachers themselves. Politics again intervened and with a new government of a different political hue in 2010, there was significant tension. A strong ideological government push for a locally driven curriculum in England, contrasted with strong central messages about the importance of subjects and knowledge in itself for primary school children.

Typically in primary schools in England there has been a tradition of at least some learning through cross-curricular topic work. So rather than learning in a particular subject, topics have been the vehicle for learning different knowledge and skills. A variation of this approach leaves subjects still as the central means for teaching and learning, but with different subjects being linked through a common theme. The influence for such an approach can be traced back to the constructivist, Piagetian influences of the Plowden report of 1967, in which 'At the heart of the educational process lies the child.' Her report viewed the main educational tasks of the primary school as building on and strengthening children's intrinsic interest in learning and to lead them to learn for themselves rather than from fear of disapproval or desire for praise. The report's recurring themes were individual learning, flexibility in the curriculum, the centrality of play in children's learning, the use of the environment, learning by discovery and the importance of the evaluation of children's progress. The liberal progressive doctrine of Plowden was that teachers should not assume that only what is measurable is valuable. As a direct riposte to Plowden's child-centred rhetoric was the rise of curriculum as economic engine. The school curriculum is at the heart of education, not the child (DfE 1981). While much of Plowden's emphasis on the Piagetian view of cognitive development has been discredited, there is some justification to the notion that young children especially are highly influenced by the context of learning (Donaldson 1978).

The following case study explains how many primary teachers present learning in highly contextualised ways to engage children in authentic and motivating ways. Few teachers would know the intricacies of the rationale, but a cross-curricular approach to learning is seen as providing opportunities for children to experiment, investigate and develop skills, knowledge and understanding at the their own pace through discovery-led learning.

 Classroom case study

A class of six-year-olds is learning through a cross-curricular topic. The linking topic is the film *Toy Story 2*. The teacher and teaching assistant have planned a unit of work for two weeks which provides children with the opportunity to:

- Learn how to build a rocket;
- Create space-shape poems;
- Investigate different ways of measuring the height of each rocket.
- This is linked to a visit to a local space centre, where the children learn how to make and launch rockets; where they find out about the European space programme, especially the early days of space flight.

The classroom is decorated with images and objects on the *Toy Story 2* theme, with rockets and stars dangling from the ceiling. 'Space words' are dotted around the classroom to facilitate reading and spelling. This is a really motivating setting and the children have been very engaged with the topic. The unit of work culminated in a 'class assembly' in which the children introduce some of their rockets, singing a song from the *Toy Story 2* film.
What subjects have been touched on in this cross-curricular unit of work?

An important advantage for children in cross-curricular learning is that it can provide a meaningful and authentic context within which to develop good attitudes and dispositions to learning. Cross-curricular learning enables topic areas to be tailored to the interests and needs of children while building bridges from the practices of the early years. Many primary schools in England have placed additional emphasis on the teaching of English and maths since these basic skills are central to progress in all learning. For instance, reading and writing are the fundamental tools for accessing the world beyond the classroom and expressing the internal world of feelings and imagination. Good subject teaching, combined with cross-curricular studies, enables children to learn not only what to study but also to develop independence in the application of core skills. While cross-curricular learning has long been seen as a excellent way of teaching the wider curriculum, there has been a tendency in English primary schools to focus on discrete teaching of the core subjects of literacy and numeracy.

The tyranny of learning objectives: a critique

It has been argued that the 'objectives model' is more suitable for training or instruction than for education (Stenhouse 1975). Training is a concept conceived of as the acquisition of skills and the capacity for human performance. Bloom et al. (1956) suggested objectives to be explicit formulations of ways in which learners are expected to be changed by the educative process. An objective describes an intended result of instruction, rather than the process of instruction itself (Mager 1962). The Mager model recommended that objectives should be specific and measurable. Mager specified the three parts of an objective as follows: it should have a measurable verb (an action verb); a specification of what the learner is given; and a specification of criteria for success or competency. For example, 'the learner will read aloud a list with 50 per cent real words and 50 per cent non-words using their phonic knowledge, achieving at least 60 per cent accuracy'. An objective-based curriculum has been criticised in relation to the systematic teaching of synthetic phonics in England. Teaching a child reading skills is not the same as teaching a child to become a reader. McKernan (2010) highlighted the following criticisms of an objectives-led curriculum:

- **Objectives do not exist in reality**: they are artificially created and atomistic account of skills and knowledge which are in themselves far greater than the sum of the learning objectives.
- **Educators are asked to accept objectives uncritically**: either in the choice of objectives or in the way they are ordered. This deprofessionalises the role of the teacher by reducing the professional judgement about what they should teach and how they should teach children.
- **Objectives reduce education to an instrumental-utilitarian activity**: achieving objectives alone tends to reduce learning to an atomistic activity: schools risk becoming 'learning factories'.
- **Breaking education down into targets is destructive of the epistemology of disciplines and subjects**: subjects are much greater

than the sum of their learning objectives. Learning objectives fail to recognise the holistic nature of the subject and its cultural tradition.

- **Objectives are often stated as low-level trivial recall items**: assessment leads the development of objectives, perhaps resulting more on a focus on the observable and testable.
- **Predetermination prevents 'teachable' moments and pursuing inquiries thrown up by the process of teaching and learning**: learning objectives can become a tyranny, preventing teaching at the point of need and interest, when opportunities arise.
- **It is not democratic to set targets in advance of instruction**: while there has been a developing tradition of children becoming involved in the setting of objectives, it has been argued that over-specification of learning objectives can be limiting of learning and expectations, reducing learning to the lowest common denominator.
- **Objectives often set the agenda for hegemonic group interests to be served**: largely by ideologically driven experts, with a commercial or government group as its covert source.
- **Objectives represent poor models of teacher–student interaction**: it can lead to didactic forms of teaching, dominated by the teacher, when all recent research into learning suggests that learning is a constructivist activity by children.
- **Empirically speaking, teachers do not plan by starting the curriculum with objectives**: they generally focus on content and pedagogy, while also recognising the role of progression in general terms from younger to older children.
- **The limits of discourse act as a constraint on objectives: centralised curricula can be worded in a particularly opaque way**: for example, 'Year 5 objectives for spelling – To spell unstressed vowels in polysyllabic words'. This objective has a fascinating ring for linguistics but amounts to a foreign language for most children and many of their teachers.
- **Objectives are often perceived as having equal value when in fact some are of greater importance and of varying significance**: this is often unwritten, changeable and therefore unhelpful at a practical level for teachers who often have to infer this information from powerful figures in the education establishment.
- **Unanticipated outcomes are always being achieved and sometimes they are the most valuable results**: this is the difference between education and training.

Kliebard (1986) suggested that pre-specifying objectives amounts to indoctrination in the sense that it purports to stipulate how a person is to behave and then attempting to control the environments so as to manipulate students into behaving as the teacher wishes them to. We argue for wider educational aims to secure progression. This allows for greater experimentation, professional decision-making by teachers and a more holistic view of learning. In the chapter on planning and assessing for innovation (Chapter 10) we will return to the idea of wider educational aims as the basis for planning. However, in the following section we analyse the current context for a curriculum for innovation.

Curriculum context

As societies are constantly changing, it is important that a curriculum is responsive to the current and future needs of the children and of society. The curriculum has to respond to national and demographic factors, such as the nature of children and their needs. For instance, medical advances now mean that many more children survive having been born at around 28 weeks of their mother's pregnancy. But many of these children are born with severe and complex learning difficulties. Many of these children will also be educated in mainstream schools in the future. This and similar challenges for the curriculum are identified below.

Globalisation: cultural awareness, communication and heritage. The increasing economic, social, political, environmental and cultural challenges of globalisation mean that schools have a responsibility to support young people to understand and respond to these complex global issues in their everyday lives. Global learning means preparing young people for the future by fostering self-awareness and open-mindedness towards difference, an understanding of global issues and power relationships, optimism and action for a better world, and critical thinking.

Diversity, immigration and war: in 2010 the UK population stood at 62 million of which approximately 7 million were born abroad. Of those, approximately 4 per cent were born outside of the European Union. While it is impossible to be accurate, there are estimates of illegal migrants to be in the range of 500,000 people. Of the refugees and asylum-seekers in Britain, many have come from war-torn countries such as Afghanistan and Somalia and countries with difficult political regimes such as China and Iran. Britain's Commonwealth ensures the strong links to the former colonial countries and there are similarly around 5 million British people who live in countries such as Hong Kong and Australia. The simple fact therefore is that children in English schools, like those of many countries in the world, need a curriculum which helps them live in a multiracial and multi-ethnic society. Many children will go on to live and work abroad. They must be prepared to communicate with people from different cultures and in different languages.

Fragmentation of family: the core of the family unit (an adult partner-ship and children) remains the same for two-thirds of families in the UK, but families now most often consist of fewer dependent children who stay in the family home for longer. The core family unit remains intact for a longer period of time before new families are formed. In 2010 the divorce rate is reducing, but the number of lone female parents remains relatively high at 22 per cent. There is absolutely no reason why good parenting cannot be assured by a two-parent or a one-parent family. However, the fact that lone female parents earn substantially less than male employees means that female lone-parent families are more likely to suffer economic deprivation than traditional fam-ily structures. Curricula must therefore be sensitive to the variety of family structures and the acknowledged link between economic deprivation and educational achievement. In a progressive society which seeks to facilitate achievement by all learners, curriculum innovation needs to acknowledge the diversity of family structure.

Changing school structures: in England as in many European countries different types of schools have been encouraged by various governments. Free schools, academies and studio schools all now have the power to step outside of the statutory national curriculum. It is argued that this flexibility encourages innovation because schools can make their own decisions about the curricu-lum. It should also be recognised that many of these new school structures are sponsored by larger chains of academies, business and educational sponsors. Of itself, this encourages different opportunities for developing the curricu-lum in line with the particular specialist interests of the sponsor bodies. The Royal Society for Arts has developed the 'Open Minds Curriculum' with the intention of encouraging curriculum innovation, in particular through its chain of academies.

The special challenge: the number of pupils with special educational needs in England decreased from around 1.70 million (21.1 per cent) of pupils in 2009/10 to 1.62 million (19.8 per cent) in 2011/12 after a rise between 2007/08 and 2009/10 (DfE 2012). The number of pupils with statements of spe-cial educational need increased slightly from around 224,000 pupils in 2009/10 to 226,000 pupils in 2011/12 (DfE 2012). The increase in numbers of children and young people with complex learning difficulties and disabilities (CLDD) is widely recognised. The numbers of children with severe and complex needs in one local authority more than doubled between 1981 and 2001. Between 2004 and 2009, the total number of children with severe learning disabilities (SLD) increased by 5.1 per cent, and the total number of those with profound and multiple learning disabilities (PMLD) rose by an average of 29.7 per cent (DfE 2012). Emerson et al. (2008) estimate that the prevalence of PMLD in the older child/young adult age range is increasing by 4–5 per cent annually.

Populations in most Western countries are becoming increasingly older: every day the average age of the UK population becomes more elderly. In the last 50 years the 65+ years population has tripled and it will triple again in the next 50 years (NESTA 2007). An ageing population presents challenges and opportunities for innovation. Families may well be living with and caring for more elderly relatives. An increasing proportion of elderly people also provides a fantastic resource in society and especially for working with younger children in schools. Therefore in terms of skills in the curriculum, the notion of 'lifelong learning skills' becomes even more important. However, the idea that learning to learn is a skill for children, changes to learning how to learn for a lifetime of learning and a lifetime of new challenges.

A curriculum for liberation

Faced with a challenging and changing societal and educational context, should we look forward or should we look back? Current reforms to the National Curriculum in England (DfE 2013) are seen by some as a nostalgic but misplaced attempt to turn back the clock to the 1950s. Refocusing on a more traditional view of knowledge taught in subjects, often through more didactic approaches, has been said to be the wrong approach. A leading headteacher in a Cambridge school articulated one such view. Tricia Kelleher (*The Guardian* 2008) accused the education secretary of 'pressing the rewind button' and warned that attempts to chase global education-league rankings will lead schools into a creativity-free 'cul-de-sac' of learning. However, it could be argued that those educated between the 1950s and 1970s and fed on a diet of facts, knowledge and didactic teaching, haven't done so badly. Another view might suggest that an inspiring, motivating teacher able to foster a good relationship with the class manages to do so regardless of the actual statutory curriculum. Ultimately, a good teacher will take the curriculum and make it work for their class, whatever the official view. Unfortunately, this view is not supported by the reality of recent research into the curriculum. For example, when answering questions in the international PISA survey about the types of activities they do in class, British students report doing many more 'traditional' activities than 'progressive' ones (*The Guardian* 2008). Half of British students reported that their teacher tells them what to do in every lesson, compared to just a quarter of students in Hong Kong and Finland. Kogan and Maden (1999) alluded long ago to the detrimental influence of a national monitoring and compliance framework for schools. Their suspicions were well-founded. It is widely recognised that England now has a centralised model of teaching and learning monitored by an inspection system based on an evaluation of performance in certain key skills (*The Guardian* 2008).

The issue of accountability is an important one. While it is acknowledged that the spending of close to £100 billion every year in the English state education system warrants close examination, there is a balance to be had between promoting learning in itself and the framework by which it is monitored and evaluated. When evaluation takes precedence over learning then we know we have a problem.

We argue that the curriculum is important in itself, in that it creates a very powerful context for learning in school. The particular form of learning is also important. Every choice in the curriculum is an ideologically motivated choice. We are quite open in our emphasis on learning as being important in itself: a good education is its own reward. Of course, a good education prepares you for life but it also allows you to enjoy the present. Especially in primary schools, this is essential. An early education in primary schools might provide superficial gains in short-term political and institutional performance targets. However, it may also have a long-term impact, shutting the gate on a generation of learners through an irrelevant curriculum, which does not promote understanding of the world as it is and as it can be. Many in the creative arts and industries argue for the development of learners who are able to apply using problem-solving and core skills in a variety of contexts. In short, this is a curriculum which promotes curiosity, a love of learning and a humanistic view of education. NESTA (2007) identified innovative learning as providing individuals with confidence based on their mastery of the basic skills that are the building blocks of all good education allied with the deep subject knowledge that allows them to create new ideas. Such learners are not the docile participants identified by Foucault in his analysis of the educational framework for compliance, alluded to in Ball et al. (2012). The alternative view of education for compliance is education for liberation. In this view, learners seize the initiative, challenge accepted norms and have the soft skills they need to develop and exploit these ideas.

An education for liberation lifts learning to focus on an analysis of the issues of today, providing learners with the skills, knowledge and motivation to become active, compassionate and successful citizens for today and tomorrow. This is an ambitious aim for the curriculum. It promotes pupils' and teachers' classroom experience as being important in itself. Every time we learn, we learn something about learning (Wells and Claxton 2002). Learners must be learners for life: for a future career in areas as yet unseen and towards a longer period of old age in which employment in itself may not be a central concern. Developing an education for compliance, providing politicians with the opportunities to generate political capital, simply is not good enough. This leads to a culture of performance rather than a culture of learning (Dweck 1990). A culture of performance and compliance in itself will not provide the context for innovation, which NESTA identifies is important for the present and the future school curriculum. Since curriculum and accountability are inextricably linked, a curriculum for liberation needs a particular form of accountability. Since curriculum outcomes are closely linked to the school and national assessment frameworks, these will also need close examination to identify approaches which foster enduring learning rather than a mere performance of understanding. This will be discussed in some detail in Chapter 10.

In this chapter, we have argued for a curriculum for liberation, which goes beyond the distorting stranglehold of accountability and inspection. An objectives-based curriculum, which leads to a highly regulated and monitored culture of performance, in itself, does not promote innovative learning and learning for innovation. It promotes compliance. We believe that education must transcend compliance. In the next chapter we explore the role of different forms of technology to promote learning. These offer exciting and different forms of learning. Innovation is synonymous with the Internet and new technologies.

Chapter summary

- Innovation should promote individual as well as collective growth, recognising the contribution of new technologies to what we learn and how we learn.
- A curriculum for innovation highlights the learners' contribution to society in terms of their new thinking, experiences and engagement with society.
- An innovative curriculum encourages teachers to experiment with new forms of knowledge, taking different approaches to knowledge and school learning.
- Innovative teachers take risks: they experiment with different teaching strategies which engage learners.
- As societies are constantly changing, it is important that a curriculum is responsive to the needs of the children as they are at the moment and of society as it is and as it will be.
- Education across the world is experiencing significant changes: there are different school structures, family and societal structures are changing, school communities are increasingly diverse, partly as a result of globalisation and the movement of peoples due to war and economic necessity.
- An education for liberation lifts learning to focus on an analysis of the issues of today, providing learners with the skills, knowledge and motivation to become active, compassionate and successful citizens for today and tomorrow.

Further reading and research

Bloom, B.S., Engelhart, M.D., Furst, E.J., Hill, W.H. and Krathwohl, D.R. (eds) (1956). *Taxonomy of Educational Objectives – The Classification of Educational Goals – Handbook 1: Cognitive Domain*. London: Longmans, Green & Co. Ltd.

Dweck, Carol S. (1990). Self-theories and goals: their role in motivation, personality, and development, in Richard Dienstbier (ed.), *Perspectives on Motivation: Nebraska Symposium on Motivation*. Lincoln: University of Nebraska Press, 38, 199–235.

McKernan, J. (2010). A critique of instructional objectives. *Education Inquiry*, 1(1): 57–67.

NESTA (2007). *Education for Innovation*. Available at: http://www.nesta.org.uk/futureinnovators (accessed December 2013).

Wells, G. and Claxton, G. (eds) (2002). *Learning for Life in the 21st Century: Sociocultural Perspectives on the Future of Education*. Oxford: Blackwell.

CHAPTER 7

INNOVATIVE LEARNING TECHNOLOGIES

Chapter guide

In this chapter you will learn about:

- The added value of using technology to support learning
- What does being digitally literate mean?
- The role of the teacher and technology
- The impact of mobile, digital technologies on learning and teaching

---

The last decade has shown a significant shift with the adoption of technology becoming interwoven into the very fabric of our lives. Consider for a moment your own personal use of digital technology. How often do you 'connect' to some form of technology, whether it is checking e-mails, booking flights, ordering groceries or playing games? We are constantly besieged with information in multiple formats and enticed into communicating with strangers about what we are doing, in real time. It is not difficult to understand when

Craft (2012) claims that we have a 'parallel existence in virtual space' that has become 'seamlessly integrated with our lives' (p. 174). We live in a very different world compared with fifteen years ago. By the time they begin school, today's children will already have encountered an array of different technologies used in everyday life, which play an important part in the technological landscape in which they are growing up. They are 'digital natives'.

When Prensky (2001a) introduced the term 'digital natives', he was referring to those brought up in a society with the digital language of computers, video games, and the Internet who have been totally immersed in vast amounts of multimedia information such as film, audio, text and image. These 'natives' are what we may call information savvy or digitally literate and are able to interact naturally with technologies such as the social networking tools Twitter and Facebook. They are able to write blogs and engage with computer games, moving seamlessly between them, simultaneously chatting, often across the continents, researching and working on assignments in a coherent and logical way. Such enviable familiarity with these technologies brings freedom to move around in what seems to the 'digital immigrant', those *not* born into the digital world but who may have engaged in some aspects of the new technologies, to be an unstructured but instinctive way (Knobel 2008). These 'natives' are in fact, our children.

An explanation for this ability to interact so easily between technologies could be the multitude of different experiences children are exposed to while growing up, which can lead to changes in brain structures (Prensky 2001a). In Chapter 3, we noted that the cognitive structures of a child's brain are continuously shaped by their experience and the brain has the potential to change (Sutton-Smith 1997; Goswami and Bryant 2007). Further research has also suggested that as a result of total immersion and interaction with our technology-rich environment, children think and process information in a less linear and fundamentally different way; their thinking patterns have changed. Children flit from one thing to another in the virtual environment and develop what could be described as a 'hyper-text' or 'hyperlinked' minds. 'It's as though their cognitive structures were parallel, not sequential' (Prensky 2001b: 3). Research has shown that brain cells are constantly replenished and the brain has the potential to change and reorganise itself differently throughout our lives, based on the inputs it receives. This is known as 'neuroplasticity', which refers to any changes in neural pathways and synapses. These changes are the product of changes in behaviour, environment and neural processes (Prensky 2001b). There is no doubt that the thinking patterns of our digital natives have changed as they have developed.

What does being digitally literate mean?

Digital literacy is having the capacity to understand information, interpret it, and evaluate and integrate the information into multiple formats; these skills are essential in this technological era (Gilster 1997). Being digitally literate empowers our society to be able to create, collaborate and communicate effectively using digital technologies and to understand how and when they can best be used to support learning (Hague and Payton 2010). It also allows children to understand how to use technology both safely and meaningfully in a growing digital world. To be digitally literate is not just an issue that faces young people, but teachers too. Technology is continually evolving and changing at such a rapid pace that it is becoming increasingly difficult to keep up with developments. This change does of course bring with it both opportunity and challenge to educators, as being 'digitally literate' is now seen as a positive entitlement for young people (Hague and Williamson 2009; Beetham et al. 2009), and is also a fundamental part of the new computing curriculum.

Access to digital tools and the capability to interact with them is part of a changing skill set that embraces a much broader variety of 'complex cognitive, motor, sociological and emotional skills'. In order for young people to be able to achieve or make sense of these new, digital environments and technologies, 'digital literacy needs to be taught and learned so that children are able to benefit and participate in this digital world' (Gilster 1997; Eshet 2004: 93). For that reason, opportunities must be provided for children to share their ideas creatively in multiple formats for diverse audiences, and to use different information from an extensive range of sources and devices.

It is without doubt that digital technologies offer opportunities for innovation in teaching practice, such as the use of the interactive whiteboard (IWB), or video conferencing such as Skype. However, opportunities for how technology can be used to support learners to *learn* needs to be at the forefront of teaching and where it can be the most powerful. Rather than being used discretely in isolated learning activities, the use of technologies needs to be thoroughly embedded across the curriculum so that for learners, it becomes the 'norm' to be able to *choose* which technology to use to support them in their learning, and also to have opportunities to use them in a much more creative and innovative way. To become proficient users of digital technologies, children not only need to make use of these technological tools for communicating and creating, but they also need to *understand* how they are used.

This will only become apparent through the development of skills using digital tools, application and practice and, of course, opportunity. There is no single technology that is 'best' for learning (Luckin et al. 2012), so we need to listen to the pupils when selecting ways of presenting ideas to demonstrate learning. With careful planning and scaffolding of learning, development of knowledge and skills, as teachers, can we take a leap of faith and allow our learners to make their own choices? We believe so.

An important consideration is what value will using digital technologies bring to the learners? Will it help and support the children to learn more effectively? Will it empower them so that they can express themselves more successfully, or promote a more inclusive classroom? If the answer to any of these questions is 'no' then you need to question why you are using these technologies in the classroom. Though we are advocators of the use of technology, we believe that not all learners benefit from using digital technologies. Each child is a unique individual and needs to be given the choice whether to use technology to represent their ideas, or not.

Teachers and technology

The use of digital technologies has become more prevalent in schools and is seen as a 'technological tool' with which to facilitate both teaching and learning. For some practitioners it may be a case of denial, for others, acceptance. Whichever it may be for you, technology in our classrooms is here to stay. For the sakes of the children, it is our duty to embrace this and the only question now is how this might be.

Findings have indicated that 'students expect to use a variety of technologies in their learning as many students use technologies as a natural tool in their everyday life' (Geer and Sweeney 2012: 294). Children are already immersed in the digital technologies that schools may be struggling to embrace and their expectations are that they continue to have access to them when in the classroom. This however can vary hugely as schools struggle to both understand what a twenty-first century learning environment might look like and how to support their learners in this new and changing environment on limited budgets.

How do we know that learning is being supported by these tools? Every new technology brings with it the promise of improved learner experience and raised standards, but sadly, more often than not it becomes a passing craze or promise, with equipment being hastily thrust to the back of the cupboard, never to see the light of day again. This then raises the frequent and slightly contentious issue of additional training for teachers in order to be able to use this equipment in practice. Due to the rapidly developing digital world, some teachers will not have had previous experience of using technology in their classroom practice, nor had any training. This can make the challenge for these teachers all the more difficult (Vrasidas et al. 2010).

The benefits of embedding technology to improve practice are undisputed. More importantly, the ability to teach pupils the skills and knowledge required to be able to use technology to support their learning, is also recognised. However, there is an initial cost to teachers in terms of time to learn these new tools. Potential will only be realised through innovative teaching practice, and to achieve this, additional training may indeed be required. Teachers need to be empowered by these new technologies, not compromised by a lack of support and training. Burden et al. (2012) suggest that requirements for 'formal' training of teachers could be minimal, and instead, other opportunities for professional development should be considered, in particular experiential learning, sharing best practice or developing virtual networks and communities of practice. However, time and support is still essential from senior management in order to allow teachers to explore the full potential of such technologies and their impact on learners.

The role of the teacher

With the emergence of new digital technologies and the growing potential for peer learning, it could be argued that the traditional role of the teacher is changing. The teacher is no longer the centre of attention, the one who imparts knowledge and information at the front of the classroom, but rather one of 'facilitator', guiding and questioning, setting goals and providing support and resources for the task. A more familiar and emerging scenario is to see many pupils 'coaching and teaching their peers without the intervention of the class teacher' (Burden et al. 2012: 10).

Following a report in 2012 by the University of Hull, it was found that when used effectively, technology can enhance the effectiveness of peer learning. In particular, it was noted that following the integration of digital technologies into the learning environment, learners with English as an additional language significantly benefited from their use alongside peer coaching and by using technology to develop podcasts in their own language to share and speak with each other, this also increased both confidence and independence (Burden et al. 2012).

Traditional approaches to learning such as 'tutorial' and 'exposition', two kinds of interaction between learner and teacher, are commonplace in the classroom and at the heart of classroom practice. If used appropriately, digital technology can support these interactions. The first interaction, 'tutorial', is the dialogue between learner and teacher (Luckin et al. 2012: 16). Supported by evidence from Bloom (1984), it was suggested that 1:1 teaching is a more effective way to learn and children achieve significantly more than they would in a traditional classroom setting. In recent studies, Luckin et al. (2012) observed that the use of technology is indeed beginning to make the 'personal tutorial' more accessible for pupils. A tablet computer that may contain specific digital tools, or apps, particularly suited to the needs of a learner becomes a very powerful and mobile 'personal learning partner'. Other free digital tools such as Twitter and Skype could be considered as powerful ways for live discussion or feedback, as this can take place even when participants are not in the same location. It was also noted that technology has the ability to 'enhance dialogue with visual aids, such as the interactive whiteboards' or tablets, the latter becoming much more commonplace in today's classroom (Luckin et al. 2012: 16). In a number of classrooms tablets have been seen to encourage children to engage in focused talk and conversation, or what Alexander (2006) would term constructive dialogue. Technology may be seen to facilitate dialogue that will in turn enhance learning. However, technology should not be seen as a teacher 'replacement'.

The second form of interaction observed by Luckin et al. was the structure and presentation of learning material described as 'exposition'. Undoubtedly the emergence of new digital technologies brings with it new, interactive and dynamic ways of presenting information such as film, animation, podcasting and ebooks. However, it was found that while these resources are easily accessible and engaging, 'the learner's role can often be passive', and that learners still need the support of 'teachers to interpret those ideas and to convert that information into knowledge' (Luckin et al. 2012: 16). Learning should be an active process rather than passive, and caution needs be taken when replacing traditional methods with digital ones. Consideration must be given to how these digital resources are used and we must question whether or not the learners are active and learning, or merely engaged.

Though it has been suggested that there is a shift from the typical 'teacher–learner dynamic towards coordinating peer learning', learners will still need the support of a teacher to scaffold learning and to convert that information into knowledge (Luckin et al. 2012). The role of a 'more knowledgeable other' (Vygotsky 1978), or 'expert' outside that of a peer, to guide and scaffold the learners should never be underrated. The use of digital technologies such as tablets can provide a 'link between the students and teachers, with the role of "expert" continually shifting between them resulting in the development of a positive rapport' (Department of Education and Training [DET] 2011: 18).

Interactive whiteboards

One of the greatest digital revolutions of the modern day classroom was initiated by the introduction of interactive whiteboards (IWBs) and typically, primary classrooms are more than likely be equipped with one. Considerable investment was made as part of the UK government's plan to invest and install IWBs into schools. This was partly in response to the need to enhance understanding, and use, of information and communications technology (ICT), but more importantly, it was a reaction to evidence from research that highlighted the growing need for pedagogic change from didactic to interactive teaching and learning, and the use of multimedia as a visual stimulus for learners (Gillen et al. 2007).

Over the last decade, it has become apparent that there are obvious benefits to the use of this technology because it has the capacity to transform teaching techniques from the ordinary, to an innovative multimodal delivery of information in a pacey and interactive style. However, careful consideration needs to be given to the use of the IWB, as this alone cannot transform learning, nor is it a technological fix that will change the pedagogy of whole-class teaching (Smith et al. 2006). To be effective, it needs to be integrated and thoroughly embedded into teaching, rather than a technological add-on, otherwise the use of IWBs becomes driven by the technology rather than by the needs of the learners (Smith et al. 2006).

Studies have shown that interactive whiteboards were mainly being used as 'a data projector that can navigate to multiple screens; as a surface which can generate a dynamic rather than static form of display; to enhance presentation in front of the class' (Moss et al. 2007: 5). If they are used exclusively as a conventional whiteboard and merely projected onto, this will not develop the interactivity that is essential to enhancing children's learning, and unfortunately, in some schools, teachers are making little use of such technologies and pupils have limited access to them (McCormick and Scrimshaw 2001; Russell et al. 2005).

As with anything new, time, familiarity and confidence are essential to be able to develop skills and knowledge of using an IWB so that there is a move from purely supporting teaching, to extending and finally transforming pedagogy as teachers gradually find out what the technology can do (Moss et al. 2007: 6). Once this has been achieved, the full potential of this digital tool can be released and embedded seamlessly into teaching. As Gillen et al. (2007: 12) observe, using IWBs effectively will most likely involve 'striking a balance between providing a clear structure for a well resourced lesson, and retaining the capacity for more spontaneous or provisional adaptation of the lesson as it proceeds'.

Mobile technology

In the past decade, technologies have shifted from being complex and very expensive to being mobile and much easier to use (Hedberg 2011). Consequently, considerable amounts of money are being invested in digital technology for educational use (Luckin et al. 2012).

A report on the increased uptake of emerging mobile technology in education across Australia, New Zealand, the UK, and South America (Johnson et al. 2012) suggests that tablet computing not only presents new opportunities to enhance learning experiences, but with the higher definition and larger screens, pupils are able to share content, images, music and video much more easily than was possible before, fostering key skills such as collaboration, problem-solving, critical thinking, communication, creativity and innovation. Evidence shows that schools are beginning to see tablets as an affordable, 'feature-rich' environment for learning, collaboratively or one-to-one, that can be applied across the curriculum and which will replace the traditional expensive and often cumbersome devices and equipment (Clark and Luckin 2013). Whether or not the use of such technology impacts on learning or pedagogical skills in the classroom still remains to be seen, and it cannot be assumed that new technology means better learning. New technologies cannot, in themselves, improve learning: so much depends on the context in which they are used.

It is becoming more apparent in schools that mobile technologies, with their simple access to digital tools, enables 'a wider range of learning activities to routinely occur in the classroom' (Clark and Luckin 2013: 3). In a trial to determine the suitability of the iPad as a learning tool for teaching and learning, it was found that the 'iPad was viewed unanimously by participating teachers as a cross-curriculum device that is not constrained to a specific subject area'. This is demonstrated 'by the range of apps available and mobility of the device' (DET 2011: 25). The effortless use of technologies such as this can support the role of teachers more effectively, helping them to manage resources with greater ease, compared with the traditional desktop PC system of complex logins and potential network issues. However, this is not to say that there are no issues of their own in using this technology.

As a professional tool, teachers who engaged with tablet technology believed it to be a significant benefit because it transformed access to the use of technology. They no longer had the worry of trying to find a computer that would support their lesson and expressed the importance of personal ownership of a tablet. It was felt that this enabled them 'to use the tool not only to support teaching and learning but also for administration and data purposes such as taking registration, planning lessons, facilitating target setting and enabling students to see immediately the results of their learning' (Clark and Luckin 2013: 21). Evidence was also found to show that, in terms of the learners, this technology had the potential to 'promote independent learning, to differentiate learning more easily for different student needs and to easily share resources both with students and with each other' (Clark and Luckin 2013: 21).

Digital technology and the learning environment

While learning has traditionally been within the primary classroom, digital technology has begun to change our way of thinking about learning spaces. A key benefit of these new digital technologies is their mobility and ability to be used in many different learning environments, even outdoors.

 Classroom case study

An example using QR codes

QR codes are barcodes which, when scanned with the mobile device, connect users to web links, text or other digital content very quickly and easily. A Derbyshire primary school used QR codes in a simple but effective way. As part of their school development plan to improve the use of technology in learning, they wanted their curriculum to reflect innovative use of digital technologies from Reception through to Year 6. In the Year 1 class, teachers were able to engage children interactively in their lessons by creating treasure hunts using QR codes around the school, with the focus being on shapes in the environment. Children were able to interact with the mobile device and engage in their learning in a fun and interactive way, rather than passively looking at the interactive whiteboard.

For older children in the school, QR codes were being used around the classrooms with links to photographs of, for example, different features of rivers, or links to short video clips that help to explain a specific geographical process.

Learning is no longer confined to within the school and more innovative use of virtual learning spaces is emerging in some schools, using free Web-based tools such as Skype. This has the potential to provide many different contexts anywhere in the world where learners can be linked with other learners or 'experts' with relative ease, as long as there is sufficient broadband available. Learning experiences could include anything from sharing book reviews to learning a new sport from a different culture, to linking with different, diverse communities. To offer these innovative learning and teaching experiences, consideration needs to be given to the learning environment. It should no longer be confined to the classroom but linked to the whole world as a learning place that can be easily accessed by all (Luckin et al. 2012). This can be achieved using technology and extends the reach of teaching with technology.

Classroom case study

Skyping an author

During an author visit to the school, the children were enthused and inspired by the tales of becoming an author and subsequently wanted to write themselves, which of course was why the visit was arranged. During conversations with the author, it transpired that he was already an enthusiastic advocator of Skype, and with very little coaxing, agreed to a follow up with a 'virtual visit' for a group of children.

As with any activity, it is important that there is a purpose for learning. What will the children learn from this? They had already written stories based around the author visit and so something different that would involve feedback and interaction during the Skype call was required. In this case, it was to learn about writing book reviews.

The author had just completed a new book due to be released for World Book Day, which was unread by anybody else and still in manuscript form. The author suggested that the children should be allowed to read the manuscript and write a book review for it which would then be used for the book on his website. However, this had to remain top secret, not even the parents would be allowed to read the manuscript.

In line with the whole school improvement plan for improving writing and challenging the more able writers, a group of key stage two children from across the year groups were selected as part of the project. Excitement was high as the author presented the challenge by first making a video of himself explaining the 'top secret mission' on a YouTube video link. A date was then set for the book review Skype link with the author himself.

During the ensuing Skype call, the children read out their book reviews to the author who was delighted with the response of the children to his new book, making this very clear with his enthusiastic response, much to the delight of the children. They were also able to talk with him to find out why he had written about specific things in the book, why he had chosen the location for the story, where his inspiration had come from and much more. It was a very honest, relaxed and informative question and answer session.

The author benefited from the interaction with the children, his audience, and the children felt they too had made a difference and their self-esteem rose immeasurably. In terms of learning, the children had a real-life context for their book reviews and an invaluable opportunity to use technology to link with an expert, and gain a unique insight into the thoughts and journey of an author and his book.

Using iPads for learning

Since the first generation of iPads was introduced in 2010, there has been a steady uptake of their use in education. As more research is undertaken, findings are beginning to report that these devices are having a positive impact on pupils' engagement with learning (Clark and Luckin 2013). Notably, it was found that if pupils had their own individual iPad, they were considerably more confident and able to manage their own learning. This was a result of being able to personalise the device with digital tools and resources that would specifically help and support their particular needs (Gasparini 2011; Heinrich 2012). Learning can be differentiated, scaffolded and customised using built-in tools such as text to speech apps, allowing pupils who might previously struggle to learn in other ways (Burden et al. 2012). The provision of instant and easy access to tools and information is a major strength, with very little time being lost on setting up or logging on (Henderson and Yeow 2012).

Co-founder of Apple, Steve Jobs, declared in a speech in 1983 that their strategy was a simple one: 'we want to put an incredibly great computer in a book that you can carry around with you and learn how to use in 20 minutes' (Panzarino 2012). What seemed to be an inconceivable but highly innovative dream back in the 1980s is now a reality, and one which we almost take for granted now. The iPad is that vision of portable technology with easy access and connectivity to data worldwide, but more importantly, one where the user interface is so simple to use, that within 20 minutes the user is able to do something extraordinary.

Due to its portability, responsiveness and ease of use, it was found to be a powerful collaborative tool; once information was found or created it could be passed around to others very quickly and easily. The essence of a socially constructivist classroom has social interaction, or collaboration, at the heart of learning and highlights that children learn better through interaction and conversation with peers and teachers, developing learning communities to work collaboratively in problem-solving and the co-construction of knowledge (Churchill et al. 2011; Oluwafisayo 2010). Learning is viewed as an active process where children construct their own meaning and knowledge based on prior knowledge. They are encouraged to seek out and solve problems for themselves based on their own way of thinking and of solving the problem (Brewer and Daane 2002). Learners construct their own understanding rather than receiving it passively from others; and this becomes most effective when shared. Digital technologies such as the iPad are well placed to support the constructivist classroom.

Greater consideration is being given to the iPad as one of the more inclusive tools for helping children to construct their own knowledge, due to its multifunctional array of tools that support learning. It has the capacity to facilitate a much more collaborative way of learning, whether the user is connecting with other learners, either in their own learning environment or elsewhere, or indeed support independent learning. Studies have also shown that pupil engagement remains high, even after the novelty effect has worn off. Children generally became more engaged in their learning, with pupils feeling empowered by what they were working on and willing to spend more time and effort on their work, thus resulting in the creation of higher level of presentations (DET 2011; Henderson and Yeow 2012). The iPad was also seen as the contributing factor to an improvement in learning as it allowed pupils to break tasks down into more manageable chunks, and notably, in terms of boys' perception, they felt that they were having fun while working (DET 2011).

All technologies used in the classroom come with particular issues of their own, such as setting up the devices, budgets for purchasing and maintaining equipment, or managing the learning environment so that pupils do not dominate the use of the device and stay on task without being distracted. This, however, could be said for any portable, technological device and careful management of the learning environment is advised to ensure that this does not occur.

The SAMR model

Digital technologies potentially play a major role in learning tasks to enhance, augment and support deeper learning. However, to simply substitute a

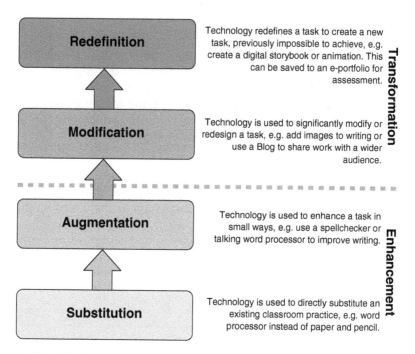

Figure 7.1   The SAMR model

Adapted from Puentedura (2013)

traditional activity such as writing using pencil and paper with digital technology, just because it is new and digital, should not be the motivation or rationale. The Substitution–Augmentation–Modification–Redefinition model (SAMR), developed by Ruben Puentedura (2013), was designed to help teachers understand how such technologies can be successfully integrated into existing teaching practices and learning, so that the *use* of the technology is not the focus, but rather the *support*, to meet pupil needs. The SAMR model is twofold: it guides educators to consider more carefully their use of technology to allow them to accomplish pedagogical goals that may previously have been inconceivable; to use technology to significantly improve pupils' achievement.

The integration of digital technologies is represented in the SAMR model as a continuum of four significant levels of change that moves from substitution through to redefinition of a classroom activity. Puentedura's original model does not demonstrate a sense of progression through these stages, and we have therefore developed this further, adding arrows to Figure 7.1 to more clearly indicate that the integration of digital technologies works most effectively on a continuum.

An example using the SAMR model (based on Puentedura 2013)

1. Substitution

This is the use of technology as a direct tool substitute for an existing classroom practice that improves efficiency. There is no functional change and it does not in any way significantly impact student outcomes. For example, rather than the pupil using pencil and paper to write, this is substituted with a word processor. It does the same task but there is no modification of the task, only the introduction of technology. There is no real gain to be had from the computer technology.

2. Augmentation

This is still a direct tool substitute and the task has not changed, but it uses technology to enhance the task in small ways such as the use of specific features to accomplish the task in a more efficient way. This could be quicker and easier access to the Internet, using a spellchecker or a talking word processor to improve writing.

It is at this level that it goes beyond the efficiency level and pupils may begin to become more engaged in the task while using the technology.

3. Modification

At this level technology can be used to significantly modify or redesign the task, which allows some learners to be able to accomplish new goals they previously struggled to accomplish. This could be as simple as adding images or, having used technology to write an essay, this can be easily shared by a wider audience by using a blog or Google docs, or even Skype. This provides the opportunity to critique the work and allows for feedback they would not have had before. At this point, significant improvements in pupil outcomes start to be seen.

4. Redefinition

Technology completely redefines the task by either partially or fully replacing the original task to create a new task, previously impossible to achieve without the use of technology. It allows the teacher to accomplish pedagogical goals that were previously inconceivable. The use of the technology allows pupils to convey deep analytical thought and meaning in other media, for example, creating a digital story book or an animation, or using an app on the iPad such as 'Explain Everything' to annotate and document problem-solving strategies which can then be saved to an e-portfolio for assessment. At this level, there is a dramatic improvement in pupils' outcomes and new technologies may transform the nature of a subject at the most fundamental level (McCormick and Scrimshaw 2001).

When following the SAMR model and using technology to reach the final 'redefinition' level, it leads to the transformation of classroom and student workflows and the technology is used in its most effective and powerful form. Puentedura (2013) also suggests a series of probing questions to ask when considering the integration of technology into the learning activity and breaks them down into the four different levels.

The SAMR ladder: questions and transitions (Puentedura 2013)

Substitution:

- What will I gain by replacing the older technology with the new technology?

Substitution to Augmentation:

- Have I added an improvement to the task process that could not be accomplished with the older technology at a fundamental level?
- How does this feature contribute to my design (of the learning experience)?

(Continued)

(Continued)

Augmentation to Modification:

- How is the original task being modified?
- Does this modification fundamentally depend upon the new technology?
- How does this modification contribute to my design?

Modification to Redefinition:

- What is the new task?
- Will any portion of the original task be retained?
- How is the new task uniquely made possible by the new technology?
- How does it contribute to my design?

The SAMR model in practice

When considering the many diverse digital technologies, the impact of the iPad in schools was found to be considerable, even at the augmentation, or enhancement, stage of the SAMR model. The research showed that it not only made the classroom 'a more efficient pedagogic place', but 'had significant impact on the attitudes of the students to learning allowing them to develop in some key skills areas as autonomous learners and self-managers of their own learning' (Burden et al. 2012: 95).

The adoption of the 'Brushes' application for the iPad was used extensively by teachers in schools in a pilot study in Scotland, and epitomises the modification and redefinition levels in the SAMR model. Utilisation of this app enabled learners 'to extend and modify normal art practices', and in some cases, 'to undertake activities which would previously have been inconceivable at the school level' (Burden et al. 2012: 95). In this instance, the use of technology in art was recognised as going beyond 'substitution' for a traditional art technique and more as 'modification' and 'redefinition'. For example, pupils were able to use techniques of filtering and image manipulation that would normally be impossible to achieve using conventional techniques. Pupils' work could also be very easily retrieved and assessed using the powerful step-by-step feature within the app that records the whole process. Therefore, the technology utilised here, the iPad and 'Brushes' app, transformed the activity and redefined it, allowing pupils to engage in 'learning activities which would previously be difficult or even impossible to undertake, in the context of a classroom' (Burden et al. 2012: 96).

A significant feature of this technology is the provisionality. The use of such an app can give pupils greater confidence to take creative risks, experiment more than they would if they were using traditional methods and remove the fear of failure by using a feature as simple as 'undo'. If their ideas do not work, they can discard them, or re-visit earlier ideas to evaluate and refine them. Having that freedom to experiment, play or take risks are essential for creative learning and can have a positive effect on the learners' self-esteem.

 Classroom case study

Transformational learning

Many schools not just in the UK, but in other parts of the world, have introduced a 1:1 iPad initiative for pupils. Over a period of time, the iPad has been introduced in most subject areas with key uses being brainstorming, research, note-taking, presentations, homework and study, creative arts and game design.

Areas where iPads have improved efficiency and provided a major improvement to what can be achieved were reported by pupils to be ease and speed of access to the Internet; use of iBooks; access to learning tools to support learners such as the text-to-speech app and translation tools; digital mind mapping and annotation tools; and easy access to educational games. iPads were found to be an easily accessible tool for accessing learning content in the form of ebooks or Web-based materials.

Parents stated that home–school communication was improved dramatically and that having less books to carry around was a major benefit.

However, funding is potentially an issue in the UK, as costs of rolling out 1:1 tablet initiatives are high, with no consistent model amongst schools: some provide devices for a minimal cost and others require greater outlay of costs from parents.

Based on a study of the introduction of iPads at Longfield Academy in Kent (Heinrich 2012).

 Reflection point

- Reflect on a technology-based activity you have observed in your school.
- Consider how you could have approached this differently using the SAMR model?
- Using the different levels in the SAMR model, consider how you could take your activity from 'enhancement' to 'transformation'?
- Was there an improvement to pupil outcomes?

The use of technology for documentation

The use of technology for assessment in the classroom is a developing area with considerable opportunities to make assessment more efficient, dynamic, effective and supportive. Educators already use smartphones or iPads to record images, video and sound as learning unfolds, integrating them into school blogs, e-learning journals and online e-portfolios for assessment, so that assessment is not restricted to the end of a learning episode but more of an ongoing process (Parnell and Bartlett 2012).

As an essential part of teaching and planning for next steps in learning, the use of a digital documentation process to gather records of learning experiences for assessment does not need to be restricted to the teacher. In fact, there are significant opportunities for the learners themselves to be involved in the assessment process. With greater opportunities to use mobile, hand-held devices, assessment has the potential to become more child-driven and help children to make more sense of their own learning and ultimately build on their learning.

 Classroom case study

Using tablets for group self assessment

A class of 32 children in upper primary school were required to set up their own investigation to explore the forces of attraction and repulsion between magnets and the forces of attraction between magnets and magnetic materials. This in itself was a challenge, as there was only a class teacher to support all groups of learners and it was important to capture evidence of both understanding and how to set up the scientific investigation. The teacher also wanted to evaluate whether each group could work collaboratively.

A solution was to use a multifunctional screen casting tool on the iPad called 'Explain Everything'.

An iPad was placed on each table for the children to use. They were asked to work as teams to capture their discussions about how they might set up the investigation, including predictions, with the video feature. They were then asked to use the app to capture their science investigation and explain their scientific thinking using any of the features of the app.

Each group carefully planned and organised their investigation and documented their progress either as digital photos with annotations, or using video. They then used the screen casting tool to talk the audience through their findings referring either to the images or the video. The pupils were asked to reflect on their learning experiences and share their findings with the whole class, using the app to model.

The class teacher was able to watch each video back and see the learning develop, noting down progress made by individuals, next steps for learning and teamwork. Importantly, the teacher was also able to learn about how and why learning occurs.

This method of recording the children's work also had other unexpected advantages. It was noted that by involving the learners themselves in the recording and assessment process, they began to view their learning differently, making more sense of it, and consequently their learning became more pupil-led.

 Reflection point

- Consider how you could use technology to support assessment in your learning environment.
- What will you do with the evidence collected for the next steps in learning?
- Consider how you might involve the children in the assessment process.

Digital documentation tips

- Record the process (rather than product) of learning.
- Include the children's words.
- Add your own reflections.
- Document with children present and engaged with you in the documentation process.
- Ask the children about their process either while recording or when they're viewing the documentation later.

Based on Parnell and Bartlett (2012: 52).

Chapter summary

- Research suggests that as a result of immersion and interaction in a technology-rich environment, children think and process information in a less linear and fundamentally different way.
- For both educationalists and learners, digital literacy is having the capacity to understand information, interpret it and be able to evaluate and integrate the information into multiple formats.

- Whether or not the use of such technology impacts on learning or pedagogical skills in the classroom still remains to be seen, and it cannot be assumed that new technology means better learning. New technologies cannot, in themselves, improve learning.
- There are benefits to the use of IWBs because they have the capacity to transform teaching techniques from the ordinary to the innovative multimodal delivery of information. However, careful consideration needs to be given to the use of the IWB, and they should not be seen as a 'technological fix' that will change the pedagogy of whole-class teaching.
- There has been an increased uptake of mobile technology in education which presents new opportunities to enhance both personal and collaborative learning experiences.
- Learning is no longer confined to within the school and more innovative use of virtual learning spaces is emerging in some schools.
- When following the SAMR model and using technology to reach the final 'redefinition' level, it leads to the transformation of classroom and student workflows and the technology is used in its most effective and powerful form.

Further reading and research

Churchill, R., Ferguson, P., Godinho, S., Johnson, N.F., Keddie, A., Letts, W., Mackay, J., McGill, M., Moss, J., Nagel, M.C., Nicholson, P. and Vick, M. (2011). *Teaching: Making a Difference*, 2nd edn. Milton, Queensland: John Wiley and Sons Australia.

Clark, W. and Luckin, R. (2013). What the research says – iPads in the classroom. Available at: http://www.thepdfportal.com/ipads-in-the-classroom-report-lkl_61713.pdf

Gasparini, A.A. (2011). Touch, learn, play – what children do with an iPad in the classroom. Masters Thesis, University of Oslo. Available at: https://www.duo.uio.no/handle/123456789/9015

Hedberg, J.G. (2011). Towards a disruptive pedagogy: changing classroom practice with technologies and digital content. *Educational Media International*, 48(1): 1–16.

Heinrich, P. (2012). *The iPad as a Tool for Education*. NAACE and 9ine Consulting. Available at: http://www.naace.co.uk/get.html?_Action=GetFile&_Key=Data26613&_Id=1965&_Wizard=0&_DontCache=1341555048.

Puentedura, R. (2013). *SAMR: Getting To Transformation*. Available at: http://www.hippasus.com/rrpweblog/archives/2013/04/16/SAMRGettingToTransformation.pdf

CHAPTER 8

WORKING WITH OTHERS AS PART OF A TEAM

Chapter guide

In this chapter you will learn about:

- Change management and leadership towards innovative learning and teaching
- Working with teaching assistants: developing communication and trust through collaborative planning, teaching and assessment
- Illustrative examples from schools

This chapter explains how teachers and managers can change the culture in school from learned helplessness to innovation. The principles of change management are explained with illustrative examples of classroom and school practice. Collaborative working between teachers and teaching assistants is particularly important. School-to-school arrangements are now more commonplace due to the changing nature of local authorities: an example from schools working in trusts is provided as a framework for school-to-school collaboration.

Introduction

At the individual and institutional level change is ever present; and educational change should always focus on promoting the needs of children. Change for the sake of it is not a good enough reason for change. Many would argue that the changes which have led to the emergence of different school structures have been politically motivated, rather than being educationally driven and therefore child-focused. Changes which result in new ways of working in the classroom can be good or bad. By implication, the word 'innovation' suggests a positive change, with a positive outcome and overall a positive process for change. The process of change is often challenging and there may be short- to medium-term negative experiences for staff, but the long-term picture may be more positive. For this reason, it is important to explore change management in relation to school pupils, teachers and other school professionals. Positive outcomes do not always justify a very negative experience by which the changes have been achieved. These complex and problematic problems always imply a balance of issues, which leaders in a school must consider.

Normally we consider the headteacher to be the main leader in a school; however, careful consideration should be given to the leadership qualities of all the participants in educational change. While there is significant evidence of the role of a headteacher in school developments, leadership is clearly a quality which is encompassed in all adults and learners in a school. It is a characteristic for successful change in the class teacher as well as the class themselves. By recognising the power of all participants to lead new developments in school, we encourage greater engagement and responsibility for enacting change. Importantly, this must include children. If children are marginalised in the process of educational change then there is a risk they will not be engaged in the new developments. As such we should be more positive about the voice of children in developing innovative approaches to learning in school. Since children and young people are the *raison d'être* for schools, it is essential that we listen to their views and include them in any developments. It encourages involvement, ownership and the taking of responsibility at an early stage. The role of children and professionals in the development of innovative practice is explained further in the next section with examples for illustration.

 Reflection point

Consider your own setting in school. What is the range of people you work with in school? These might for instance include:

People you may work with in school	What contribution do these people make to day-to-day learning in your class?
Business managers	
Businesses	
Charities	
Complementary therapist	
Conservation and environmental groups	
Educational psychologists	
English as an additional language specialist teachers	
Inspectors/advisory teachers	
Lunchtime supervisors	
Occupational therapists	
Parents, foster parents and other carers	
Police	
School nurse	
Social workers	
Special education specialist teachers	
Speech and language therapist	
Sports coaches	
Teachers	
Teaching assistants	
Voluntary groups	
Youth and community workers	

As you can see there are many different people, with many different roles, with whom you may work in school. There are probably even more that you can think of beyond the list above.

The list has been written in alphabetical order to allow you to make your own judgements about the relative contributions of each group of people. Some people make a daily contribution. Others touch on the lives of a school infrequently. In some cases, there are opportunities to develop their role and these are discussed in this chapter.

Participants and processes in school innovation

People in school contribute to children's learning in different ways. This can be quite direct as a teacher, but more subtly as a specialist teaching assistant as a learning mentor. On the one side, the teacher teaches, developing skills, knowledge and understanding; on the other, the learning mentor encourages motivation, emotional development and an understanding of how to make progress against given tasks. While it is quite easy to see that the teacher can have a very direct impact on children's learning, we must be open to the idea that different professionals beyond the teacher can have a very important impact on children's learning. The key question in today's schools is, given the limited resources available to schools, what is the best balance of different professionals in the classroom? In order to make this judgement, we need to evaluate the relative contributions of all those who work with children.

Evaluating the contribution of different professionals in school

The evaluation of educational impact is itself an ideological and professional minefield. This is explored in the section below on teaching assistants. For teachers and leaders in school a very useful resource is the Educational Endowment Funds Toolkit (http://educationendowmentfoundation.org.uk/toolkit/). This compares the relative benefits of different professionals with their respective costs. Top of the list comes the contribution of good feedback to children. For a cost of something like £100 per pupil, taking into consideration the expenditure for professional development of teachers and teaching assistants, it is calculated that this can lead to around an eight-month improvement in children's learning. Of course, critics of this approach to evaluating the contributions of different staff would question all the quantitative data presented in support of this analysis. How can a 'per child' cost be analysed and in reality what does 'an eight-month improvement' mean in practice?

The value of the Educational Endowment Foundation resources, we would argue, is less in a rigid calculation of impact, but the ideas and discussion presented should alert teachers and schools to new ways of working which might help them to change things for the better in their schools. Clearly, finding out about different ways of working can be a stimulus for educational innovation.

While professionals can have a direct, and sometimes indirect, impact on children's learning, this can operate on a short- or long-term basis. For example, a very effective way of working with children with additional needs involves teaching teams identifying particular skills of concepts which children need to develop. Certain aspects of the skill or concept can be a barrier to learning.

For example, if you are teaching science, the language itself may be a barrier as a knowledge of the vocabulary is essential in a scientific discussion. One approach to facilitating learning in this case is through pre-teaching aspects of the language so that children are acquainted with the vocabulary involved. For instance, for younger children exploring the properties of different materials, knowing the way to describe materials such as transparent, translucent, opaque, rigid, elastic, floating, or sinking provides some of the language to discuss, explore and communicate the properties of different materials. The important point here is that a decision about short-term learning needs to be made by the teacher and where appropriate the other staff working with children. A pre-teaching activity like this might be undertaken by the teacher, a teaching assistant, a speech and language therapist or learning mentor, depending on the context. A decision about who undertakes this task generally resides with the teacher. This important point recognises the delineation of roles and responsibilities in schools on a day-to-day basis. Generally, the class teacher will take this responsibility, but the ground-rules for making such decisions should be agreed and transparent. Whereas a seamless interchange between a special school teacher and a speech and language therapist can lead to quick and responsive changes to the role they both take in class, such dynamic interplay is quite difficult to foster without highly qualified professionals who are experienced in working together.

Pre-teaching activities can impact on the success of learning within the day and the week of a teaching unit; but other roles and activities within school take longer, with also potentially a longer impact. One such role is in the use of adults to facilitate social and emotional well-being in all children. This can be through a taught programme, such as the Social, Emotional and Affective Learning (SEAL) programme evaluated in DCFS (2005) or through broader school arrangements such as a nurture group. This latter is a short-term, focused, small-group intervention strategy, which addresses emotional and social issues through the development of secure and happy relationships. The SEAL programme can be taught by a teacher to the whole class, but the nurture group is almost always managed by a teaching assistant, extracting children from class at different times of the week according to need. This same 'extraction' arrangement is used in some schools to remove children from their usual classroom activities where they have additional special educational needs and those who speak English as an additional language. The argument is that working in a small group away from the class is more effective, because it provides children with the opportunity to develop learning and language which is essential for accessing the main school curriculum. Others would argue that this marginalises children from the main curriculum, which they have an entitlement to access like any other children.

Regardless of the merits or demerits of working with 'extraction' groups, the key skills which all professionals need in this situation is the ability to work together. This involves good communication skills, the ability to plan together and report back the outcomes of individual groups and programmes of learning.

 Reflection point: professional communication

This section encourages you to reflect on the skills which all professionals need for effective communication. At each stage, consider your own context and how well you would rate yourself in your own skills or understanding.

What is communication?

- Having something to say, a way of saying it and the desire to say it.
- Communication always takes place in a social context and part of this context is the network of professional and personal relationships of those working together.

The quality of relationships is perhaps one of the most important factors in schools and individual classrooms, whether this is with senior leaders, teachers, teaching assistants, parents and senior leaders.

Good communication

- Put simply, successful communication involves a speaker communicating a message to a listener.
- A successful listener engages actively in the process of communication both verbally and non-verbally.

These might seem like simplistic ways of describing a complex act. Of course, professional communication involves an interchange between two or more professionals. They might not always agree; but eventually through a process of compromise, they reach an agreement. Problems occur when the speaker fails to explain their thoughts sufficiently and the listener fails to genuinely listen to the speaker. Poor communication leads to misunderstanding and resentment in either the speaker or listener. Of course, minor communication issues are sustainable when the quality of relationships is sufficiently good to accept the breakdown. Too many of these, and the quality of the professional relationship will itself be compromised.

Good listening

- To truly listen, we must engage in deep listening.
- Deep listening involves listening to others with no preconceptions and not interrupting.
- Listening is an active process, involving verbal and non-verbal cues to facilitate communication.
- Listening involves knowing when to speak and importantly, when not to speak.

Questions can often impede good communication when they close off communication, channelling the topic or discussion in the direction the listener wants and away from that intended by the speaker.

Ground-rules for good communication

Any professional team and working relationship will benefit from starting with an effective set of ground-rules. On committees these might be called 'terms of reference', but effectively they all function as a way to determine an agreed way of working.

Ground-rules should be established at an early stage in any team. While there are many 'downloadable' ground-rules, it is essential that these are negotiated and agreed with the staff involved. Writing down ground-rules and returning to them enables a team to evaluate successes and to avoid pitfalls. The following provides some ideas for focusing your ground-rules for successful communication:

- Open expression by team members
- Include all team members in discussion
- Respond quickly
- Communicate with openness
- Value other's contributions
- Be constructive
- Listen to other people's constructive criticisms
- Respect everyone in the team.

There is some criticism of ground-rules. First, if they are to be useful then sufficient time must be allocated to their development. They should not be seen as a vacuous management tool for controlling a team. If they are to be successful, ground-rules should provide recognisable behaviours and ways of working, to which team members should be accountable. While regulation should never be the focus in good communication, there must be accountability for individuals if the ground-rules are to be in any sense meaningful. For this reason, teams may prefer to identify a set of 'guiding principles' for good communication. This avoids the connotation of 'top-down regulation'. Ultimately, good communication is a central tenet of innovation in schools. Leadership is another key element.

Leadership in schools

Teams involve different people adopting different roles. Plato defined 'justice' as the right person doing the right job. Some people have specialist skills, knowledge or qualities, which make them best suited for particular tasks or roles. This is no less the case in schools. So what is leadership and why is this important for innovation in schools? Thrift (2000) argues that schools, along with Western society, have become focused on short-term performativity, in which leaders must be able to respond quickly to ever-changing demands, often with limited resources and subject to regular monitoring. Inspection in English schools is now recognised as being a dominant theme in headteacher and school concerns in terms of the workload and challenges for the development of their school. This is important because the short-term, short lead into drop-in inspections in England with one or two days' notice can lead to a very flat hierarchy so that change in school is quickly implemented, rather than mediated through a hierarchy of management. Another approach is to delegate the decisions for change and evaluation to other people in school. The role of the headteacher in this situation is to facilitate the structures by which responsibilities and roles have been delegated. In either context, leadership is an important skill.

In his ground-breaking book on school leadership John MacBeath (2002) identifies key aspects of successful leadership, which are also linked to aspects of innovation below.

- **Breaking rules**: research suggests that successful leaders know when to break the rules. Innovation therefore is partly about knowing what the rules are and when to break them.
- **Setting unattainable goals**: managers set SMART targets (Specific, measureable, achieveable, realistic, time-referenced), but leaders, by setting high expectations, can develop a culture of true excellence which goes beyond the expected parameters of the context. Too often we are the victims of our

own limited expectations. Innovation requires going beyond what you think is currently possible, to consider different ways of tackling issues, outside of your current approaches.

- **Leaders have learned how to be led**: by listening to others they demonstrate the ability to grow and go beyond their own initial successes. According to David Hopkins (2001) schools are less machines to be driven and more boats to be sailed through the educational landscape. Of course, the balance between listening to others and maintaining a focus when others are saying differently is not an easy one to achieve. Innovation like leadership requires courage.
- **Being managed**: leaders often sail close to the wind and they can be subject to the tyranny of urgent matters, unless they have others to manage key aspects of their work. Innovation can only happen with the support of others. Having ideas is one thing, but to enact new approaches is as much an act of persuasion of colleagues at all levels.
- **Good leaders behave like grown ups**: those ruled by inflated egos or distorted needs on the basis of difficult past relationships and social development can lead to conflict. While innovation is often driven by powerful personalities, the outcomes for children's learning are of central importance, not the success of the leader;
- **Preferred leadership styles are 'female'**: good communication, the ability to listen, good intrapersonal and interpersonal skills are commonly seen as qualities of women. It is interesting therefore that only in recent years have women become more represented in positions of school leadership. It is as much a function of the societal structures which have sustained men in such leadership positions, that overly authoritative, aggressive approaches to team leadership can be effective in the short term, but is this really a way that we would want to relate to our fellow human beings? Fighting for what is right also means treating people decently on the journey towards innovation.

Change is a significant aspect of both leadership and innovation. The types of change which individual teachers and schools must deal with are multiplying across the world. For instance, the people you work with come and go. New staff are recruited and all come with different personalities, experiences and skills as professionals. The knowledge and skills we need as teachers changes as new government policies and curricula are introduced. The world itself is changing: war and economic necessity drives people away from their homelands. The children of these families come to your school and may well have different experiences of education which can bring new ideas and attitudes for the better and sometimes challenges which drive the need for change. For some teachers, teaching children with English as an additional language is an educational first, for which they are not equipped. Schools across the world are currently considering the impact of globalisation and the nature of knowledge and skills in the design of their school curricula. This is a classic example of change and must be managed carefully by school leaders. Handled well, it also provides an opportunity for curriculum innovation. The aspects of change are outlined using a curriculum development project as an example.

 ## Case study for change

Church Summerton Primary School Curriculum

Following a government-sponsored change in the national curriculum in England, Church Summerton Primary School approached a local university to work towards a new school curriculum. There is no easy template for change but the work of Brundrett et al. (2010) has been useful to frame the actual steps taken to devise and implement a new curriculum at Church Summerton Primary.

Involving the whole school: teachers, teaching assistants, governors, parents and of course children all have important contributions to what should be studied in school. Setting up parent and pupil discussion sessions and an electronic survey all helped to gather information on what the curriculum for Church Summerton Primary should contain and how it should be delivered. This requires time and the ability to delegate the leadership of change. It took courage to bring the whole school staff to the local university to explore ideas for the new curriculum over several days. This gave everyone the time to discuss ideas and really test out what the school wanted in its new curriculum. The involvement of two university educators provided a degree of challenge, asking 'why' questions, when teachers often wanted to know 'what, when, where and how'.

Research: the school spent some time working to really understand what it wanted and what it actually did at the moment, before exploring what the new government policy was. The reality following a period of curriculum development in Church Summerton Primary was that the proposed school curriculum, known in England as the Rose curriculum, was dropped as a national policy following a change of government in 2010. This is not uncommon in England and around the world, where politically motivated changes to the school curriculum are almost always quite transient. Finding out about the new curriculum back in 2008 provided opportunities, but always had the risk that this information would be subject to change. For this reason, it is worth emphasising that research starts with self-awareness and understanding your own context. Exploring the values and visions of the school was a very important step. Some members of the school team were at first resistant to this; wishing to 'get on with designing the new curriculum from a week-to-week basis'. Of course, knowing yourself as a school is the first step in any change and therefore was essential whatever the current government policy.

Ethos-building: any change is as much an emotional step as it is a professional and physical process. People will not do things if they do not want to. The role of the headteacher in Church Summerton Primary started with convincing the staff and community that there was a need for change. In short, the first step in change management is selling the problem, rather than a solution. In this case, the government policy context combined with a desire to change the nature of learning from 'spoon-feeding' to educational empowering pedagogy, was compelling. Of course, there can always be naysayers in any development who do not accept the need for change. Those DUCKS (people who 'Don't Understand Can Kill Silently') can sabotage new innovations. One such teacher in this context was wedded to a didactic teacher-led approach to the curriculum, very much at odds with the vision of the headteacher and the school more generally. Change management should be a humane process, but ultimately once a decision to enact a new school curriculum had been made by the school, then a refusal to take part in the development is an issue of performance and competence. Ultimately, leaders have a responsibility to develop the motivation and skills for change as part of the school ethos, but they also have a job to do to ensure that every member in the school is accountable. Communication, both listening and explaining the problem, as well as guiding the team in developing curriculum solutions is critical. Again there is a balance to be had between reasonable and unreasonable resistance to change. No one is perfect, but individuals cannot choose to go it alone in defiance of the wider school community. Being part of an organisation means that one has an individual responsibility towards the wider community. Ultimately, the DUCKS in this situation left and now teaches in a school more suited to their professional approach.

Trialling: to bring in a new curriculum without really testing it out is potentially very dangerous. Change is often a long thin process, especially when bringing in a new curriculum. Church Summerton Primary tested out some really innovative units of work, long before the new curriculum was finally implemented. This helped staff to understand in concrete terms what the new curriculum might look like, what worked, how things could be improved and making the implementation of the new curriculum more manageable. In reality, researching, building ethos, building the team, trialling and implementing the curriculum happen in parallel. Schools cannot afford to wait for a long process of research and trialling to be

(Continued)

(Continued)

completed before implementing new changes. It may be more useful therefore to see these steps for curriculum innovation as being phases, possibly being managed by different individuals or different teams.

Implementation: making sense of the timescale for changing the curriculum was important for Church Summerton. As a small school, they had to map out the experiences of children throughout the school to ensure that there was continuity and progression from 5 to 11 years of age. This included an experience of the old and newly designed curriculum. What resources, training and steps were needed to ensure a successful implementation of the new curriculum? This became the focus for a school curriculum implementation plan. This was probably more like a set of aims than a tool for micro-managing the implementation of the new curriculum, but it certainly provided a route map with key milestones for a successful new curriculum. With any change there is likely to be a difficult initial phase where staff confront and solve problems. This leads to something called the 'implementation dip'. This is where the early ethos-building, coming back to the central reasons and benefits for change, have to be reasserted by the headteacher. Leadership at this stage requires perhaps even more courage and the will to maintain a focus on what is right, even when things appear to be falling apart. This is where evaluation and recursive small step changes to reinforce the central focus is an essential skill for leaders of innovation.

Evaluation: change in many respects is a continuous process. This is no less the case at Church Summerton. The proof in the success of the new curriculum is in the feedback from children and parents: as well as a sustained improvement in the children's learning. One brilliant example of this curriculum innovation lies in the West End musical project, whereby children raised money through an auction of their own artwork, which funded a visit to a London West End musical production. The musical performance became the stimulus and focus for a whole term of work building on core skills in literacy and numeracy as well as wider related themes in the performing arts, nature and the environment.

Ironically, with a new government in England in 2010, there is a new politically inspired National Curriculum for 2014. But for Church Summerton, the hard work of self-research and forging new skills in curriculum development has already been undertaken. The challenge again is that the former staff team has changed and the cycle continues. In the above case study, curriculum development was a whole-school approach. This involved teaching assistants as well as teachers.

Working with teaching assistants

Teacher numbers have been growing steadily in recent years, increasing by 32,000 (7.9 per cent) between spring 2000 and November 2011. The total number working in England's state school system is now 438,000. Meanwhile, the number of teaching assistants in schools has almost trebled since 2000, rising to 219,800 in November 2011 (Blatchford et al. 2009). Teaching assistants therefore make up a significant part of the school workforce, especially in English primary schools. There have been several recent evaluations of the work of teaching assistants in school: for example, Blatchford et al. (2009) reported on the *Deployment and Impact of Support Staff*. While there has been considerable support for the role of teaching assistants some research, like that of Blatchford, suggests that their impact on children's learning is quite limited. Appreciation for the work of teaching assistants is universal amongst teachers and headteachers: providing pupils with increased individual attention, prompting pupils' more active role in interaction with adults, helping to increase classroom engagement of pupils, and helping to make classroom control easier. They achieve this by offering specialist help, for example with technology skills, counselling, or careers advice; offering advice about literacy learning of pupils who don't speak English; allowing more teaching by the teachers by helping with classroom management; increasing the range of curriculum, tasks and activities offered, such as giving small groups of children one-to-one support on reading and spelling; and creating more teacher time for planning lessons by taking responsibility for dealing with resources and practical equipment. Every single aspect of the work of the teaching assistant therefore has the potential to support innovation!

On the other hand, Blatchford et al.'s (2009) report on the deployment and impact of support teachers rather suggested that far from supporting progress in learning there was a consistent negative relationship between the amount of support given and the progress children made in English and mathematics in 2005–6 and 2007–8, even after controlling for pupil characteristics such as prior attainment and SEN status. The same could be said of science in 2007–8. The steps for successful working with teaching assistants are no different than in working with any professional in school:

- **An overall focus on learning rather than task completion**: defining success based on the degree of activity of the professional may actually lead to over-engagement in the class by the teaching assistant, when the actual focus is the children's learning outcomes not the completion of tasks.
- **Communication between professionals to exchange classroom information**: in order to maintain a focus on learning, it is important that the

teaching assistant as well as the teacher has a good understanding of progress in the child's learning. The Reggio Emilia approach to early years
professional communication suggests that time must be set aside for teachers
and teacher assistants to discuss past and future learning.

- **Active engagement of teaching assistants in collaborative planning
  and assessment**: by giving them ownership and involvement for new developments, this provides a new voice with different ideas but also a sounding
  board for the teacher to discuss classroom innovation. Planning for the
  involvement of teaching assistants is particularly important in whole-class,
  teacher-led activities. Good planning means that teaching assistants will contribute to the agreed focus for learning but in ways which contribute to
  mastery and progression in learning, rather than 'learned helplessness'.

- **Subject knowledge development through whole-school practice**:
  including teaching assistants in whole-school professional development
  means that they will not only develop the knowledge necessary to promote
  children's learning, they will do this alongside fellow teachers, and therefore
  develop a common understanding of learning, teaching and assessment in
  the school.

- **Using and accessing technology not only for the benefit of children,
  but also for professional purposes**: technology has the potential to make
  learning better, easier or different. It is vital that teaching assistants have this
  opportunity to innovate alongside their qualified counterparts. For instance,
  training a teaching assistant to monitor learning through the use of an electronic portfolio of digital still, moving images and sounds. Of course,
  involving children in this aspect of recording progress is also important.
  Children could easily upload examples of work they are particularly proud
  of, providing a review of the degree of independence they have had in the
  completion of the task.

Teaching assistants are often employed from the community within which they
work, so they are frequently highly attuned to the wider school culture and views
of families. Teaching assistants are often at the heart and soul of the local community. Innovation often starts with an understanding of the views of the local
community, in relation to opportunities for change and improvement. Teaching
assistants are therefore well-placed to make a positive contribution to innovative
problem-solving by developing dialogue with parents and the community in
relation to school developments.

Recent research by Peter Blatchford (DfE 2012) suggests that teaching assistants work best in school when they focus on children's learning rather than
the completion of tasks. What innovations are possible in this area? There has
always been a tension between identifying different ways of working with teaching assistants in class and the limitations of their contractual role and the level

of their remuneration. So the argument goes: why should teaching assistants do more or work differently when they are not paid to do that? UNISON (2013), the union in England which represents many teaching assistants, reported that while many love the work they do, there were significant concerns around pay, unpaid work and lack of training. New and different types of schools, such as academies and free schools, which do not have to follow nationally recognised pay agreements, can be seen as providing opportunities to raise the bar for teaching assistants, but is this likely to create uncertainty that can further damage confidence? While schools have to make their own decisions based on agreed policies when it comes to pay and conditions, we make the following suggestions about innovation and the role of the teaching assistant.

One potential innovation lies in the generalist and specialist roles of teaching assistants. It is vital in defining the role and responsibilities of a teaching assistant, so that these are clear and transparent from the start, and the right person is employed for the right role. A generalist role provides flexibility for the future, while individuals with specialist knowledge can make a very significant contribution in specialist areas. Again we reiterate that expectations must be clear from the start, so as not to take advantage of individuals. But it is clear that while some teaching assistants do not want to be fully-fledged teachers, they often come from other professions with a great deal of specialist skills and knowledge which are vital and hugely beneficial for schools. For example, professionals from the health and social care sector could provide significant support for social, emotional and affective learning in school. The role of the learning technologist is now well-embedded in higher education but the greater use of blended learning and technology-enhanced learning in schools provides opportunities to further develop the role of learning technologists in schools. These professionals need to understand the use of technology to enhance learning. Just being an IT technician alone is insufficient in this role, though the ability to solve hardware and software issues is important.

There is clearly a distinction between those who take on the teaching assistant role as a career choice in itself, and those who take on the role as a means to gain valuable experience in school prior to eventually going on to train and qualify as a teacher. For many young graduates who lack school experience, this can be a very attractive proposition. They gain experience, contacts and possibly the chance to utilise specialist skills and knowledge from their degree, such as language skills, sports, music and the wider creative arts. Schools, be it on a temporary basis, attract energetic and quite flexibly minded graduates who are able to deliver new programmes in school with appropriate training. This for instance has included language intervention programmes for speakers of English as an additional language and literacy development programmes, such as Read Write Inc. The important point here is that these are paid staff, who are suitably trained. While schools always attract unpaid voluntary helpers, there has been resistance to engage with unpaid internships, which are common in the commercial sector. It is very likely that this will become an attractive approach for the future as a route to gain experience for graduates who want to go on to train in particularly school-based teacher training programmes (such as School Direct in England). If a teaching assistant appointment comes with a significant training package, which is a step on the way to train and qualify as a teacher, this could be a very innovative way of identifying new talent. It recognises that the teaching assistant role can be seen as only a temporary medium-term role. However, there will still be a need for long-term permanent appointments. Flexibility within that role, will only come when there is sufficient and appropriate training available for teaching assistants. Professional development which provides an experience, but no evidence of impact on professional learning and children's outcomes, will naturally be doomed to failure. Again a blended approach to learning using technology and face-to-face taught sessions with school-based assessment is essential if impact on learning is to be evaluated. This can come through audits of subject knowledge and pedagogical understanding, allied with teacher and headteacher feedback on classroom learning.

Going beyond the school

Innovation can come from the internal workforce of a school, but also by expanding the nature of the actual 'team' itself. This is the focus for community and commercial developments in a school. By this we mean the type of learning-centred projects which engage with community groups, charities, sports associations and enterprise. Here the skills of the team are important. Teachers and leaders in school need to be able to negotiate and communicate with non-educational professionals. Increasingly, this also means being able to write commercial bids and manage community–school-related projects, which provide funds or other resources, such as materials, people, and technology. Some schools have used such funding to provide really innovative forms of learning. For instance one school, through a new teacher employed for her former journalistic skills and contacts, was able to fund a school-based radio station with visiting sound engineers and radio professionals to show children how to operate a radio station. There was some funding from local television companies, but this was relatively small. By far the greatest resource was the time made available to the school. To be successful in these arrangements, schools need to recognise the potential benefits to the community or business partner. Both have wider aims than just delivering their community service or a business profit. The community relationship is an important marketing tool for a business. Philanthropy or corporate social responsibility (CSR) in some firms goes beyond compliance with legal and business principles and engages in actions that appear to further some social good, beyond the interests of the firm and that which is required by law. CSR is a process with the aim to embrace responsibility for the company's actions and encourage a positive impact through its activities on the environment, consumers, employees, communities, stakeholders and all other members of the public sphere who may also be considered as stakeholders. Schools are important local stakeholders in any community.

Educational and commercial bids for funds often by necessity have a short lead in time prior to the submission of the bid. Schools commonly complain that potential funds are made available via a local, national or international bidding process. This can provide important funding for short- and medium-term innovations. Quite simply, it is important to find the time to write such bids and to develop the capacity for developing school income through government and charitable educational bids. If you don't bid for the funds, then your school won't receive the money. Identifying members of staff who have the experience, skills and desire to engage in external developments is an important element of delegating leadership. Since many individuals who qualify as teachers come from business and non-educational backgrounds, prior experience and contacts with external groups is a significant potential resource for school. Far-sighted headteachers will recognise the rewards for children and the school, when staff are given the time and appropriate training to accomplish such bids.

It seems that more finance for schools is provided directly to schools, cutting out intermediary institutions like local authorities. However, since more and more schools internationally are organising themselves into locally and nationally recognised networks, there is an opportunity for schools to develop educational projects and bids in collaboration with other schools. Inter-school bids and educational planning is an important next step for many schools and will be explored in particular in the concluding chapter to this book.

Chapter summary

- Educational change should always focus on promoting the needs of children.
- Since children and young people are the *raison d'être* for schools, it is essential that we listen to their views and include them in any developments.
- The key question in today's schools is, given the limited resources available to schools, what is the best balance of different professionals in the classroom?

- While professionals can have a direct and sometimes more indirect impact on children's learning, this can operate on a short- or long-term basis.
- The quality of relationships is perhaps one of the most important factors in schools and individual classrooms, whether this is with senior leaders, teachers, teaching assistants, parents or senior leaders.
- Questions can often impede good communication when they close off communication, channelling the topic or discussion in the direction the listener wants but away from that intended by the speaker.
- Ground-rules should be established at an early stage in any team. While there are many 'downloadable' ground-rules, it is essential that these are negotiated and agreed with the staff involved.
- Managing change often involves whole-school issues and requires research of the problem, ethos-building amongst staff, trialling of potential solutions, implementation and evaluation.
- Recent research emphasises that effective teaching assistants focus on learning rather than task completion per se.
- As with all professionals it is important that teaching assistants feel part of class planning and assessment; this requires good communication between the class teacher and their assistant.
- Commercial and financial opportunities arise from commercial and community-group funding and resourcing for school. This can focus on short-term projects which can provide energising innovations in school.

Further reading and research

Blatchford, P., Bassett, P., Brown, P., Koutsoubou, M., Martin, P., Russell, A. and Webster, R. with Rubie-Davies, C. (2009). *Deployment and Impact of Support Staff (DISS) in Schools*. London: HMSO.

Brundrett, M., Duncan, D. and Rhodes, C. (2010). Leading curriculum innovation in primary schools project: an interim report on school leaders' roles in curriculum development in England, *Education 3–13: International Journal of Primary, Elementary and Early Years Education*, 38(4): 403–19.

MacBeath, J. (ed.) (2002). *Effective School Leadership: Responding to Change*. London: Sage Publications Ltd.

CHAPTER 9

INCLUSION AND CLASSROOM BEHAVIOUR

Chapter guide

In this chapter you will learn about:

- Inclusion: achievement and engagement of all learners
- Context for innovative inclusive classrooms and schools
- Classroom strategies for inclusive teaching, learning and behaviour

---

Introduction

A theme running through our investigation of innovation in education has been the foundations and rationale for education in society and schools. Is education merely for children's learning, or is the fundamental aim of education to produce citizens who will contribute to the economy and wider society? Few would argue that both aspects are important, but what is the balance between the needs of society and the needs of the child? While many teaching professionals would prefer not to consider the political aspects of these questions, these are indeed relevant to the discussion. In this chapter, concepts such as inclusion, discipline and behaviour will be examined both from a practical professional point of view but also on a more political level. It is our view that in order for innovation in schools to take place, we should ask different questions of inclusion and behaviour. This is not a manifesto for educational anarchy, but a recognition that innovation requires us to ask difficult questions.

For example, we could ask inclusion of whom, for what ends and how? Stereotypes of 'inclusive education' often suggest a limited medical model which sees deficits or deviance in individuals and groups of learners, which will be addressed by one or more professionals, often working in a multi-professional capacity to address particular diagnosed needs. Alternatively a focus on individual differences and learning styles suggests that differentiation for different learners is simply a case of employing particular teaching methods. Often in opposition to a medical model of inclusion, the 'social model' suggests that educational special needs and to a certain extent disability in general is a cultural and social construct. While it is quite common to look at how society perceives the learner with particular educational needs, there are few analyses of the teacher's role as an agent in the learning process and the impact of their own psychosocial reality on that of the children. By challenging the perceived common view of learning and learners, we can redefine the very nature of learning, needs and disability. Innovation therefore can be simply a redefinition of the problem and a reanalysis of our common concepts in learning.

Guðjónsdóttir et al. (2007) suggest such an innovation in their analysis of transformative teaching for inclusion. In this process, the teacher should analyse their views of the reality of inclusion. Only through such an analysis can teachers fully understand the nature of learning, teaching and learners in their school. This takes place at three levels: examining the reality of schooling, issues around knowledge and professional pedagogical issues.

- **Ontological inquiry**: the school students and their relationship with schooling. How does the school, including the teachers, understand school learners' engagement in learning? Is significance given to students' socio-economic location? Inquiry of this kind can lead to an emotional response; for example, moral outrage at education's reinforcement of social division.
- **Epistemological inquiry**: learners and their relationship with knowledge and the school curriculum. For example, what do students appear to be interested in? How do their interests match those of the school curriculum?
- **Technical inquiry**: a review of which school approaches to learning 'work' for all students (and which don't). To this extent, how does the school respond to the needs of all children in the school regardless of age, gender, sexual orientation, ability, class, race or faith?

Rix et al. (2013) criticise headteachers who do not critically engage with new policies in special education. The headteachers interviewed in Rix et al.'s research said that their pedagogical assignments are their prime focus. They point out that students in need of special support are prioritised and that their pedagogical leadership then becomes even more pronounced. All headteachers emphasise the importance of being pedagogical leaders and being part of the school's activities. Some headteachers may rather uncritically accept some of the premises of the requirements set out in policies, such as the strong focus on evaluating individual children. Consequently, they may not consider in much depth how to develop the larger learning context and even less on how to create learning communities (Ainscow and Sandhill 2010).

This is a good starting point when reviewing inclusion in school. Here we invite you to explore your own experiences and views of inclusion.

 Reflection point

Based on your own school or educational setting reflect on the three areas of inquiry around learning and schooling, as discussed earlier in this chapter, in your context:

- ontological inquiry
- epistemological inquiry
- technical inquiry.

Your answers may touch on different forms of learning: traditional cognitive, through to physical, emotional, social and affective forms of learning. You might have considered children from different backgrounds, children with different educational needs. Some children learn well, enjoy what they do and make good progress. Others struggle along the way and this can lead to classroom stresses and strains for children and teachers alike. Classroom behaviour, especially low-level disruption, is commonly seen across a range of countries as being the main source of stress for the majority of teachers. There is a general sense among many new teachers across the world that their pre-service teaching programmes do not prepare them adequately in this respect. A lack of understanding of the reasons behind children's reactions and behaviour in class can lead to a culture of blame. The predominant view appears to be that of educational practitioners blaming parents for the onset of behavioural difficulties in children. Croll and Moses (1985) explored teacher perspectives on blame and highlighted that parents were deemed responsible for inappropriate behaviour. Understanding classroom learning and behaviour is therefore important for teachers as a starting point in educational innovation. Without such understanding, poor learning and behaviour are attributed to child and parental deficits in a blame game.

We have avoided a simplistic review of behaviour techniques and strategies for teaching children with special educational needs as a bolt-on. Concepts like 'inclusion' and 'behaviour' are quite problematic. Innovation partly involves a questioning of received notions and current contexts.

Inclusion: achievement and engagement of all learners

Rolheiser et al. (2011) identify difference as central to the experience of learners and teachers across the world. This approach, known as inclusion, is an oft-used term to explain particular approaches to teaching and learning in a range of contexts and with a range of learner needs. As inclusion is referenced frequently by many teachers, it bears further analysis. We will explore its meaning, and how this provides opportunities for a reanalysis of classroom learning and behaviour.

Fundamentally, the objective of inclusion is to enable all learners regardless of their context and their particular approach to learning to achieve. By achievement, we mean an outcome of learning; but the process of learning is also very important. Outcomes of learning are not necessarily more important than engaged and motivated learners. It is problematic and subject to significant critique by many right-wing thinkers. Rolheiser et al. (2011) define inclusion as embracing difference as a central value to be encouraged. They regard inclusion as a starting point for the learning culture of a school, rather than as a central problem to be managed and through which culture becomes inert. Typically, inclusion references differences along certain dimensions, such as sexual orientation, gender identity and expression; racism; faith and religion; social class and deprivation; sexism; ageism; ableism.

Gender, sexual orientation, race and faith are cultural constructs, and inclusion in these areas requires societal change, which starts with individual acts of acceptance, tolerance providing equity of opportunity for learners. Rolheiser et al. (2011) rightly question that difference and disability is a negative feature of the classroom. All of us come with different strengths, abilities and conditions. There is no such thing as conditions with promising possibilities without accompanying limits. As a dyslexic, for example, there are difficulties in reading; yet these difficulties give rise to a variety of constructive classroom practices, such as reading aloud or reading more than once and with differing intonations. The teacher's experience of dyslexia brings the possibility of reading differently to the classroom, contemplating word order and significance, and potentially experiencing in new ways not only with words but also our understanding of them. Simply put, this means that just as vision and hearing do not always meet the promise of education, disability need not always be conceived as a barrier to education. This of course is as true for the learner as it is for the teacher.

A particular focus in inclusion is the support for children with different abilities. For instance, children may have difficulties in learning due to neurological problems, there may be a visual or hearing impairment, or in some cases the learner may have more complex and severe learning disabilities. Special educational needs are widely seen as an area of challenge for teachers. How do we provide an equitable environment that meets the needs of all learners? We often focus on their physical and cognitive abilities, but increasingly we are challenged to recognise the stress and mental health issues affecting schoolchildren. Broomhead (2013) identifies classroom behaviour as a challenge for teachers, pupils and parents alike. Frequently, an argument put forward by critics of the medical model of special education is that labelling children with dyslexia, autism, ADHD and other 'medicalised' educational labels only marginalises the child. So the argument goes, obtaining a label does nothing to address the particular needs of the child. The reality is that most children with special educational needs (SEN) do not present simplistically under a homogeneous profile of conditions or difficulties. It is argued therefore that the SEN label does nothing educationally to support the child. On the other hand, obtaining a diagnosis of special educational needs actually can be critical. The 'passported benefits' of special educational needs diagnoses for accessing support and resources are commonly agreed (DfE 2011). So in identifying opportunities to innovate in relation to special educational needs, we must examine closely the role of 'labels'. While those against the medical model of special educational needs argue that labels are not good, many parents believe that they serve an important function.

Broomhead (2013) investigates the feelings of parents and the relationship between teachers and parents in the diagnosis and attribution of the reason for difficulties in children's learning. If teachers do not see certain conditions such as deafness or blindness as being the fault of pupil or parent, this is not the case for children with classroom behaviour difficulties. The predominant view appears to be that of educational practitioners blaming parents for the onset of behavioural difficulties in children.

Sher (2006) defines blame as an attitude that a person takes towards themselves or another individual, due to that person 'fail[ing] to conform to some moral standard'. The issues regarding blame and SEN are situated within the wider context of parental blame, with parents being blamed for a wealth of societal problems such as anti-social behaviour and falling school standards. Recent special educational needs legislation in England proposes that behavioural emotional and social difficulties should be removed from the SEN framework and instead these pupils should be viewed as a vulnerable group due to their home circumstances (Ellis and Tod 2012; DfE 2011).

A wealth of research has also reported that parents of children with a variety of special educational needs frequently experience self-blame, or guilt, and it has therefore been proposed that the guilt process is also experienced by parents regardless of the nature of their children's special educational needs (Francis 2012). Hinton and Wolpert (1998) refer to this as a 'label of forgiveness' and suggest that parents of children with behavioural difficulties are guilty until proven innocent, in other words, guilty of causing their children's behavioural difficulties until their children receive a formal diagnosis. Key findings revolve around blame towards parents of children with behavioural difficulties, leading to much parental guilt, which is contrasted with the lack of blame or guilt experienced by parents of children with other special educational needs.

All parents of children with behavioural difficulties discussed how acquiring a 'label' for their children's behavioural difficulties was essential, the reason being to reduce feelings of blame and therefore excusing them for their children's difficulties by viewing the special educational needs as innate in their children. Parents of children with behavioural difficulties were predominantly focused on labelling to absolve their own blame and guilt. The parents were focused on acquiring labels to ensure their children received funding and support. The language of special education is vitally important. Take for example the term 'dyslexia'. Elliott and Grigorenko (2014) argues that there is consistent overdiagnosis of a range of literacy and language difficulties with the term 'dyslexia', which he sees as a complex combination of visual, auditory and processing disorders. The practical difficulty in this argument is that obtaining any assessment and consequent diagnosis is very difficult. If the catch-all term of dyslexia for a range of reading and spelling difficulties provides a way of focusing efforts and resources of educational professionals, then at least resources can be accessed. Furthermore, the anxiety of not knowing is at least somewhat assuaged by developing some understanding of a child's needs. We are not arguing for a misdiagnosis or inaccurate assessment of needs, but the recognition that language and terminology to describe educational difficulties ('labels') do serve an important function in analysing the needs of a child. Importantly we must reassert that the label is not the child!

This qualitative exploration of parental and educational practitioner experiences of blame and guilt has yielded several key findings. First, the nature of a child's SEN has a key influence on whether their parents felt blamed by educational practitioners, as well as whether educational practitioners viewed parents as responsible for their children's difficulties. Second, the nature of a child's SEN, as well as evidence of blame, appears to impact on parental guilt. Finally, parental experiences of blame and guilt consequently influence their focus on obtaining labels of SEN for their children, and their reasons for doing so.

The implications of these findings for practice are first that home–school relationships are clearly fragile due to being suffused with notions of blame and guilt, with emotions evidently running high. There needs to be a shift in focus from preoccupation with attributing blame, towards developing positive home–school relationships and supporting the needs of pupils.

Rix et al. (2013) analyse the provision for special educational needs in ten countries. Special education provision typically views the needs of the child as a continuum, supported within a continuum of provision and by a continuum of services. It is arguable that there is greater negative pressure on provision for children with special educational needs. The economic crisis of the first decade of the twenty-first century in Western countries certainly contributed to a review of what is possible in SEN provision across the world. The innovations have been less focused on delivery and pedagogy but more on the way special education is organised.

Context for innovative inclusive classrooms and schools

Stangvik (2014) analyses the influence of the neo-liberal establishment in sector-wide innovations. New management regimes emphasise that being able, which means to be self-sufficient, independent and self-reliable, is an important conditions for citizenship (Chouinard and Crooks 2005). The ideological common sense of the new management divides those who are able and those who may not become employable and economically independent. In order to become meaningful for management, 'ableness', like other management criteria, has to be objictified and arranged on a scale through classifications, examinations and assessment. When units in regular schools close and mainstream options become inadequate they report that more parents turn to special schools. Educators in special schools and units noted that parents became more interested in non-mainstream options when their child reached eight or nine years and when a child had difficulty in reading and felt isolated in a class of peers.

Internationally, studies are undertaken setting the standards for improving national educational standards (Progress in International Reading Literacy Study (PIRLS) and the Program for International Student Assessment (PISA)). This process shifts the adopted cultural and historical standards of schooling from the national to global economy and the future productivity of students. In order to ensure that these standards are met a new control regime has been adopted. Ball's work (Ball et al. 2012) on the role of high-stakes assessment as a strong measure for accountability is highly relevant here. This draws on Foucault's analysis of compliance in education through schooling. Based on financial considerations and the principles of efficacy and accountability, fragmentation of educational processes and contracts becomes an important instrument to control education at a governmental level. Results show that this model does not support the decision-making process in special education very well (Stangvik 2014).

There is a trend towards greater decentralisation of governance, with more importance given to parental choice and greater monitoring of the quality of provision delivered. This creates a tension between a focus upon learning outcomes and support for the vulnerable. Individual Educational Plans (IEPs) are used widely to provide a way of personalising support and teaching for the learner, recognising the greater social and external context for the learner. This change constitutes a shift away from psycho-medical models of thinking about children's needs. Class teachers frequently receive support from specialist staff either situated externally, internally or within special schools. Effective pedagogies for inclusion depend upon teachers' skills in understanding and responding to difference. However, there are opportunities in the IEPs to recognise the needs of the teacher in supporting the child, as in the following case study.

 Classroom case study

An IEP for teaching and learning

Sarah is a newly qualified teacher in a small rural primary school. In her new class is a boy with severe and complex needs. At the start of the year, Sarah had little understanding of the needs of the boy, but experiences gained during her training were critical in helping the boy engage and interact much more with the class.

Sarah had undertaken a work shadowing week with Ruth, a Specialist SEN teacher visiting schools and coaching teachers in how best to help children with severe and complex needs in mainstream settings.

Ruth advised Sarah from the start of the year in how to differentiate her lessons so that the boy could be consistently a part of the lesson more than he had been. Sarah's training needs were written into the boy's IEP. After all, the boy would not make progress if his teacher had not received an appropriate level of training.

The headteacher was happy to make explicit and match the resources for Sarah's training and include this in the boy's IEP. Not only did Sarah progress professionally, the boy was much more engaged in learning. Importantly, both Sarah and the boy's teaching assistant felt that a central benefit was in the developing of higher expectation by all professionals working with the boy.

Rix et al. (2013) explain that special education innovations in northern Europe have focused upon providing information on inclusive practice via in-class training; a focus upon whole-school reform, issues of leadership, service coordination, as well as multidisciplinary planning, parental involvement and capacity building through in-school support systems.

In Norway, for example, where people spoke with absolute conviction about the need for inclusion and the right for inclusion, a focus upon learning outcomes and traditional classroom methods overrode the need for a collaborative, less teacher-centred pedagogy, with assumptions and practices carried over from an earlier policy context and long-established theoretical positions. The values practice gap in 'inclusive' practices is common in northern Europe. In many cases, teachers and schools complain that there are insufficient resources to teach children with special educational needs. Unfortunately, the level of resource associated with special education encourages the use of 'special' as a solution and acts as a barrier to a mainstream response. Frankly, this is about pushing responsibility for a child outside of the school, family and community. In England several major research reports culminated in questions about the use of teaching assistants to support children with SEN. In some cases poor training for teaching assistants meant that children made less progress than if they had not been employed at all. In fact several headteachers state that they now have reduced the number of teaching assistants in order to be able to have two teachers in the classroom more often and also reduce the number of children in each class.

Support for children needs to be individualised and specialised. Frequently, certain children were seen as the responsibility of special education, even if both the class and special teachers had similar qualifications and formal responsibility for the whole class. The need for early identification and prevention was much in evidence. However, delays in identification, assessment and intervention are frequently noted, as are high levels of bureaucracy and inconsistency or inaccuracy in assessment outcomes. The over-reliance upon medical services for diagnostic or evaluation purposes was noted as well as over-medicalised placement procedures, which encouraged a teacher focus upon medical assessment (Rix et al. 2013).

Multisensory teaching and learning

Commonly accepted as being effective in teaching all learners, including those with special educational needs, is the so-called 'multisensory' approach to teaching and learning. Gifford (2004) explores the idea of situated cognition (Lave 1988), which challenges the extent to which children or adults 'transfer' learning from one situation to another, because the cultural context is a major part of what is being learned. The issue is one of bridging between social practices or, as Lerman (2000) has pointed out, with respect to mathematics, 'Learning to transfer mathematics across practices is the practice.' The implication is that the teacher must be aware of children's home experiences and help them to make connections in school, especially through the use of language. Dahlberg et al. (1999: 49) have proposed a 'post-modern paradigm of childhood', in which children are: 'social actors, participating in, constructing and determining their own lives, but also the lives of those around them and the societies in which they live and contributing to learning as agents building on their own experiential knowledge'.

 Reflection point: multisensory learning in early mathematics

Gifford (2004) explains the important role of physical resources, using active teaching strategies which involve all the senses in teaching mathematics:

- outdoor activities;
- large-scale resources;
- fingers and patterned images for number, including number lines;
- music and rhythmic action;
- technological resources.

The role of the teacher is to facilitate learning

- helping children make connections;
- challenging misconceptions;
- providing opportunities for representation and discussion;
- instructing and demonstrating;
- thinking aloud;
- providing immersion and apprenticeship opportunities;
- sharing and scaffolding problem-solving;
- giving feedback.

Sensitive teaching strategies help develop cognition as well as social, emotional and affective aspects of mathematics:

- avoid anxiety and exposure to public failure by encouraging safe risk-taking;
- foster success, build mathematical confidence and positive self-image;
- allow children ownership of goals and some control in activities;
- make the purpose of learning explicit;
- take children's interests into account.

Inclusion and accountability

Provision for SEN is most effective when the class is not seen as a particular group in a single space, but as a range of groups, who can work in different ways with different peers for different activities and come back together throughout the day for academic and social purposes. Creative, collaborative solutions are sought which begin with the needs of the child. Here the emphasis is to support the child with the most difficulties in accessing the curriculum. In both Italy and Norway, more localised control allows more flexible management of resources, in a way that could be more responsive to the school context. Rix et al. (2013) assert that mainstream schooling marginalises those with SEN. The challenge is to create additional time and space within the mainstream to minimise marginalisation. Lindqvist and Nilholm (2014) argue that inclusion can be threatened by external measures of accountability. Demanding that schools achieve academically, as we have seen in previous chapters, is not the same as seeking achievement for all.

Innovation is stifled in a culture of performativity. Hodkinson (2013) criticised integration and inclusion as a policy that failed to account for individual need. He argues that it is society that disables people, not individual pathologies. From this perspective, educational exclusion is generated by policy-makers' and professionals' practices, attitudes and policies and leads to the educational and social marginalisation of people with impairments. Inclusion here operates within a regime of accountability, which locates inclusive education as an obligation rather than as a right. Innovation in 'inclusive' education must move from student needs to student performance and from the school voice to the student voice (Apple 1996). There has been significant innovation at the sector level, but many people would argue that this has resulted in greater control and conformity and runs completely counter to the needs of children.

Classroom behaviour has long been seen as a challenge for many teachers; and especially for newly qualified teachers. In the remainder of this chapter we analyse best practice in teaching children. We argue that there is only good teaching: not separate routines for children with special educational needs, behavioural difficulties or underachieving children. While it is important to understand the source of educational difficulties, there are common approaches to good teaching, which develop good learning, in a positive classroom atmosphere with good discipline and behaviour.

Classroom behaviour of learners and teachers

In this section we discuss some commonly agreed approaches to good teaching. However, before doing so we invite you to reflect on the role of the learner *and* also the teacher in each dimension. Hart's (2010) investigation of educational psychologists' views of good classroom behaviour-management strategies identifies the following important approaches:

Rules: firm but fair rules are an essential element of any classroom management. Hart (2010) identifies certain qualities associated with good rules, such as using positive, specific and simple language, and having as few rules as possible (he suggests a maximum of five). However, for learners to value the rules, it is important that they take part in their development. A sense of justice, and what is commonly agreed as being right, often pervades their contributions. Of course, having rules for children means nothing if there is a perception of double standards. Teachers must also be subject to the agreed rules; and they must be applied consistently and equitably across the class.

Reinforcement of appropriate behaviour: behavioural strategies aim to increase desirable behaviour using reinforcement. The application of a consistent and fair reinforcement of good behaviour is probably more important than responding to poor behaviour. According to Hayes et al. (2007: 162), 'Verbal reinforcement is possibly the most fundamental tool available to teachers and arguably the most powerful and meaningful for pupils.' However, an emphasis on the use of rewards to promote positive behaviour can lead to a reduction in intrinsic motivation for a task and reduced task performance once a reward is withdrawn.

Further criticisms of behavioural approaches to learning and classroom management include contentions that the use of rewards to reinforce behaviour are potentially coercive, diminish pupil autonomy and do little to foster appropriate social skills (Nie and Lau 2009).

Response to undesired behaviour: behavioural strategies aim to decrease undesirable behaviour using extinction (withdrawal of reinforcement through ignoring unwanted behaviour or using 'time outs') and by focusing on antecedent setting conditions for unwanted behaviour in the class environment.

Staff–student relationships and interactions: psychodynamic approaches based on attachment theory emphasise the importance of secure and trusting relationships, as well as emotional containment and expression (Frederickson and Cline 2002). The importance to children of stable, caring and trusting relationships with adults is emphasised within attachment theory, which provides the basis for nurture groups as an intervention to help children to learn developmentally appropriate behaviours (Boxall 1976). 'Classic' nurture groups were developed and described by Marjorie Boxall in the 1970s and involve children attending a class of up to twelve pupils with two adults within a structured and supportive environment. Of course, nurture groups can be used for a range of groups of children: for instance to facilitate learning in gifted and talented children. But what is the value of nurture groups for staff? Supervision to ensure staff well-being is commonplace in many of the professions, such as counselling, social work, and psychiatry, but this is rarely in place for teachers. While newly qualified teachers have a mentor and all teachers have a line manager, perhaps we need to take seriously the feelings of staff in classroom interactions.

Van Tartwijk et al. (2009) interviewed a number of teachers who had been identified as being successful at creating positive working environments in their classrooms. The majority of these teachers identified the importance of creating and maintaining positive relationships with their students.

Expectations: Hattie (2012) reinforced the notion of high expectations as central to success in school. Of course, high expectations are important for both the teacher and the learner. Where a learner expects to achieve a low grade, invariably they will achieve a low grade. School inspectors report that in lessons where staff have high expectations about the behaviour of children and young people, students' behaviour is better than in lessons where such expectations are not in evidence (Ofsted 2005).

Procedures for chronic misbehaviour: humanistic perspectives attach great significance to the relationship between teacher and pupil. One example is learner-centred education, where the teacher displays empathy, unconditional positive regard, genuineness, non-directivity and the encouragement of critical thinking (Cornelius-White 2007). Care is a key element in facilitating student self-determination (Nie and Lau 2009). At the heart of the humanistic approach is the idea that students' motivation, and consequently their behaviour, is underpinned by certain basic psychological needs, such as needs for competence, relatedness, and autonomy (Nie and Lau 2009). External (teacher) control is said to diminish motivation (Nie and Lau 2009), and foster powerlessness. Behavioural approaches tend to encourage adults to control children's behaviour because children are not capable of controlling themselves. In this approach to behaviour adults must decide what is right and wrong for children because they are not capable of deciding this for themselves. Self-regulation and personal responsibility are seen as important characteristics of recent approaches to learning and behaviour such as socio-cognition and self-theory (Dweck 1999).

Determining a shared, consistent approach to responding to chronic and more severe behaviours is seen as a key element in classroom behaviour management programmes which have been positively evaluated (Algozzine et al. 2005).

Classroom environment: systemic approaches, which focus on the social interactions where problematic behaviour occurs, emphasise the behaviour, the social environment's reaction to that behaviour and social cognitions or skills (Frederickson and Cline 2002). An effective learning environment is key to promoting positive behaviour, and this is identified as the first site for intervention within the framework when concerns are raised about pupil behaviour. From a systemic perspective, behavioural strategies based on reinforcement and punishment are important, but these should be allied to preventative strategies which promote a positive climate, pupil self-discipline and social problem-solving strategies (Bear 1998). Displays celebrating children's work, clean and bright classrooms, good acoustics, having sufficient space to store equipment and having dedicated spaces for special equipment or activities are all conducive to improved behaviour.

The following box summarises advice on good classroom management strategies.

Strategies for promoting effective classroom behaviour management

At the school level ...

- Rules should be clear, positive, and negotiated with pupils
- There should clear, agreed policies for rewarding good behaviour and responding to negative behaviour
- Teachers should be supported by school leadership in applying policies
- The school should foster and support the emotional well-being of staff

At a class level ...

- Rules should be displayed and referred to
- Expectations should be negotiated, shared and upheld consistently
- The classroom should be arranged with resources available and clearly labelled; space for people to move about; organised
- Children should have ownership of their environment, and be involved in its planning
- The class should be calm and nurturing
- Lessons should be well-planned with clear objectives, a variety of activities, clear instructions, effective pacing and use of time, managed transitions between activities
- Learning activities should be varied, interesting, accessible to all, relevant, and differentiated to meet the needs and build on the strengths of learners
- Support should be available to all children and young people encountering difficulties with respect to learning, behaviour and social and emotional issues

The teacher ...

- Should use language that is clear and positive; that is 'performance' rather than 'labelling' language
- Should give clear explanations of tasks, behaviour and learning expectations, and seek feedback from learners

---

- Should move around the class, scan visually and be vigilant, looking for potential triggers of unwanted behaviour such as anxiety
- Should be confident, authoritative and enthusiastic
- Should use non-verbal means to prevent or reinforce behaviour, as appropriate
- Should model desired behaviour: respect, manners, interest, and tone of voice and language use
- Should develop positive relationships with learners; get to know their strengths, weaknesses and interests; communicate warmth, positive regard and respect, and value others' opinions
- Should look for opportunities to give praise – 'catch 'em being good'

Children and young people ...

- Should be given opportunities to have ownership over their learning and their environment, and should be given choices
- Should be involved in agreeing rules and expectations, and in making decisions
- Should have opportunities to express their thoughts and feelings
- Should be encouraged to monitor their behaviour and learning, and their progress in relation to agreed targets
- Should know how to ask for help if they require it

Responses to behaviour ...

- Appropriate behaviour should be reinforced through a variety of means: verbal praise, non-verbal signals (such as thumbs up, an approving look), and tangible rewards
- Praise should be specific, genuine, age-appropriate, realistic, linked to rules/expectations, fairly distributed, immediate, and for both behaviour and learning
- All children and young people should be praised
- There should be a clear, hierarchical system of rewards, consistently applied
- There should be vicarious reinforcement of appropriate behaviour through the use of proximal praise
- Teachers should use 'low-level' strategies for dealing with inappropriate behaviour, such as planned ignoring, take-up time, 'fair pairs', giving choices
- Inappropriate behaviour should be responded to quickly, quietly and calmly, and the response should be linked to the rules, or expectations
- There should be a clear school policy for responding to more serious, or persistent, misbehaviour that is understood by all and followed consistently

The curriculum itself offers important opportunities for developing the learner and good behaviour. A curriculum innovation of the 2000s in England was the government-approved scheme for teaching social emotional and affective learning (SEAL). It has been widely used in primary schools and is generally quite popular. However, this innovation has received some criticism, which is explored by Gillies (2011). She explains the context in which the SEAL materials were developed as a cultural preoccupation with therapy. Ecclestone and Hays (2008) highlight a new significance attributed to feelings and introspective analysis as a means of understanding and addressing long-standing social issues and problems. By implication, they do not agree with this approach, despite the popularity of SEAL materials in school. One view is that schools have an important role in developing children who are responsible citizens, who can make an ethically acceptable contribution to society. While many people would argue that such a view implies that social and emotional development is fundamental to such an education, others argue that this prevents a more objective and rational view of society. Fundamentally, we would maintain that ethical and more judgement is central to the life of a citizen and therefore should be central to their education (Gillies 2011). The argument against SEAL materials is that they do not actually support development of emotional and affective learning, but they do manage the development of these characteristics in a way which is consonant with a government conception of the compliant child and school. The focus on emotional literacy builds on a recent but more established concern with well-being, and more specifically self-esteem. On the other hand, Ginsburg and Allardice (1983) pointed to children's difficulties in mathematics resulting from 'anxiety, poor self concept and defensive cognitive style'. McLeod (1992) argued that attitudes were formed by repeated intense emotional reactions, suggesting a need to avoid anxiety and exposure to failure.

The role of the teacher in education is contentious and problematic. Knowledge and understanding themselves can be analysed as merely the teaching of bald facts or a broader concept of emotional intelligence. Our position is that teaching is much more than the transmission of knowledge from adult to child. Relationships, empathy and problem-solving are all important processes and objectives of education. How this is achieved is also open to some debate.

Chapter summary

- A medical model sees deficits or deviance in individuals and groups of learners, which will be addressed by one or more professionals, often working in a multi-professional capacity to address particular diagnosed needs.

- The 'social model' of inclusion suggests that educational special needs and to a certain extent disability in general is a cultural and social construct.
- The objective of 'inclusion' is to enable all learners regardless of their context and their particular approach to learning to achieve.
- Home–school relationships are clearly fragile due to the fact that they are suffused with notions of blame and guilt.
- In order to become meaningful for management, 'ableness', like other management criteria, has to be objectified and arranged on a scale through classifications, examinations and assessment.

Further reading and research

Broomhead, K. (2013). Blame, guilt and the need for labels: insights from parents of children with special educational needs and educational practitioners, *British Journal of Special Education*, 40(1): 14–21.

Gifford, S. (2004). A new mathematics pedagogy for the early years: in search of principles for practice, *International Journal of Early Years Education*, 12(2): 99–115.

Gillies, V. (2011). Social and emotional pedagogies: critiquing the new orthodoxy of emotion in classroom behaviour management, *British Journal of Sociology of Education*, 32(2): 185–202.

Graham, A., Phelps, R., Maddison, C. and Fitzgerald, R. (2011). Supporting children's mental health in schools: teacher views, *Teachers and Teaching: Theory and Practice*, 17(4): 479–96.

Hart, R. (2010). Classroom behaviour management: educational psychologists' views on effective practice, *Emotional and Behavioural Difficulties*, 15(4): 353–71.

Hodkinson, A. (2013). Illusionary inclusion – what went wrong with New Labour's landmark educational policy? *British Journal of Special Education*, 39(1): 4–11.

CHAPTER 10

INNOVATIVE APPROACHES TO EDUCATIONAL ASSESSMENT AND PLANNING

Chapter guide

In this chapter you will learn about:

- An introduction to educational planning and assessment
- Planning for education
- Assessment for education
- Educational planning, assessment and the central purpose of education

Introduction

This chapter reiterates the importance of an education for children which has high ambitions and expectations for the quality, range and depth of education for children in primary schools. We take a fresh look at planning and assessment with a focus on education rather than learning. Education is a broader term than learning but still reflects the development of learning in cognitive, social and emotional terms. Education is an important term in relation to planning and learning, because it suggests that the development of the person is a cultural and intergenerational transmission of knowledge, skills and values which takes place in and outside of school, in formal schooling as well as recreation. Jacks (1932) wrote that a master in the art of living draws no sharp distinction between his work and his play, his labour and his leisure, his mind and his body, his education and his recreation.

While this chapter will focus on innovations in planning and assessment rather than acting as a primer for these topics, some simple principles are summarised below.

Educational assessment

Assessment of the curriculum and development: while the curriculum may aim to follow developmental progression, this is not always the case. There can be a disconnection between curriculum progression and developmental progression. This has often been the criticism of the English reading curriculum in the National Curriculum, for instance in the area of phonics and phonological development.

Assessment of learning: summative assessment allows pupils, teachers and their parents to understand achievement in learning at certain stages: typically at the ages of 5, 7, 11, 16 and 18. However, it is not necessary that summative assessments, often via formal, standardised tests, are reported or even assessed so regularly. In the Finnish education system first formal exams take place only at the age of 18 years of age. The standard argument is that summative assessment is often staged for the sake of school accountability and compliance checks, rather than for the benefit of learners.

Assessment for learning: typically this is formal and informal assessment to inform teaching and learning. James and Pedder (2006) suggest that there is a range of practice in England in relation to assessment for learning. They identify versions which track and record numerical progress on an industrial scale: primarily focused on accountability and quite out of the learner's control. On the other hand they distinguish versions which emphasise pupil voice, self-regulation and assessment for emancipation. While teachers might value one of these versions of assessment for learning over others, their practice can be unduly influenced by compliance and control exerted by external agencies and the push for progress to meet the demands of accountability

Assessment as learning: when 'assessment is the learning', we have a problem. This is an extreme, industrial form, in which assessment becomes the means and end of learning in school. This is illustrated by a headteacher reporting a discussion with some of her pupils at the age of seven. She asked them why they were involved in a writing activity. The children replied that it would enable them to achieve a certain level in a test four years hence. This saddened the headteacher. Where was the motivation for writing and the joy of self-expression in the written form? While some would argue that this is an educational innovation, it is probably one that most people would abhor.

The question for us then is what is the nature of assessment and planning for educational innovation? Clearly, planning, teaching and assessment are inextricably linked.

Educational planning

In order to analyse the complex picture of planning in schools, we have chosen to adopt the term 'educational planning', of which planning for learning is one important element. Educational planning however is a significantly more comprehensive concept. The timescale and purpose of planning is important as well as the focus for planning. Educational planning includes:

Planning for learning: typically short-, medium- and long-term planning against curriculum objectives, potentially from a statutory document. Individual teachers and teams of teachers try to balance the requirements of the curriculum with the needs of children in order to provide a positive but challenging and enjoyable learning experience in itself. In terms of lifelong learning, there is a sense that planning needs to ensure continuity and progression of learning. Learning which fades on the short- to medium- and long-term is not effective. Likewise, planned learning which impacts negatively on the learner's motivation and curiosity for learning is likely to inhibit engagement with future learning and the skills which enable learners to learn in the future. As Claxton (1990) says, 'every time we learn, we learn something about learning'. A turgid and unengaging planned learning experience is self-limiting and not sustainable. Planning for learning therefore not only considers assessment information to ensure that the learning activities are well matched at a cognitive level. It is also important that planning is informed by the interests of the child to engage them on a social and emotional level. That is not to say that planning should be limited by the immediate interests of the learner, as new experiences and looking beyond the horizons of learning are critical when children explore the world of knowledge. Assessment of learners should evolve into a learning conversation, which informs planning at all levels. Discussion with all school stakeholders provides opportunities to include the topic and programmes of study. This is planning for relevance.

Planning for professional development: we assume that teachers and teaching assistants have all the knowledge in order to plan, teach and assess for a particular class. Of course the reality, particularly in the primary years, is that teachers often teach children with a range of abilities, with challenges across a multiplicity of subjects and curricula. It is a wonder that teachers and children do so well given the complexity and enormity of the task. It is wrong to assume that the knowledge, skills and understanding of teaching professionals is appropriate to the task at hand. For this reason, alongside a plan for learning there should be a plan for professional development. There was an excellent example of this in the case of a newly qualified teacher who was planning lessons for six-year-old children. One of the children had severe and multiple learning difficulties. Initially, the teaching team struggled to know how to plan for the learning of this child and the rest of the class in order that all children were included and engaged. The solution came from an advisory special needs teacher who helped the teaching team assess their own professional needs to enable successful teaching of the whole class. Therefore in this context planning and assessment meant analysing the professional needs of the teaching team. This re-analysis therefore sees planning as an enabling process for both learners and teaching professionals. Of course, teachers are learners in class as well and this approach provides a professional development plan which is aligned with the plan for learning in the class.

Planning for school development: while we question the balance and emphasis of accountability measures in many schools in England, we fully accept that the school is a public (or increasingly private) entity and has an obligation to develop a sustainable and good value education of the highest quality. This requires planning and assessment of the school's position in respect of key aims and indicators. Again the balance errs from innovation to compliance. Importantly, the school planning must align with that of learning and professional development. By starting with the educational plan for learning we maintain a focus on the prime aim of education in schools. Innovation at the level of learning then has a knock-on impact on professional development and whole school aims. The timescale for planning at these different levels accordingly impact on the possibilities for innovation.

Strategic educational planning: at this level, starting with children's learning the teaching team identifies the educational aims of the school, its values and visions, the curriculum and the needs of the children and makes choices about the priorities, approaches and tone of learning across the whole school. This must involve all the stakeholders: the wider community, governors, the teaching team and children. It often happens on a long-term basis and acts as a route map for children's learning, professional development and the wider school development. It can be quite time-intensive; but if carried out on an inclusive basis it engages everyone involved and the benefits far outweigh the costs. Most organisations suffer from the tyranny of the immediate and urgent; long-term innovation requires time to step back and reflect.

Incremental educational planning: any long-term educational plan will struggle to predict the educational landscape of the future. Uncertainty in English schools is replicated across the world, so strategic plans are only a route map, but must be open to shorter-term adjustment and interpretation, following professional reflection. This means that the teaching team should work closely together to reflect on the short-term assessment of learning and teaching experience. The teaching team need time to plan for such incremental planning and the school leadership team need to monitor the success of planning not only at the strategic level but also at the incremental level.

While we do not deny many of the important principles of planning and assessment for learning (Black and Wiliam 1998), we believe that the use of assessment information to inform learning and for the purposes of accountability needs to be rebalanced. Teachers, learners and schools should always be accountable for educational outcomes, since there is an expectation of high quality and effective use of public funds. But when education is reduced to assessment and the central focus for learning, then compliance has become an end in itself rather than an educational means.

Progress in learning can only really take place where teaching is in advance of development and learner independence is emphasised. This must however recognise the importance of starting from good understanding of the current starting point for the learner. It is argued that assessment which puts the learner at the centre of the process, emphasising responsibility for understanding their own learning and the next steps for progress, is essential for innovation. This builds on James and Pedder's (2006) work questioning the current principles of assessment for learning. Industrial and regimented forms of assessment result in industrial and regimented forms of learning. Different ways of educational planning and assessment are provided as possible innovations, but first some of the issues for planning and assessment are explained below.

Personalised learning emerged in the 2000s as a political approach to provision in the public services. There was a rhetoric of choice; in schools this meant that personalised learning partly provided choice through different educational structures. Free schools, academies and, more widely, specialist secondary schools provided parents with potential choices in terms of the quality and particular type of school they might want to send their child to. Educational planning for parents therefore includes choosing a specific school to educate their child. How much the choice extends to younger children in primary school is questionable. There has always been choice at fourteen and sixteen years of age, in terms of GCSE and A level qualifications. But why should children in primary schools not have an element of choice within their curriculum? Of course, in smaller schools there is an argument that with fewer teachers, it would not be possible to extend the range of choice to younger children. However, now that schools are starting to coalesce into more or less formal clusters, federations, and academy networks the opportunities for sharing expertise and staff across schools are more manageable. While the interchange of staff between schools may be impractical, other ways to provide choice in learning for children have always been available. For instance, primary school timetables are often arranged with literacy and numeracy in the morning and mainly topic work in the afternoon. Topic work is a vehicle for exploring the wider curriculum as well as an important opportunity to apply core skills such as reading, writing and number. While teachers might have been dictated to by a centralised curriculum which identified particular topics which schools must cover, the latest advice in England is that schools should be unshackled from a centralised curriculum. This being so, children should be involved in the planning process so that they have some choice in the topic work and how they will approach the learning. The danger in pupil consultation is that it can be tokenistic and superficial. However, giving children an authentic voice in planning pays dividends in terms of learning, behaviour, motivation and ultimately standards in school (Ofsted 2010).

Personalised learning itself seems to have been appropriated to include any approaches which suggest innovation for more effective learning. The Teaching and Learning Research Project (TLRP 2004) suggests that personalised learning includes:

- **Assessment for learning** and the use of evidence and dialogue to identify every pupil's learning needs.
- **Teaching and learning strategies** that develop the competence and confidence of every learner by actively engaging and stretching them.
- **Curriculum entitlement and choice** that delivers breadth of study, personal relevance and flexible learning pathways through the system.
- **A student-centred approach to school organisation**, with school leaders and teachers thinking creatively about how to support high-quality teaching and learning.
- **Strong partnership beyond the school** to drive forward progress in the classroom, to remove barriers to learning and to support pupil well-being.

This chimes with much of the literature on innovation and innovative learning. A focus on individual needs, with a student centred-approach within a strong learning community, is completely in tune with the concept of an innovative education outlined in this book. However, we emphasise this approach in the sense of wider educational aims, rather than simply a meaningless objectives-led curriculum divorced from the realities of children's lives. Educational planning is strongly reliant on a rigorous and effective educational assessment framework. When these two aspects of learning come together we say that educational planning and assessment are constructively aligned. Constructive alignment involves all aspects of the educational planning and assessment framework working in a sympathetic way to promote outstanding educational aims in school. This is encapsulated in the diagram in Figure 10.1.

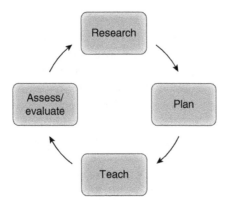

Figure 10.1 The educational cycle: assessment and planning

Many teachers will be familiar with the cycle shown in Figure 10.1. Trainee teachers have a tendency to go straight to planning in the preparation for teaching. More effective is to consider assessment data and where children are at that moment in their learning. We introduce the idea of research in the planning and teaching cycle, to reflect the need to consult children and the wider community on their views and children's interests in the chosen topic area. The starting point in the learning cycle is therefore between assessment, evaluation and research. This provides information about the learner and the wider world, so that teaching and learning are aligned appropriately to provide a challenging but enjoyable educational experience for the learner. Of course, now that we have a wider view of educational planning and assessment, this should include research, planning, teaching, assessment and evaluation for learning as well as professional development and school development. Only when all three dimensions of educational planning and assessment come together can we say that we have true constructive alignment.

Educational planning, assessment and the central purpose of education

In 1997 Tony Blair in a pre-election speech made clear his political intentions in respect of education in Britain. 'Education, education, education' was how Tony Blair set out his priorities for office, as Labour campaigned to put classrooms at the top of the political agenda. It would be incredibly cynical to say that politicians only implement educational policies, such as school assessment, for political capital. However, there have been too many short-term changes of direction in national testing and assessment and planning regimes to encourage genuinely innovative ways of working. For instance, the Labour Governments from 1997 to 2010 introduced a succession of very costly central programmes for literacy and numeracy development as well as centrally driven intervention programmes to increase achievement in English primary schools. If micromanagement is too harsh a critique of this approach, it is certainly the case that the level of guidance for assessment and planning originating from central government multiplied vastly, with some limited impact on reported outcomes in school. Interestingly, Scottish, Welsh and Northern Irish educational approaches started to move away from such an intensive focus on planning and assessment, especially in English and mathematics (Education Scotland 2014).

More recently the rhetoric of 'localism' in education has been a driving force behind many changes in the school curriculum (DfE 2010). The focus of Britain's standing in international educational league tables seems to be a long way off the aims of the original aims of the National Curriculum (DfEE 1989. In England a radically reduced new school curriculum (DfE 2013) provides little concrete guidance to teachers and schools as to how to plan and assess the curriculum. While there has been a strong emphasis in the past on the use of levels to designate progress in planning and assessment, the current Secretary of State for Education has questioned the validity and reliability of such assessment. Others (for example James and Pedder 2006) would argue that the industrial scale of National Curriculum assessment using levels is a direct consequence of the use of assessment information to feed the accountability machine. Free schools and academies now do not have to follow National Curriculum planning and assessment frameworks published by central government. In any case, the centrally published curriculum is but one aspect of the school curriculum. Critics of a central approach to planning and assessment say that educational innovation will only follow from a more flexible, locally mediated and slimmed-down curriculum. However, if schools are given the opportunity to set their own assessment framework, then this also calls into question the data-driven approaches of national inspection systems such as Ofsted in England. Comparing schools' diverse forms of planning and assessment will be a challenge. It could be argued that this will reduce the reliability of school inspections. But many would say that the accountability agenda now drives assessment and education; so this may be a positive.

 Reflection point

Life after levels

The English assessment framework from 1988 to 2014 has been based on a series of levels of attainment in each subject area of the National Curriculum (DCFS 2006). In practice, every subject of the National Curriculum was

(Continued)

(Continued)

broken down into separate areas of study. Each of the areas of attainment were then broken down into eight levels. Each level, especially for primary schools, was subsequently broken down into three sub-levels to aid formative assessment. These were meant to be broadly progressive. In recent years, assessment using these sub-levels was enshrined in an approach called 'Assessing Pupil Progress' (DCFS 2006). While there are many supporters, it is the ongoing assessment and reporting of progress by levels (often converted to numerical points) which has been criticised both by teachers and politicians.

Your reflection:

- Why do teachers sometimes complain about the use of ongoing assessment?
- Is it an effective use of teachers' time to constantly monitor and report progress in children's learning?
- Would children still make progress if assessment levels were not reported?

In the US, tests which supposedly result in objective and reliable assessments of learning are routinely used to gauge progress in learning and are used strategically to evaluate the effectiveness of schools. Standardised tests typically give a statistically reliable definition of progress, often articulated as a score with 100 being the average. Performance year-on-year can then be compared using the standardised tests to evaluate progress.

How do we know if assessment is effective?

The question then with the fragmentation of nationally set planning and assessment approaches is: how do we judge which framework to use for the future? There are a number of useful concepts in education which are relevant here:

- **Validity**: to what extent does an assessment approach represent the reality of a learner's understanding?
- **Reliability**: does the assessment represent learning in an accurate and useful way: does it help the teacher, child and parent understand learning for different purposes (such as diagnosis, evaluation, and summary) in assessment?

- **Manageability**: is the balance right between the benefits of using the assessment and planning framework, compared with the time taken?
- **Communication**: the assessment frameworks must provide information which can be used to communicate effectively to all concerned in school. This includes pupils, the teaching team and of course parents.
- **Promotes progression and continuity**: from Early Years Foundation Stage (up to 5 years) to Key Stage 4 (from 15 to 16 years) it is important that different professionals and different schools come to some arrangement for commonly agreed standards. Typically disagreement occurs between schools where children are assessed at one point to have achieved a certain stage of learning, but on transition to another school the language of assessment and interpretation of standards is different.

Whether or not learning is assessed by levels or using a standardised test, there are some concerns about the impact of assessment on teaching and learning:

- Is there 'teaching to the test'?
- Does the assessment regime lead to an emphasis on compliant learners and teachers, or ones who go beyond the form of stated learning and expectations set by the teacher, school and wider sector?
- How independent is the learning during the assessment process?
- Do children continue to function at that level of learning beyond the point of assessment?

Learning as process and product

How much does assessment focus on learning as a process, compared with assessment of learning as a product? This may seem to be a rather erudite question, but it reflects the value of a good education as being important in itself. How well children tackle a problem is as important as the final outcome. This again harks back to the value of the learning experience in comparison with learning outcomes. Theoretical support comes from sociocognitive approaches to learning. If learning is a social and cognitive experience, then the quality of relationships and the manner of learning will have a significant impact on the outcomes of learning. Learners and teachers who are overly focused on the achievement of outcomes can lead to an approach to learning called 'performance orientation', while those who value deeper understanding aspire to a mastery orientation to learning: 'Students with mastery orientation seek to improve their competence. Those with performance orientations seek to prove their competence' (Dweck 1999: 122).

Ultimately, educational assessment and planning is an issue of ethics. The general yardstick of ethical behaviour is 'do no harm, do good'. Recent publications suggest that educational tests and formal assessments in the UK have an impact on children's welfare. For instance, the Whitlam Institute in Australia identified as many of 40 per cent of families and children who perceived that national testing arrangements in Australia contributed to unacceptably high levels of stress. Unexpectedly, a survey of 1000 English children revealed that they generally did not mind being tested, since they saw it as being useful to inform their learning. However, in common with their Australian counterparts, there was a rejection by children of high-stakes national testing arrangements in England (*The Guardian* 2010). The central concern with children was that having a mark (level, pass or fail) was just not useful. A test which provided genuine feedback was seen by pupils as being more likely to inform and improve future learning. Innovations in assessment and planning therefore need to provide a platform for progress. It is clear that children are capable of reflecting on assessment and planning. While assessment of learning per se is not rejected, there is widespread criticism of the formal testing regime in England, as evidenced by the vast evidence base of the Cambridge Primary Review (2007).

Assessment in different subjects

It is worth reflecting on the application of assessment protocols across the primary curriculum. Feedback from schools suggests that assessment is not a homogeneous mechanism across the curriculum. For instance, most primary teachers would recognise decreasing levels of engagement from higher to lower in the following subjects: English, maths, science and foundation subjects (PE, history, geography, art, music, design, computing). Furthermore there is a continuum of assessment engagement within subjects. For example, one school reported that this probably runs from higher to lower for writing (sentence structure and punctuation), reading (phonics then comprehension), talk, maths then science. These subjects and aspects of subjects are most likely to be the object of formal assessment approaches, with recording and some moderation taking place, but it is unclear how much moderation to ensure consistency of assessment judgements is taking place across other subjects.

Assessment often involves making qualitative judgements, which have to be validated through moderation. This is frequently the case in areas such as English. The close analysis of a child's writing requires good knowledge of sentence and text structures. In writing there is often a written product the teacher can use as evidence of a child's independent ability to apply certain skills. How often the teacher collects evidence of the process of accomplishing that independent writing is debatable. However, observation can be a very useful tool to capture performance in more ephemeral activities like sport. Technology now allows us to capture sporting and dramatic performance on camera and to analyse this in some detail: a process which is commonplace in the sports sciences, but potentially not manageable for a class of twenty-five or more children. The point we make here is that these are all choices teachers and schools have to make. Innovations in early years assessment include the use of tablet computers to record assessment artefacts in still images and movies to build up a better picture of a child's learning journey through an electronic portfolio. This is very much an evolution of a common approach to early years assessment using notes to record performance. By observing the learning in class, the teaching team will have opportunities to evaluate progress but also the effectiveness of classroom pedagogies. So much is tied up in the links between assessment, planning and teaching. We should not ignore the self-reflection of professionals on their own role in the learning process: assessment is of progress in learning but also progress in teaching. What is common between the two approaches is the importance of time for professionals to collect the information and then most importantly to discuss and reflect on the status of the information to inform future teaching and learning. This is what the Reggio Emilia approach to learning in Italy conceives of as 'the teacher as researcher'. This approach sets important aims for education, but also translates these into a conception of the teacher, their work and the use of their time in school. These issues are encapsulated in the concept of 'assessment literacy'.

Assessment literacy

Assessment literacy is the knowledge, skills and set of values associated with educational assessment. It is a feature of individual teaching teams, schools and wider networks of educational issues. To summarise, and linking to the Teachers' Standards of England, assessment literacy involves the following:

- **Values**: underpin successful assessment. Assessment is always an issue of ethics, since any assessment depends on professional honesty, integrity, responsibility, objectivity and the recognition of bias. For example, professionals must recognise the need for accountability if assessment is to be valid and reliable. However, there is a wider responsibility in the profession to ensure quality in the educational experience. This involves ensuring a balance between assessment for learning and assessment for compliance. In their daily work teachers make choices which influence the balance between the two.

- **High expectations** for all children: this is central to a high-quality educational experience.
- **Progress**: focus on all children's educational progress. For example, in their motivation and engagement with independent learning.
- **Knowledge and understanding**: across different subjects which underpins good assessment for all children. For example:
  - Subject knowledge per se: the letters /oar/ are/ a trigraph which represents the same vowel sound in 'for' and 'saw'
  - Subject knowledge for development: from week to week and from year to year
  - Subject knowledge pedagogy: knowing how to teach split digraph
  - Subject knowledge attitudes: reflecting on and developing further subject knowledge.

- **Planning and teaching**: using assessment information to inform planning and to evaluate the success of educational approaches for all children. For example in planning next steps for children in Y1 from CCVC (consonant, consonant, vowel, consonant) words to split digraphs (phase 4 to phase 5 phonics).
- **Assessment strategies**: such as observation and the ability to analyse learning in both formal and informal ways. This inevitably must include the use of assessment data for the purposes of accountability and compliance.
- **Personalised learning**: involves using assessment information for diagnostic and formative purposes to personalise learning and teaching for a range of learners. For example, this will include children who come from different language backgrounds, and may have different ways of learning.
- **Assessment of behaviour for learning**: for example, supports the social, emotional and motivational progress of a learner.
- **Working with the wider teaching team**: for the benefit of your class and the wider educational network. For example, this involves teamwork, good communication and project management skills which are all central to successful assessment. For example, moderation of work assessed by teachers for the purposes of consistency is central to valid assessment judgements. Likewise an assessment framework is necessary but not sufficient. It must be accompanied by a robust framework for validating, developing and monitoring assessment decisions. This cannot be external to the teaching and learning community; but should involve external professionals from teaching schools, universities, educational authorities and national agencies. One focus for the assessment community is in the calibration of assessment interpretations. Essentially this is the process of ensuring a common interpretation of educational standards in school.

Teachers and schools should never operate alone. This is important in relation to planning and assessment. A 'closed loop' approach is not effective or desirable where this comes to making judgements about standards. Teachers and schools should not do this on their own, but neither should they be subject to external systems which they do not understand or for which they do not have a voice. For all the reasons explained above, it is suggested that teachers are part of an assessment community: involving learners, parents, professionals and external agencies. Teachers may be more or less engaged in a system, which is more or less coherent and cohesive across the community of assessment. However, the best way to ensure a valid and reliable assessment approach in schools is to ensure that there is common agreement and understanding around assessment judgements. We believe that this is best achieved across a network of schools and educational organisations in an 'assessment consortium'. The idea of an assessment consortium is explained through the following case study.

 Case study

ABC Schools – university community of assessment

This is a fictionalised case study based around several examples of assessment networks being developed across England at the moment. A community of assessment and learning essentially aims to develop educational assessment literacy in professionals across a network of schools. In this example:

- An educational network of primary schools has a developing approach to moderation across nine schools: in years 2, 4, 6 starting with writing and maths.
- There is an annual moderation event with all Year 6 and Key Stage 3 teachers for writing. This involves cross-school moderation of samples of written work, mediated by a university teacher education English team.
- Different schools are at varying stages in the implementation of assessment moderation approaches. Some teachers have skills and expertise which allows them to take a lead in the moderation, while others are benefiting from benchmarking effective assessment practices in other schools.
- The value of coordinated assessment and management across the network of schools validates standards of educational achievement. This

(Continued)

(Continued)

has been recognised in external validations of the school standards, for instance through school inspections.

- There is a strong formative component to the moderation of assessment since it provides the opportunity to discuss the steps which lead to certain educational outcomes: essentially a dialogue about effective teaching pedagogies. One school for instance emphasises the importance of oral communication and practice for grammatical development. This is recognised in the quality of sentence structure and writing more generally. Other schools have learned significantly from this approach.
- Development of assessment-rich activities and opportunities which could be used across the network no matter what the national assessment framework.
- Parents are involved in the development of the assessment process through a network educational forum.
- Using different technologies to promote assessment literacy within the schools. For instance, electronic portfolio, YouTube and podcast training for moderation can encourage greater engagement and understanding in children and staff.
- The quality of the assessment practices or a school or groups of schools should be subject to peer review and external inspection agencies.

Useful questions

- Is there a common approach to assessment across the network? What is the value in that? How do we best approach that development?
- Is there a need for an overall assessment approach across the network?
- What would be the criteria for a good assessment framework across the network?
- What would be the most effective assessment framework to encourage the best education for all children?
- What will assessment on entry to school look like? How will it be measured?
- What do we know about the approaches to assessment within the current and new curriculum?
- What do we know about national external agencies' approach to inspection?
- Who can we identify and draw upon for networking opportunities?
- How do we manage assessment change in schools?
- What are the resource implications for assessment changes?

This assessment community is a model for other assessment consortia. A collaboration of university teacher education departments provides an opportunity to embed principles of assessment literacy in both school network and university teacher education departments. School leadership and modelling the principles of assessment literacy is essential if schools are to take ownership of assessment. Professional development led by school teachers from a network school community of assessment professionalises the role of the teacher and enables local schools to strengthen standards in education through a rigorous and reliable educational assessment.

Educational planning and assessment is a much wider concept than is traditionally used to talk about planning and assessment in schools. It provides a broader framework for organising a broader education for children. It also provides alignment of learning with professional development and whole-school aims. This is more than semantics. A focus on wider educational aims is broader than just a focus on learning. Within a school or a wider educational network such as a trust, academy chain, teaching school alliance or professional network it is important that the broader aspects of educational planning and assessment are promoted through a management-led standards committee. This provides the headteacher and senior leadership team in a school with the opportunity to monitor and set the agenda in terms of educational standards more broadly within the school. It also provides a sober voice in setting the tone for assessment and planning. Broader educational values go beyond mere compliance to become the focus for educational development in the school. In short such a group will uphold the educational ethics of the school – do no educational harm, do educational good!

Chapter summary

- Educational assessment provides information about the broader learning of children, highlighting professional development needs of the staff and issues which should become the focus for whole-school developments.
- Educational planning involves planning for learning, professional development and whole-school development.
- The education cycle involves research, planning, teaching and assessment/ evaluation of classroom learning, professional development and wider whole-school issues.
- Constructive alignment involves all aspects of the educational planning and assessment framework working in a sympathetic way to promote outstanding educational aims in school.
- Giving children an authentic voice in planning pays dividends in terms of learning, behaviour, motivation and ultimately standards in school.
- Effective assessment is reliable, valid, manageable, promotes continuity and progression with good communication of the information made available to all the participants.

- Learners and teachers who are overly focused on the achievement of outcomes can lead to an approach to learning called 'performance orientation', while those who value deeper understanding aspire to a mastery orientation to learning.
- Assessment literacy is the knowledge, skills and set of values associated with educational assessment. It is a feature of individual teaching teams, schools and wider networks of educational issues.
- The best way to ensure a valid and reliable assessment approach in schools is to ensure that there is common agreement and understanding around assessment judgements. This is best achieved across a network of schools and educational organisations in an 'assessment consortium'.
- A community of assessment and learning essentially aims to develop educational assessment literacy in professionals across a network of schools.
- Broader educational values go beyond mere compliance to become the focus for educational development in the school.

Further reading and research

Black, P. and Wiliam, D. (1998). Assessment and classroom learning, *Assessment in Education*, 5(1): 7–71.

DCSF (2006). *Assessing Pupil Progress*. London: HMSO.

Dweck, C.S. (1999). *Self-theories: Their Role in Motivation, Personality and Development*. Philadelphia: The Psychology Press.

Guardian, The (2008). High stakes testing. Available at: http://www. theguardian.com/theguardian/2008/may/14/4 (accessed January 2014).

Jacks, L.P. (1932). *Education Through Recreation*. New York: Harper and Brothers, pp. 1–2.

Nusche, E.D., Maxwell, W. and Shewbridge, C. (2012). *OECD Reviews of Evaluation and Assessment in Education: New Zealand 2011*. Paris: OECD Publishing.

Ofsted. (2010). *Creative Approaches Which Raise Standards*. London: HMSO.

TLRP. (2004). *Personalised Learning*. London: ESRC.

CHAPTER 11

INNOVATION: TODAY AND TOMORROW

Chapter guide

In this chapter you will learn about:

- Innovation in action
- Implications for the future of the country: lifelong learning
- Illustrative examples from schools

This final chapter considers the wider implications for education and schools of more innovative approaches to learning. It cautions against the rhetoric of innovation, when this is a top-down response by government. A strong argument is made for an evidence-based practice for innovation, which is constantly questioning the nature of learning as society evolves. Teachers must aspire to understand the children they teach, the local area within which they work and the wider professional teaching community. This is a call to the highest standards of teaching professionalism, based on strong values and a professional ethic. A professional ethic goes beyond compliance with government educational policy to ensure that children's education is at the centre of school. Any innovation in school must focus on such wider notions of education. It might seem merely a matter of semantics to focus on education rather than learning, but as has been explained in earlier chapters this wider conception promotes wider dimensions of children's achievements beyond mere demonstrable attainment of a narrow band of skills and knowledge. Not everything that is important can be tested.

Watt (2002) invites a view of innovation focused on a model of leadership, school structures and processes and cultures; together with the people who work in a school. The interaction of these elements is suggested as the creative crucible of innovation:

- Do the same thing with less (*resource reduction*, for example: reducing the time, capital costs or staff needed for an activity);
- Do better with the same, or less (*quality enhancement*, for example: do things faster, better or cheaper);
- Do things differently (*reconceptualisation*, for example: using new technologies to teach the curriculum);
- Do different things (*transformation*, for example: using online learning to engage students in learning activities from different locations).

〰 Reflection point

Consider how the above processes (Watt 2002) have either supported or impeded innovation in your school in the following four forms of innovation:

Resource reduction: how can you do the same thing with less?
Quality enhancement: how can you do better with the same, or less?
Reconceptualisation: how can you do things differently?
Transformation: how can you do different things?

Examples:

- Promoting better leadership with fewer resources: a headteacher acts as an executive head overseeing several schools.
- Enhancing the quality of leadership: ensuring that senior leaders focus on developing classroom learning through staff coaching, rather than completing mundane administrative tasks.
- Developing a cooperative trust of schools: in this way schools can do things differently by working together as a group, each taking responsibility for the wider achievement of the other schools.
- Planning and assessment with children: by emphasising the voice of learners in the planning and assessment process it transforms classroom

> responsibilities and encourages greater ownership of learning amongst
> the students.
> - Developing school community information evenings: changing the
>   culture of the parent and school communication evening helps to
>   educate parents in the wider principles of learning, which they might
>   reinforce at home.
> - Employing an extended school coordinator provides opportunities to
>   make more effective use of out-of-hours school facilities. In one very
>   good example, the emphasis for development was placed on parents to
>   lead innovations: 'If you think this is a good idea, bring me another ten
>   parents who will participate in the project, and we'll look to fund it.'

In the following section we look at some examples of school innovation
through different school structures.

Changing school structures

It has been long argued that teachers and schools do make a difference to
children's education. Rutter et al.'s (1979) famous study of secondary schools
suggested that schools and individual teachers can and do make a difference
to the learning and behaviour of their pupils. Of course, schools in England
and across the world have changed along with society since the 1970s. The
research and professional view seems to maintain that schools and teachers
still do make a difference but the degree of influence is somewhat at question.
Evidence over many decades and from many countries seems to show that
family background continues to be a major determinant of educational outcomes: the poorer a child's family is, the less well they are likely to do in the
education system (Cassen and Kingdon 2007). It is claimed that a good education provides a route out of poverty for the most disadvantaged young
people. A significant question arises therefore from these studies. How do
teachers and schools encourage effective learning, particularly when there are
significant challenges for more disadvantaged children? In this chapter, we
explore the contribution by individuals and schools in developing innovative
approaches to meet these challenges. After all, the greatest resource of any
organisation is people. People have the power to help or hinder the present
and future path of education through their everyday responses to classroom
challenges. Whether we like it or not, change happens. Decisions can be made
to continue current classroom approaches or to consider different and better
ways to respond to existing and new problems. Educational innovation involves

human decisions, which provide new ways of acting in school for individuals and the teams they work with.

Innovation can also work at an institutional level. For instance, in the last two decades in both England and the US, the development of different types of schools has been a substantial focus. In the US, private and public collaborations led to the development of charter schools and chains of schools. The formation and history of charter schools can be traced to reform ideas, from alternative schools, to site-based management, magnet schools, public school choice and privatisation. The idea of charter schools first arose in the 1970s and is generally attributed to Ray Budde. He suggested that groups of teachers be given contracts or 'charters' by their local school boards to explore new approaches.

In the 1980s schools-within-schools were set up in Philadelphia. These were also called 'charters'. Charter schools could be characterised by three basic values: opportunity, choice and responsibility for results. Since the late 1980s there has been a similar approach in England whereby schools could distance themselves from local education authorities by becoming grant-maintained. By 1998 these eventually became foundation schools. A more radical alternative similar to charter schools emerged in the form of the 'free school', which were announced with a significant rhetoric of parent power and decentralisation. The reality in England has been somewhat different. In England just 5 per cent of the free schools approved to open in 2014 are being set up by parent groups while over half are being established by multi-academy chains, established mainstream schools or academies. In 2014, free schools are still a tiny proportion of England's schools: less than 1 per cent. A cynical view of this educational innovation suggests that the development of free schools and charter schools, more widely in the world, is a manifestation of the marketisation of schools. At best, payment by educational results could be seen as an economic response to educational improvement. At worst, it could be seen as part of a neo-liberal assault on the public sector: for no greater reason than to reduce the size of the state and to increase the size of the private sector. The net result: a channelling of public money from the public sector to the private sector.

Cross-school innovation

While schools can work closely with others to expand the possible contexts and approaches to learning, exploring the opportunities within class is a good starting point. Returning to Watt's (1999) pillars of innovation, we suggest changes to how we organise classes as one different approach which can be stimulating for children. De Lemos (1999) highlights the fact that most children in England are taught in mixed-age classes. Often lower numbers of children entering school or low numbers of a particular age range mean that a multi-age class is a practical way to organise classes. For example, children of similar ages (say five–six years of age) may be taught for all or most of their lessons in the same class. Variations of this approach allow for differently organised classes, depending on different subject areas and different abilities. Research is inconclusive as to whether mixed-age classes promote or detract from achievement. There is, however, little evidence of the impact of children working in vertically arranged classes. By this, we mean classes which have children of the youngest age through to children of the oldest age in a school. In a primary school, this might mean children of 5 years of age being taught alongside children of 11 years of age. The arguments against this tend to focus on the role of the teacher and the difficulties of differentiating for such a wide band of ability. On the other hand, such an organisation need not be applied for every lesson in the week.

There are many schools which organise teaching interventions for children who need more support in their reading. The use of systematic synthetic phonics is widely promoted as one such approach to developing children's reading. Different schemes can be applied in different ways but phonics teaching often involves teaching children in small groups for about 20 minutes each day. Some schools organise these groups on a vertical basis. This means that according to the progress the child is making and following detailed assessment, they are placed in a group according to their stage of development. In extremis, this can lead to children of 5 and 11 years being taught in the same phonics group. This approach has been criticised on the grounds that the grouping of children according to so-called stages of development risks reinforcing educational failure. If an older child has been taught alongside younger children for most of their school career, clearly they have not made progress and a different approach is needed.

  ## Classroom case study

University school vertical classes

One school decided to change the way it organised the school week. Discrete teaching of literacy and numeracy remained, with topics being taught traditionally in a base class. However, once a week, normally on a Friday afternoon, children were organised into vertically arranged groups with younger and older children in the same group for enrichment activities: these were craft-, sports- and arts-based.

Activities were taught by all staff in the school, including teaching assistants, office staff and caretakers. The children very much enjoyed working in their 'university school' groups.

(Continued)

(Continued)

The experience of learning was different. There was recognition of the pastoral strength of older children caring and supporting younger pupils. Younger pupils clearly benefited from learning with more able children who represented excellent role models. Teachers enjoyed working with different children in smaller classes.

A variation of vertical age arrangements involves teaching across usual age phases. For example, schools in England are traditionally organised as primary (5–11 years) and secondary (11–16 years). However, there is long-standing evidence that the transition point between these two phases can be difficult for some children. Evangelou et al. (2008) suggested that only a minority of children did not feel positive towards the support offered at transition from primary to secondary school: 16 per cent did not feel prepared when they changed schools, but only 3 per cent of children were worried or nervous a term after starting their secondary school. Some new schools have sought to iron out even this small level of anxiety by organising their intake from 3–19 years of age. The various phases of the school, such as infants (5–7 years), junior (7–11 years), secondary (11–16 years) and sixth form (16–19 years) are able to maintain their identity as part of the 'school campus'. However, there is much greater exchange of staff, with subject specialist teachers from the secondary school teaching in the primary setting; and where there is a need for early skills specialists in literacy and numeracy supporting children in the secondary setting. This was called a learning campus in a recent evaluation of a proposal for 3–19 schools in Wales: providing education, training, and a range of children's and community services in an integrated campus. Pupil Voice Wales (2014) called this 'a holistic model of provision bringing together education, social services and community and leisure services'.

Developing learning in school through lesson study

Collaborative working between schools is a powerful way to improve learning and the broader culture of education in a school. However, there are some effective and less effective ways of doing this. There has long been a tradition in England of seeing teaching as a craft, which can be learned by observing an experienced and qualified practitioner. This learning through apprenticeship was recently articulated by the Secretary of State for Education (DfE 2010). His policy and recent changes to teacher education have reduced the role of universities in both teacher training and continuing professional development, by passing much of the state funding in this area to a new cadre of teaching schools. Fundamentally, as Hargreaves (2011) explains, this will have limited success in developing professionals. Most 'sharing of good practice' does not amount to practice transfer, unless the practice is very simple. As one of the major means of improving teaching and learning, it is a relative failure.

Lesson study attempts to develop deeper understanding through collaborative, planning and evaluation of classroom learning. Hargreaves (2011) emphasises the power of joint professional development, in which teachers take ownership of learning outside of their own class. Typically in a pair or trio, teachers will identify a focus for development and discuss planning for a teaching episode to address this focus. Teachers will then observe learners within the respective classes to identify the impact of the planned teaching, with a view to drawing conclusions for their own practice and that of the wider professional community.

 Classroom case study

Joint professional development for assessment

There is a great value in coordinating assessment activities across schools to ensure that standards of assessment judgement are valid and reliable. Typically, such assessment moderation activities are carried out by externally appointed peer-moderators. As explained in the previous chapter, a cooperative trust has chosen an innovative alternative to this approach. The trust, along with a local university, moderates the assessment of writing across nine schools in Years 2, 4, 6 writing and mathematics.

Moderation is seen as a continual process throughout the year, with an initial moderation in the autumn followed by an annual meeting to review standards at the end of the year in June. In the final event, the university writes a formal report based on feedback and judgements made by the teachers. This works summatively to validate judgement made at the moderation meeting, but also, it provides a feed-forward to the next year:

- The annual moderation cycle comprises moderation and blind assessment of a range of written work for English, by Year 6 and Key Stage 3 teachers;
- Cross-school moderation of the sample is mediated by a university teacher education English team;
- Teachers from the secondary school were also involved in moderating judgements about National Curriculum-level assessments made by teachers in each school.

(Continued)

(Continued)

There are significant benefits to this approach. Teachers have been given the responsibility and ownership of the moderation process. Assessment moderation is now seen as an opportunity for professional development rather than external moderation. The 'back-wash' from the assessment moderation involves schools analysing how particular pedagogies have influenced particular assessment outcomes. For example, one school in the trust places great emphasis on the role of oral rehearsal in the development of sentence structures for variation in sentence openers. This has been proven to generate better quality outcomes in the pupils' writing. Other schools have adopted this pedagogical technique.

In this concluding chapter, we have seen a number of innovations in action in real schools. A central theme of this book is that school can make a difference to the lives of young children. This is a question of social justice. Ultimately, schools have a choice to promote deeper forms of learning for wider educational success. Success in schools includes achievement in learning in a range of subjects as well as developing the values and learning dispositions central to a life of learning. The innovators of tomorrow are the scholars of today. There is some danger in the move to a compliance culture in education. Creative learning requires creative teachers. Everyone agrees with the need for accountability in schools. However, when the focus on assessment data takes over from a focus on the quality of the actual learning, teachers and learners become risk averse and innovation is stifled.

Chapter summary

- Watt's (2002) model of school innovation focuses on leadership, school structures and processes and cultures; together with the people who work in a school. Opportunities for innovation focus on resource reduction, quality enhancement, reconceptualisation and transformation.
- Charter schools are characterised by three basic values: opportunity, choice and responsibility for results.
- Vertically arranged classes and cross-phase school structure such as 3–19 through schools offer creative and innovative solutions to issues linked to transfer and transition between age phases.
- Most 'sharing of good practice' does not amount to practice transfer, unless the practice is very simple. As one of the major means of improving teaching and learning, it is a relative failure.

- Lesson study attempts to develop deeper understanding through collaborative planning and evaluation of classroom learning.
- When the focus on assessment data takes over from a focus on the quality of the actual learning, teachers and learners become risk averse and innovation is stifled.

Further reading and research

Barber, M. (2003). Deliverable goals and strategic challenges – a view from England on reconceptualising public education, in *Networks of Innovation: Towards New Models for Managing Schools and Systems* (Schooling for Tomorrow series). Paris: OECD, pp. 113–30.

Hargreaves, D. (2011). *Self-improving School Network*. Manchester: NCTL.

Hopkins, D. (2003). Understanding Networks for Innovation in Policy and Practice, in *Networks of Innovation: Towards New Models for Managing Schools and Systems* (Schooling for Tomorrow series). Paris: OECD.

Rutter, M., Maughan, B., Mortimore, P., Ouston, J. with Smith, A. (1979). *Fifteen Thousand Hours: Secondary Schools and Their Effects on Children*. London: Open Books; Cambridge, MA: Harvard University Press. Reprinted 1994, London: Paul Chapman Publishers.

Watt, D. (2002). *How Innovation Occurs in High Schools Within the Network of Innovative Schools: The Four Pillars of Innovation Research Project*. The Conference Board of Canada. Available at: http://www. schoolnet.ca/nisrei/e/research/pillars/index.asp, accessed 20 March 2002.

BIBLIOGRAPHY

Adair, J. (2007). *Leadership Skills*. London: Times.

Ainscow, M. and Sandhill, A. (2010). Developing inclusive education systems: The role of organisational cultures and leadership, *International Journal of Inclusive Education*, 14(4): 401–16.

Ainsworth, M.D.S., Blehar, M.C., Waters, E. and Wall, S. (1978). *Patterns of Attachment: A Psychological Study of the Strange Situation*. Hillsdale, NJ: Erlbaum.

Al, S., Sari, R.M. and Kahya, N.C. (2012). A different perspective on education: Montessori and Montessori school architecture, *Procedia – Social and Behavioral Sciences*, 46: 1866–71.

Alexander, R.J. (2004) Still no pedagogy? Principles, pragmatism and compliance in primary education, *Cambridge Journal of Education*, 34(1): 7–33.

Alexander, R.J. (2006). *Towards Dialogic Teaching: Rethinking Classroom Talk*, 4th edn. Hong Kong: Hong Kong Institute of Education with Dialogos.

Alexander, R.J. (ed.) (2010). *Children, their World, their Education: Final report of the Cambridge Primary Review*. London: Routledge.

Algozzine, B., Audette, R.H., Marr, M.B. and Algozzine, K. (2005). An application of Total Quality principles in transforming the culture of classrooms, *Planning and Changing*, 36: 176–92.

American Psychological Association (2014). *The road to resilience*. Available at: http://www.apa.org/helpcenter/road-resilience.aspx (accessed September 2014).

Andrews, M. (2012). *Exploring Play for Early Childhood Studies*. London: Sage Publications.

Apple, M. (1996). *Cultural Politics and Education*. New York: Teachers College Press.

Austin, J.T. and Vancouver, J.B. (1996). Goal constructs in psychology: structure process and content, *Psychological Bulletin*, 3: 338–75.

Ball, S., Maguire, M. and Braun, A. (2012). *How schools do policy: policy enactments in secondary schools*. London: Routledge.

Barber, M. (2003). Deliverable goals and strategic challenges – a view from England on reconceptualising public education, in *Networks of Innovation: Towards New Models for Managing Schools and Systems* (Schooling for Tomorrow series), pp. 113–30. Paris: OECD.

Barblett, L. (2010). Why play-based learning? *Every Child*, 16(3): 4–5.

Baron-Cohen, S. (1991). Precursors to a theory of mind: Understanding attention in others. In A. Whiten (ed.), *Natural theories of mind: Evolution, development and simulation of everyday mindreading* (pp. 233–51). Oxford: Basil Blackwell.

Baron-Cohen, S., Leslie, A.M. and Frith, U. (1985). Does the autistic child have a 'theory of mind'?', *Cognition*, 21(1): 37–46.

Bear, G.G. (1998). School discipline in the United States: Prevention, correction, and long-term social development, *School Psychology Review*, 27(1): 14–32.

Beetham, H., McGill, L. and Littlejohn, A. (2009). Thriving in the 21st century: Learning Literacies for the Digital Age (LLiDA project). Available at: http://www.earlychildhoodaustralia.org.au/nqsplp/wp-content/uploads/2012/05/Why_play_based_learning.pdf.com (accessed September 2014).

Benson, C. (2004) Creativity: Caught or taught? *Design and Technology Education: An International Journal*, 9(3): 138–45.

Black, P. and Wiliam, D. (1998). Assessment and classroom learning, *Assessment in Education*, 5(1): 7–71.

Blanchette, I. and Richards, A. (2010). The influence of affect on higher level cognition: a review of research on interpretation, judgement, decision making and reasoning, *Cognition & Emotion*, 24(4): 561–95.

Blatchford, P., Bassett, P., Brown, P., Koutsoubou, M., Martin, P., Russell, A. and Webster, R. with Rubie-Davies, C. (2009). *Deployment and Impact of Support Staff (DISS) in Schools*. London: HMSO.

Bloom, B.S. (1984). The 2 sigma problem: the search for methods of group instruction as effective as one-to-one tutoring, *Educational Researcher*, 13(6): 4–16.

Bloom, B.S., Engelhart, M.D., Furst, E.J., Hill, W.H. and Krathwohl, D.R. (eds) (1956). *Taxonomy of Educational Objectives – The Classification of Educational Goals – Handbook 1: Cognitive Domain*. London: Longmans, Green & Co. Ltd.

Boud, D., Keogh, R. and Walker, D. (1985). *Reflection: Turning Experience into Learning*. London: Kogan Page.

Bowman, R. (1982). A Pac-Man theory of motivation. Tactical implications for classroom instruction, *Educational Technology*, 22(9): 14–17.

Bowman, R. (2007). How can students be motivated: A misplaced question? *The Clearing House*, 81(2): 81–6.

Bowman, R. (2011). Rethinking what motivates and inspires students, *The Clearing House: A Journal of Educational Strategies, Issues and Ideas*, 84(6): 264–9.

Boxall, M. (1976). The nurture group in the primary school, *Therapeutic Education*, 4(2): 13–18.

Bransford, J.D., Brown, A.L. and Cocking, R.R. (eds) (2004). *How People Learn: Brain, Mind, Experience and School*. Washington, DC: National Academies Press.

Brewer, J. and Daane, C.J. (2002). Translating constructivist theory into practice in primary-grade mathematics, *Education*, 123(2): 416–17.

Broomhead, K. (2013). Blame, guilt and the need for labels: insights from parents of children with special educational needs and educational practitioners, *British Journal of Special Education*, 40(1): 4–11.

Brown, A.S. and Palinscar, A.L. (1984). Reciprocal teaching, *Cognition and Instruction*, I(2): 117–75.

Bruce, T. (2011). *Learning through Play: Babies, Toddlers and the Foundation Years*, 2nd edn. London: Hodder Education.

Bruce, T. and Meggitt, C. (1999). *Child Care and Education*, 2nd edn. London: Hodder & Stoughton Educational.

Brundrett, M., Duncan, D. and Rhodes, C. (2010). Leading curriculum innovation in primary schools project: an interim report on school leaders' roles in curriculum development in England, *Education 3–13: International Journal of Primary, Elementary and Early Years Education*, 38(4): 403–19.

Bruner, J.S. (1972). Nature and uses of immaturity, *American Psychologist*, 27(8): 687–708.

Bruner, J. (1991). *Acts of meaning*. Cambridge, MA: Harvard University Press.

Bruner, J. (1996). *The culture of education*. Cambridge, MA: Harvard University Press.

Brunton, P. and Thornton, L. (2010) *Science in the Early Years: Building Firm Foundations from Birth to Five*. London: Sage.

Buber, M. (1958). *I and thou*. New York: Scribner and Sons.

Burden, K., Hopkins, P., Male, T., Martin, S. and Trala, C. (2012). *iPad Scotland Final Evaluation Report*. Hull: The University of Hull.

Buzan, T (1993). *The Mind Map Book*. London: BBG.

Cachia, R., Ferrari, A., Ala-Mutka, K. and Punie, Y. (2010). *Creative Learning & Innovative Teaching: Final Report on the Study on Creativity and Innovation in Education in the EU Member States* (No. EUR 24675). Seville: IPTS, Joint Research Centre, European Commission.

Callaghan, J. (1976). *'A rational debate based on the facts'*. Speech given at Ruskin College Oxford.

Cambridge Assessment (2011). *Cambridge Assessment's Parliamentary Research Enquiry series: Usha Goswami* [Podcast]. Available at: http://www.cambridgeassessment. org.uk/ca/Spotlight/Detail?tag=learn (accessed 5 February 2013). University of Cambridge Local Examinations Syndicate.

Cambridge Primary Review (2007). *Independent review of the Primary Curriculum*. Available at: http://cprtrust.org.uk/cpr/ (accessed September 2014).

Camhy, D.G. (2007). *Teaching Thinking – The Practice of Philosophy with Children*. Available at: http://www.rhodes.aegean.gr/tepaes/filosofia_eisai_edo/Anakinosis/Anakinosis3.pdf (accessed 3 January 2013).

Ceredigion Council (2010): Good practice in joint working. Available at: www.weds. wales.nhs.uk/opendoc/211559 (accessed September 2014).

Cassen, K. and Kingdon, G. (2007). *Tackling low educational achievement*. London: Joseph Rowntree Foundation.

Chism, N.V.N. (2006). Challenging traditional assumptions and rethinking learning spaces, in D.G. Oblinger (ed.), *Learning Spaces*, EDUCAUSE. Available at: https://net.educause.edu/ir/library/pdf/pub7102b.pdf (accessed 23 April 2014).

Chouinard, V. and Crooks, V.A. (2005). 'Because *they* have all the power and I have none': State Restructuring of Income and Employment Supports and Disabled Women's Lives in Ontario, Canada, *Disability & Society*, 20(1): 19–32.

Churchill, R., Ferguson, P., Godinho, S., Johnson, N.F., Keddie, A., Letts, W., Mackay, J., McGill, M., Moss, J., Nagel, M.C., Nicholson, P., and Vick, M. (2011). *Teaching: Making a Difference*. Milton, QLD: John Wiley & Sons Australia, Ltd.

Clark, W. and Luckin, R. (2013). What the research says – ipads in the classroom. Available from http://www.thepdfportal.com/ipads-in-the-classroom-report-lkl_61713.pdf (accessed 18 February 2014).

Claxton, G. (1990) *Teaching to Learn*. London: Cassell.

Claxton, G. (2007). Expanding young people's capacity to learn, *British Journal of Educational Studies*, 55(2): 1–20.

Coelho, P. (1998). *The Alchemist*. London: Harper Collins.

Coelho, P. (2008). *The Pilgrimage*. London: Harper One.

Cohen, L.M. (2012). Adaptation and creativity in cultural context, *Revista de Psicología*, 30(1).

Colcott, D., Russell, B. and Skouteris, H. (2009). Thinking about thinking: innovative pedagogy designed to foster thinking skills in junior primary classrooms, *Teacher Development: An International Journal of Teachers' Professional Development*, 13(1): 17–27.

Coplin, D. (2013). *Business Reimagined: Why Work Isn't Working and What You Can Do About It*. New York: Harriman House.

Cornelius-White, J. (2007). Learner-centered teacher–student relationships are effective: a meta-analysis, *Review of Educational Research*, 77: 113.

Craft, A. (2005). *Creativity in schools: tensions and dilemmas*. Abingdon: Routledge.

Craft, A. (2012). Childhood in a digital age: creative challenges for educational futures, *London Review of Education*, 10(2): 173–90.

Croll, P. and Moses, D. (1985). *One in Five. The Assessment and Incidence of Special Educational Needs*. London: Routledge & Kegan Paul.

Csikszentmihalyi, M. and Larson, R. (1980). Intrinsic rewards in school crime. In M. Verble (ed.), *Dealing in discipline*. Omaha: University of Mid-America.

Dahlberg, G., Moss, P. and Pence, A. (1999). *Beyond Quality in Early Childhood Education and Care: Postmodern Perspectives*. London: Falmer Press.

Darling-Hammond, L. (1998). Teachers and teaching: Testing policy hypotheses from a national commission report, *Educational Researcher*, 27(1): 5–15.

Darling-Hammond, L., Austin, K., Orcutt, S. and Rosso, J. (2001). *How People Learn: Introduction to Learning Theories*. Stanford: Stanford University Press.

Darnton, R. (2009). *The Case for Books, Past, Present, and Future*. New York: Public Affairs.

De Lemos, M. (1999). *A Research-based Evaluation of the Victorian First Steps Pilot Project for the First Three Years of Schooling*. Report to the Victorian Department of Education. Melbourne: ACER.

Delors, J. (1996). *Report to UNESCO of the International Commission on Education for the Twenty-first Century.* Paris: UNESCO.

D'Angour, A. (2013) Plato and Play, *American Journal of Play,* 5(3): 293–307. Available at: www.journalofplay.org/sites/journalofplay.org/files/pdf-articles/5-3-article-plato-and-play.pdf (accessed 19 January 2015).

D'Emidio-Caston, M. and Crocker, E. (1987). *Montessori Education: A Humanistic Approach for the 1990s.* Santa Barbara: Confluent Education Department, School of Education, University of California at Santa Barbara.

Department for Children, Families and Schools (2005). *Social, Emotional and Affective Learning. SEAL materials for schools.* London: HMSO.

Department for Children, Families and Schools (2006). *Assessing Pupil Progress.* London: HMSO.

Department for Education (1981). *The School Curriculum.* London: HMSO. Available at: http://www.educationengland.org.uk/documents/des/schoolcurric.html (accessed 2014).

Department for Education (1989). *National Curriculum.* London: HMSO.

Department for Education (2011). *Support and aspiration: a new approach to SEN and disability.* London: HMSO.

Department for Education (2012). *Development Matters in the Early Years Foundation Stage (EYFS).* Available at: http://www.foundationyears.org.uk/files/2012/03/Development-Matters-FINAL-PRINT-AMENDED.pdf (accessed 6 February 2012).

Department for Education and Skills (DfES) (2005). *Harnessing Technology: Transforming Learning and Children's Services.* London: HMSO.

Department of Education and Training (2011). *iPad Trial: Is the iPad Suitable as a Learning Tool in Schools?* Queensland Government, Australia: DET.

Devon County Council (2013). *Pupil Voices Project.* Available at: http://www.devon.gov.uk/pupilvoicereport2010.pdf (accessed September 2014).

Dewey, J. (reprinted 1966). *Democracy and Education.* New York: Free Press.

DCSF (2009). *National Curriculum.* London: DCSF.

DFE (2010). *The Importance of Teaching.* London: DFE.

DfE (2012). *Special Educational Needs in England.* Available at: https://www.education.gov.uk/publications/standard/publicationDetail/Page1/DFE-00178-2011 (accessed September 2014).

DfE (2013). *The Early Years Foundation Stage (EYFS) Review: Report on the Evidence.* Available at: https://www.education.gov.uk/publications/standard/publicationDetail/Page1/DFE-00178-2011 (accessed 6 February 2013).

DfES (2004). *Excellence and Enjoyment: Learning and Teaching in the Primary Years. Creating a Learning Culture: Conditions for Learning. Primary National Strategy.* London: DfES.

Dickens, C. (2003). *Hard Times* (ed. K. Flint). London: Penguin.

Doidge, N. (2007). *The Brain that Changes Itself: Stories of Personal Triumph from the Frontiers of Brain Science.* London: Penguin.

Donaldson, M. (1978). *Children's Minds.* London: Fontana.

Drucker, P. (1993). *Post- Capitalist Society.* London: Routledge.

Dunn, J. (2004). *Children's Friendships: The Beginning of Intimacy.* Oxford: Blackwell.

Dweck, C.S. (1990). Self-theories and goals: their role in motivation, personality, and development, in Richard Dienstbier (ed.), *Perspectives on Motivation: Nebraska Symposium on Motivation*, Vol. 38, pp. 199–235. Lincoln, NE: University of Nebraska Press.

Dweck, C.S. (1999). *Self-theories: Their Role in Motivation, Personality and Development*. Philadelphia: The Psychology Press.

Ecclestone, J. and Hays, D. (2008). *The Dangerous Rise of Therapeutic Education*. London: Routledge.

Edelson, D.C., Gordin, D.N. and Pea, R.D. (1999). Addressing the challenges of inquiry-based learning through technology and curriculum design, *Journal of the Learning Sciences*, 8(3&4): 391–450.

Education Scotland (2009). *Pre-birth to Three: Positive Outcomes for Scotland's Children and Families*. Available at: http://www.educationscotland.gov.uk/Images/17play_tcm4-637902.pdf (accessed 5 February 2013).

Education Scotland (2012). *What is Enquiry in Education?* Available at: http://www.educationscotland.gov.uk/stemcentral (accessed 18 November 2012).

Education Scotland (2014). *Supporting Curriculum for Excellence*. Available at: http://www.educationscotland.gov.uk (accessed December 2014).

Edwards, D. and Mercer, N. (1987). *Common Knowledge: The Development of Understanding in the Classroom*. London: Methuen.

Elliott, J. and Grigorenko, E. (2014). *The Dyslexia Debate*. Cambridge: Cambridge University Press.

Ellis, S. and Tod, J. (2012). Identification of SEN: is consistency a realistic or worthy aim? *Support for Learning*, 27(2): 59–66.

Emerson, E. and Hatton, C. (2004). *Estimating the Current Need/Demand for Supports for People with Learning Disabilities in England*. Lancaster: Institute for Health Research, Lancaster University.

Enhancing Education: A Producer's Guide (2002). *The Five 'Es'*. Available at: http://enhancinged.wgbh.org. (accessed 18 November 2012).

Eric, C.C.M. (2005). Engaging students in open-ended mathematics problem tasks – a sharing on teachers' production and classroom experience (primary). Available at: http://math.ecnu.edu.cn/earcome3/TSG2.htm (accessed 18 November 2012).

Eshet, Y. (2004). Digital literacy: a conceptual framework for survival skills in the digital era, *Journal of Educational Multimedia and Hypermedia*, 13(1): 93–106. Norfolk, VA: AACE. Retrieved 14 August 2013 from http://www.editlib.org/p/4793.

European Commission (2008a). *Dialogue on Dialogue: A Resource Book for the Developing Dialogue through Philosophical Enquiry Course for Teachers*. MENON: Developing Dialogue through Philosophical Inquiry. Comenius 2.1 Action 226597-CP-1-2005-1-MT-COMENIUS-C21. Brussels: Europeon Union.

European Commission (2008b). *Doing Philosophy in the Classroom: A Handbook for Teachers*. MENON: Developing Dialogue through Philosophical Inquiry Comenius 2.1 Action 226597-CP-1-2005-1-MT-COMENIUS-C21 Brussels: Europeon Union.

Evangelou, M., Sylva, K., Edwards, A. and Smith, T. (2008) *Supporting Parents in Promoting Early Learning: the Evaluation of the Early Learning Partnership Project*. Research Report DCSF-RR039. London: DCSF.

Facer, K., Joiner, R., Stanton, D., Reid, J., Hull, R. and Kirk, D. (2004). Savannah: mobile gaming and learning? *Journal of Computer Assisted Learning*, 20: 399–409.

Ferriter, B. (2013). *Centre for Teaching Quality (CTQ)*. Available at: http://www.teachingquality.org/content/technology-tool-not-learning-outcome (accessed 2 March 2014).

Firestien, R. (1996). *Leading on the Creative Edge: Gaining Competitive Advantage Through the Power of Creative Problem Solving*. Colorado Springs: Pinon Press.

Flynn, N. and Stainthorp, R. (2006). *The Learning and Teaching of Reading and Writing*. Chichester: WileyBlackwell.

Forbes, R. (2004). *Beginning to Play: Young Children from Birth to Three*. Maidenhead: McGraw-Hill and Open University Press.

Francis, A. (2012) Stigma in an era of medicalisation and anxious parenting: how proximity and culpability shape middle-class parents' experiences of disgrace, *Sociology of Health & Illness*, 1–16.

Frankl, V. (1959). *Man's Search for Meaning*, 5th edn. Boston: Beacon Press.

Frederickson, N. and Cline, T. (2002). *Special Educational Needs, Inclusion, and Diversity: A Textbook*. Buckingham: Open University Press.

Freire, P. (1993). *Pedagogy of the Oppressed*. New York: Continuum.

Fullan, M. (2007). *The New Meaning of Educational Change*. Routledge: New York.

Gandhi, I. (1976). Meaning of education. Convocation address, 24 April, North-Eastern Hill University, Shillong. Available at: http://www.dialogueworks.co.uk/docs/Inquiry_based_learning.pdf (accessed 3 January 2013).

Gardner, H. (2000). *Can technology exploit our many ways of knowing?* pp. 32–5.

Gasparini, A.A. (2011). Touch, Learn, Play – What Children do with an iPad in the Classroom. Masters Thesis, University of Oslo. Available at: https://www.duo.uio.no/handle/123456789/9015.

Geer, R. and Sweeney, T. (2012). Students' voices about learning with technology, *Journal of Social Sciences*, 8(2): 294–303.

Ghiselin, B. (1985). *The Creative Process*. California: University of California Press.

Gibbons, M. (2004). 'Pardon Me, Didn't I Just Hear a Paradigm Shift?' *Phi Beta Kappan* 85(6): 461–67.

Gifford, S. (2004). A new mathematics pedagogy for the early years: in search of principles for practice, *International Journal of Early Years Education*, 12(2): 99–115.

Gilbert, I. (2013). *Essential Motivation in the Classroom*. Abingdon: Routledge.

Gillen, J. and Barton, D. (2009). *Digital Literacies: A Research Briefing by the Technology-enhanced Learning Phase of the Teaching and Learning Research Programme*. London: TLRP.

Gillen, J., Kleine Staarman, J., Littleton, K., Mercer, N. and Twiner, A. (2007). A 'learning revolution'? Investigating pedagogic practices around interactive whiteboards in British primary classrooms, *Learning, Media and Technology*, 32(3): 243–56.

Gillies, V. (2011). Social and emotional pedagogies: critiquing the new orthodoxy of emotion in classroom behaviour management, *British Journal of Sociology of Education*, 32(2): 185–202.

Gilster, P. (1997). *Digital Literacy*. New York: John Wiley and Sons.

Ginsburg, H.P. and Allardice, B.S. (1993). Children's difficulties with mathematics: Cognition in the school context, in B. Rogoff and J. Lave (eds), *Everyday Cognition: Its development in social context*. Cambridge, MA: Harvard University Press.

Glennon, F. (2008). Promoting freedom, responsibility, and learning in the classroom: the learning covenant a decade later, *Teaching Theology and Religion*, 11(1): 32–41.

Gordon, D. (2000). *The Digital Classroom: How Technology Is Changing the Way We Teach and Learn*. Cambridge, MA: Harvard Education Publishing Group.

Gordon, T., Holland, J. and Lahelma, E. (2000). *Making Spaces: Citizenship and Difference in Schools*. London: Macmillan.

Goswami, U. and Bryant, P. (2007). *Children's Cognitive Development and Learning (Primary Review Research Survey 2/1a)*. Cambridge: University of Cambridge Faculty of Education.

Gove, M. (2011). *Training our next generation of outstanding teachers: An improvement strategy for discussion*. London: DfE.

Graesser, A.C. and Person, N.K. (1994). Question-asking during tutoring, *American Educational Research Journal*, 31(1): 104–37.

Graham, A., Phelps, R., Maddison, C. and Fitzgerald, R. (2011). Supporting children's mental health in schools: teacher views, *Teachers and Teaching: Theory and Practice*, 17(4): 479–96.

Grant, L. (2010). *Connecting Digital Literacy Between Home and School*. Bristol: Futurelab.

Guardian, The (2010). High stakes testing. Available at: http://www.theguardian.com/theguardian/2008/may/14/4 (accessed January 2014).

Guðjónsdóttir, H., Cacciattolo, M., Dakich, E., Dalmau, M.C., Davies, A. and Kelly, C. (2007). Transformative pathways: inclusive pedagogies in learning and teaching, *Journal of Research on Technology in Education (ISTE)*, 40(2): 165–82.

Haddow, J. (1931). The Haddow report: Primary. Board of Education. Available at: http://www.educationengland.org.uk/documents/hadow1931/ (accessed September 2014).

Hague, C. and Payton, S. (2010). *Digital Literacy Across the Curriculum: a Futurelab Handbook*. London: Futurelab. Available at: http://www.futurelab.org.uk/sites/default/files/Digital_Literacy_handbook_0.pdf (accessed 22 February 2014).

Hague, C. and Williamson, B. (2009). Digital participation, digital literacy, and school subjects: a review of the policies, literature and evidence. Available at: http://www.futurelab.org.uk/sites/default/files/Digital_Participation_review.pdf (accessed 9 August 2013).

Hannafin, M.J., Hall, C., Land, S. and Hill, J. (1994). Learning in open environments: assumptions, methods, and implications, *Educational Technology*, 34(8): 48–55.

Hansen, D.T. (ed.) (2006). *John Dewey and our Educational Prospect. A Critical Engagement with Dewey's Democracy and Education*. Albany: State University of New York Press.

Hargreaves, A. (2003). *Teaching in the Knowledge Society*. New York: Teachers' College Press.

Hargreaves, D. (2010). *Creating a Self-improving School System*. Nottingham, National College for School Leadership.

Hargreaves, D. (2011). *Self-improving School Network*. Manchester: NCTL.

Hart, R. (2010). Classroom behaviour management: educational psychologists' views on effective practice, *Emotional and Behavioural Difficulties*, 15(4): 353–71.

Hattie, J. (2003). Teachers make a difference: What is the research evidence? Available from: http://www.educationalleaders.govt.nz/ (accessed 3 January 2013).

Hattie, J. (2012). *Visible learning. Maximizing impact on learners*. London: Routledge.

Hayes, B., Hindle, S. and Withington, P. (2007). Strategies for developing positive behaviour management: Teacher behaviour outcomes and attitudes to the change process, *Educational Psychology in Practice*, 23(2), 161–75.

Hayward, J. (2012). *Find It, Make It, Use It, Share It: Learning in Digital Wales. Digital Classroom Teaching Task and Finish Group*. WG15089 Ref: CAD/GM/0213. Available at: http://wales.gov.uk/newsroom/educationandskills/2012/120329digitalclassrooms/?lang=en (accessed September 2014).

Hedberg, J.G. (2011). Towards a disruptive pedagogy: changing classroom practice with technologies and digital content, *Educational Media International*, 48(1): 1–16.

Heinrich, P. (2012). *The iPad as a Tool for Education*. NAACE. Available at http://www.thepdfportal.com/ipads-in-the-classroom-report-lkl_61713.pdf (accessed September 2014).

Henderson, S. and Yeow, G. (2012) iPad in Education: A case study of iPad adoption and use in a primary school. *45th Hawaii International Conference on Social Sciences*.

Heseltine, P. (2013). *Play in the past*. Available at: http://www.ipa-ewni.org.uk/services/Heseltine%202013%20Play%20in%20the%20past.pdf (accessed 10 June 2013).

Hewitt, D. (2007). *Understanding Effective Learning*. London: Sage

Hinton, C. and Wolpert, M. (1998). Why is ADHD such a compelling story? *Clinical Child Psychology and Psychiatry*, 2315–2317.

Hirsch, E.D. (1988). *Cultural Literacy*. New York: Vintage.

Hirst, E. and Cooper, M. (2008). Keeping them in line: choreographing classroom spaces, *Teachers and Teaching: Theory and Practice*, 14(5–6): 431–45.

Hodkinson, A. (2013). Illusionary inclusion – what went wrong with New Labour's landmark educational policy? *British Journal of Special Education*, 39(1): 4–11.

Hopkins, D. (2001). *School Improvement for Real*. London: Falmer Press.

Hopkins, D. (2003). Understanding networks for innovation in policy and practice, in *Networks of Innovation: Towards New Models for Managing Schools and Systems*, (Schooling for Tomorrow series). Paris: OECD.

Hutchings, B. (2012). *The Centre for Excellence in Enquiry-Based Learning* (CEEBL). Available at: http://www.manchester.ac.uk/ceebl (accessed 18 November 2012).

Hutchings, W. and O'Rourke, K. (2006). Enquiry-based learning, internationality and interdisciplinarity: a case-study of a trial Anglo-American student event. Available at: http://www.ceebl.manchester.ac.uk/resources/casestudies/ceeblessay003.pdf (accessed 3 January 2013).

i-Fen Yeh, McTigue, E. and Malatesha Joshi, R. (2012). Moving from explicit to implicit: a case study of improving inferential comprehension. *Literacy Research and Instruction*, 51(2): 125–42.

Independent, The (2013). A letter from one hundred academics. http://www.independent.co.uk/voices/letters/letters-gove-will-bury-pupils-in-facts-and-rules-8540741.html (accessed Sptember 2014).

Institute of Ideas (2012). *Towards a subject-based curriculum*. Available at: http://instituteofideas.com/documents/educationforum/Towards_a_subject_based_education_IOI_Ed_Forum_April_2012.pdf (accessed September 2012).

Isaacs, S. (1929). *The Nursery Years – The Mind of the Child from Birth to Six*. London: G. Routledge & Sons Ltd.

Istance, D. (ed.) (2008). *Think Scenarios, Re-think Education, Schooling for Tomorrow series*. Paris: OECD.

Jacks, L.P. (1932). *Education through Recreation*. New York: Harper and Brothers.

Jaeckle, S. (2008). The EYFS principles: a breakdown. Available at: http://www.teachingexpertise.com/articles/eyfs-principles-breakdown-4117 (accessed 6 February 2013). Optimus Professional Publishing Limited 2006–2010.

James, M. and Pedder, D. (2006) Beyond method: assessment and learning practices and values. *The Curriculum Journal*, 17(2):109–38.

Jeffrey, B. and Craft, A. (2004). Teaching creatively and teaching for creativity: distinctions and relationships. *Educational Studies*, 30(1): 77–87. Available at: http://www.naace.co.uk/get.html?_Action=GetFile&_Key=Data26613&_Id=1965&_Wizard=0&_DontCache=1341555048 (accessed September 2014).

Jobs, S. (1996). The next insanely great thing. Available at: http://archive.wired.com/wired/archive/4.02/jobs_pr.html (accessed September 2014).

Johnson, L., Adams, S. and Cummins, M. (2012). *The NMC Horizon Report: 2012 Higher Education Edition*. Austin, TX: The New Media Consortium. Available at: http://www.nmc.org/pdf/2012-horizon-report-HE.pdf (accessed 18 January 2013).

Jones, D. (2012) (quoted in) *Cotton Wool Kids*. Issues, Paper 7. Releasing the potential for children to take risks and innovate. HTI: London. Available at: www.hti.org.uk/pdfs/pu/issuespaper7.pdf (accessed November 2014)

Kahn, P. and O'Rourke, K. (2005). *Handbook of Enquiry and Problem-based Learning: Irish Case Studies and International Perspectives. Section 1: Understanding Enquiry and Problem-based Learning*. Dublin: National University of Ireland.

Karkockiene, D. (2005). Creativity: Can it be Trained? A Scientific Educology of Creativity, *International Journal of Educology*, Lithuanian Special Issue, 51.

Karsenti, T., and Fievez, A. (2013). *The iPad in education: uses, benefits, and challenges – A survey of 6,057 students and 302 teachers in Quebec, Canada*. Montreal, QC: CRIFPE.

Katzenbach, J. (2006). Motivation beyond money: Learning from peak performers, *Leader to Leader*, 41: 59–62.

Kaufman, J.C. and Beghetto, R.A. (2009). Beyond big and little: The four C model of creativity, *Review of General Psychology*, 13: 1–12.

Kelly, A.V. (2009) *The Curriculum: theory and practice*, 6th edn. London: Sage.

Kersting, K. (2003). What exactly is creativity? Psychologists continue their quest to better understand creativity, *American Psychological Association*, 34(10).

Kliebard, H. (1986). *The struggle for the American curriculum 1893–1958*. Boston, MA: Routtledge & Kegan Paul.

Kogan, M. and Maden, M. (1999). *The Impact of OfSTED on Schools*. London: Joseph Rowntree Charitable Foundation.

Knobel, M. (2008). Digital literacy and participation in online social networking spaces, in *Digital Literacies: Concepts, Policies and Practices*, p. 49. New York: Peter Lang. Available at: http://www.academia.edu/3011380/Digital_literacy_and_participation_in_online_social_networking_spaces (accessed 8 August 2013).

Lamm, C., Meltzoff. A.N. and Decety, J. (2010). How Do We Empathize with Someone Who Is Not Like Us? A Functional Magnetic Resonance Imaging Study. *Journal of Cognitive Neuroscience*, 22: 362–76.

Lankshear, C. and Knobel, M. (2006). *New Literacies: Everyday Practices and Classroom Learning*, 2nd edn. Maidenhead: Open University Press.

Lave, J. (1988). *Cognition in practice: Mind, mathematics and culture in everyday life.* Cambridge: Cambridge University Press.

Learning and Teaching Scotland (2006). *The Reggio Emilia Approach to Early Years Education.* Glasgow: Learning and Teaching Scotland.

Legare, C.H. (2008). *The Development of Causal Explanatory Reasoning.* Michigan: University of Michigan.

Legutke, M. and Thomas, H. (1991). *Process and Experience in the Language Classroom.* Harlow: Longman.

Leithwood, K.A. (1981). The Dimensions of Curriculum Innovation, *Journal of Curriculum Studies*, 13(1).

Lerman, S. (2000). The social turn in mathematics education research, in J. Boaler (ed.), *Multiple Perspectives on Mathematics Teaching and Learning*. Westport, CT: Ablex Publishing.

Lester, S. and Russell, W. (2008). *Play for a Change. Play, Policy and Practice: A Review of Contemporary Perspectives.* London: Play England.

Lillard, A.S. (2013). Playful learning and Montessori education, *American Journal of Play*, 5(2): 157–86.

Lilley, I. (ed.) (1967). *Friedrich Froebel: A Selection from his Writings.* London: Cambridge University Press.

Lindqvist, G. and Nilholm, C. (2014) Promoting inclusion? 'Inclusive' and effective head teachers' descriptions of their work, *European Journal of Special Needs Education*, 29(1): 74–90.

Lipman, M. and Sharp, A.M. (1998). *Ethical Inquiry: Instructional Manual to accompany Lisa.* Montclair: University Press of America.

Lipman, M., Sharp, A.M. and Oscanyan, F.S. (1980). *Philosophy in the Classroom*, 2nd edn. Philadelphia: Temple University.

Livingstone, I. and Hope, A. (2011). *Next Gen.: Transforming the UK into the World's Leading Talent Hub for the Video Games and Visual Effects Industries.* London: NESTA.

Lortie, D. (1975). *Schoolteacher: A Sociological Study.* Chicago: University of Chicago Press.

Louv, R. (2005) *Last Child in the Woods: Saving Our Children from Nature-Deficit Disorder.* Chapel Hill: Algonquin Books.

Louv, R. (2010). *Last Child in the Woods: Saving Our Children from Nature Deficit Disorder.* London: Atlantic.

Louv, R. (2011). A timely truth, *National Trust Magazine*, pp. 34–7.

Loveless, A.M. (2001). *The interaction between primary teachers' perceptions of information and communication technology (ICT) and their pedagogy.* School of Education. Brighton, University of Brighton: 390.

Luckin, R., Bligh, B., Manches, A., Ainsworth, S., Crook, C. and Noss, R. (2012). *Learning: The Proof, Promise and Potential of Digital Education.* London: NESTA.

Luo, L. (2010). Web 2.0 integration in information literacy instruction: an overview, *The Journal of Academic Librarianship*, 36(1): 32–40.

Macarthur (2014). Confronting the challenges of participatory culture: media education for the 21st century. Chicago: MacArthur Foundation. Available at http://digitallearning.macfound.org/atf/cf/%7B7E45C7E0-A3E0-4B89-AC9C-E807E1B0AE4E%7D/JENKINS_WHITE_PAPER.PD (accessed September 2014).

Macbeath, J. (ed.) (2002). *Effective School Leadership: Responding to Change*. London: Sage Publications Ltd.

Mager, Robert F. (1962). *Preparing Instructional Objectives*. Palo Alto: Fearon.

Male, B. (2012). *The Primary Curriculum Design Handbook*. London: Bloomsbury.

Matijević, M. (2011). The new media and informal learning, *Digital Technologies and New Forms of Learning*, pp. 271–278. Available at: http://files.eric.ed.gov/fulltext/ED521060.pdf (accessed 25 April 2014).

Matijević, M. (2012). The new learning environment and learner needs this century, *Procedia – Social and Behavioural Sciences*, 46: 3290–5.

McCormick, R. and Scrimshaw, P. (2001). Information and communications technology, knowledge and pedagogy, *Education, Communication & Information*, 1(1): 37–57.

McGregor, J. (2003). Making spaces: teacher workplace topologies, *Pedagogy, Culture and Society*, 11(3): 353–76.

McGuiness, C. and Nisbet, J. (1990) Teaching thinking in Europe, *British Journal of Educational Psychology*, 61: 174–186.

McKernan, J. (2010). A critique of instructional objectives, *Education Inquiry*, 1(1): 57–67.

McLeod, D.B. (1992). Research on affect in mathematics education: A reconceptualization, in D.A. Grows (ed.), *Handbook of research on mathematics teaching and learning* (pp. 575–96). New York: Macmillan.

McNeil, J.D. (1977). *Designing Curriculum*. Boston: Little Brown.

Meighan, R. (1997). *Comparing Learning Systems*. London: Educational Heretics Press.

Mercer, N. (1987). (ed.) *Language and Literacy from an Educational Perspective, Vol. 1: Language Studies*. Milton Keynes: Open University Press.

Mercer, N. and Sams, C. (2006). Teaching children how to use language to solve maths problems, *Language and Education*, 20(6): 507–28.

Mercer, N., Dawes, L. and Kleine Staarman, J. (2009). Dialogic teaching in the primary science classroom, *Language and Education*, 23(4): 353–69.

Merchant, G. (2010). 3D virtual worlds as environments for literacy learning, *Educational Research*, 52(2): 135–50.

Miller, D.M. (2011). What college teachers should know about memory: a perspective from cognitive psychology, *College Teaching*, 59(3): 117–22.

Miller, H. (2009). Adaptable spaces and their impact on learning: research summary. Available at: http://www.hermanmiller.com/research/research-summaries/adaptable-spaces- and-their-impact-on-learning.html (accessed 24 April 2014).

Mohan, R. (2007). *Innovative Science Teaching for Physical Science Teachers*, 3rd edn. New Delhi: Asoke K Ghosh.

Montessori, M. (1966). *The Secret of Childhood*, translated by M.J. Costelloe. New York: Ballentine Books. (Il Segreto dell'infanzia, 7th edn, Milan, 1960).

Montgomery, T. (2008). Managing static formal learning spaces, *Active Learning in Higher Education*, 9(2): 122–38.

Moon, J.A. (2009). The Use of Graduated Scenarios to Facilitate the Learning of Complex and Difficult-to-describe Concepts, *Art, Design and Communication in Higher Education*, 8: 57–70.

Morris, W. (2003). *Creativity: Its place in education*. Belgium: JPH.com

Moss, S. (2012). *Natural Childhood*. Rotherham: National Trust.

Moss, G., Jewitt, C., Levaãiç, R., Armstrong, V., Cardini A. and Castle, F. (2007). *The Interactive Whiteboards, Pedagogy and Pupil Performance Evaluation: An Evaluation of the Schools Whiteboard Expansion (SWE) Project: London Challenge Research report no. 816*. London: Institute of Education, University of London. Available at: http://eprints.ioe.ac.uk/905/1/Moss2007whiteboardsRR816.pdf (accessed 25 February 2014).

Mumford, M.D. (2003). Where have we been, where are we going? Taking stock in creativity research, *Creativity Research Journal*, 15: 107–20.

NACCCE (1999). *All our futures: creativity, culture and education*. NAACE.

NESTA (2007). *Education for Inovation*. Available at: http://www.nesta.org.uk/futureinnovators (accessed December 2013).

Nie, Y. and Lau, S. (2009). Complementary roles of care and behavioral control in classroom management: The self-determination theory perspective. *Contemporary Educational Psychology*, 34(3): 185–94.

Nusche, D., L.Maxwell W. and Shewbridge, C. (2012). *OECD Reviews of Evaluation and Assessment in Education: New Zealand 2011*. Paris: OECD Publishing.

OECD (2003). Networks of innovation: Towards new models for managing schools and systems, *Schools for tomorrow*. Paris: OECD Publishing.

Ofsted (2005). *Managing Challenging Behaviour*. London: HMSO.

Ofsted (2010). *Creative Approaches Which Raise Standards*. London: HMSO.

Oluwafisayo, E. (2010). Constructivism and web 2.0 in the emerging learning era: a global perspective, *Journal of Strategic Innovation and Sustainability*, 6(4): 16–25. Available at: http://www.na-businesspress.com/JSIS/EnobunWeb.pdf (accessed 27 February 2014).

O'Rourke, J., Main, S. and Ellis, M. (2013). It doesn't seem like work, it seems like good fun: perceptions of primary students on the use of handheld game consoles in mathematics classes, *Technology, Pedagogy and Education*, 22(1): 103–20.

Oxford Dictionaries (2013). Available at: http://oxforddictionaries.com/definition/english/play (accessed 20 December 2012).

Palmer, Parker J. (1998). *The Courage to Teach*. San Francisco, CA: Jossey-Bass Publishers.

Panzarino, M. (2012). Rare full recording of 1983 Steve Jobs speech reveals Apple had been working on iPad for 27 years. Available at: http://thenextweb.com/apple/2012/10/02/rare-full-recording-of-1983-steve-jobs-speech-reveals-apple-had-been-working-on-ipad-for-27-years/#!xS1pw (accessed 1 March 2013).

Parker, K.R. and Chao, J.T. (2007). Wiki as a teaching tool, *Interdisciplinary Journal of Knowledge and Learning Objects*, 3: 57–72.

Parks, T. (2011): *Stop What You're Doing and Read This*. London: Vintage.

Parnell, W. and Bartlett, J. (2012). iDocument: how smartphones and tablets are changing documentation in preschool and primary classrooms, *Young Children*, 67(3): 50–59.

Payton, S. and Williamson, B. (2009). Curriculum and teaching innovation: transforming classroom practice and innovation. Future Labs. Available at: http://www.academia. edu/3270711/Curriculum_and_Teaching_Innovation_Transforming_classroom_ practice_and_personalisation.

Phillips, E. (2013). A case study of questioning for reading comprehension during guided reading, *Education 3–13: International Journal of Primary, Elementary and Early Years Education*, 41(1): 110–20.

Piaget, J. (1952). *The origins of intelligence in children*, translated by M. Cook. New York, NY: W.W. Norton & Co.

Pifarré, M. and Kleine Staarman, J. (2011). Wiki-supported collaborative learning in primary education: how a dialogic space is created for thinking together. *Computer Supported Learning Collaborative Learning*, 6: 187–205.

Plato (1955) *The Republic*, translated by H.D. Lee. Harmondsworth: Penguin.

Plato (360 BCE) *Laws*, translated by Benjamin Jowett. New York: Basic Books.

Plowden B. (1967). *The Plowden Report. Children and their Primary Schools. A Report of the Central Advisory Council for Education (England)*. London: HMSO.

Pollard, A. (2008). *Reflective Teaching: Evidence-informed Professional Practice*. London: Continuum International Publishing Group.

Powell, S.D. and Jordan, R.R. (1993). Diagnosis, intuition and autism, *British Journal of Special Education*, 20: 26–29.

Powell, S.D. and Makin, M. (1994). Enabling pupils with learnings difficulties to reflect on their own thinking, *British Educational Research Journal*, 20: 579–593.

Prensky, M. (2001a). Digital natives, digital immigrants, *On the Horizon*, 9(5): 1–6.

Prensky, M. (2001b). Do they really think differently? *On the Horizon*, 9(6): 1–9.

Puentedura, R. (2013). *SAMR: Getting to Transformation*. Available at: http://www. hippasus.com/rrpweblog/archives/2013/04/16/SAMRGettingToTransformation.pdf (accessed September 2014).

Pupil Voice Wales (2014). Local Youth Forums. Available at: http://www.pupilvoicewales. org.uk/secondary/get-involved/local-youth-forums (accessed January 2015).

Qualifications and Curriculum Authority (1999). *National Curriculum Handbook*. London: DFEE.

Qualifications and Curriculum Authority (2008). *Early Years Foundation Stage Profile Handbook*. London: HMSO.

Radunovich, H.L. and Kochert, J.L. (2011). *Creating a successful early learning environment for children who have autism spectrum disorders*. University of Florida. Available at: http://edis.ifas.ufl.edu/pdffiles/FY/FY105600.pdf (accessed 27 April 2014).

Rasmussen, K. (2004). Places for children – children's places, *Childhood*, 11: 155–73.

Reh, R., Rabenstein, K. and Fritzsche, B. (2011). Learning spaces without boundaries? Territories, power and how schools regulate learning, *Social & Cultural Geography*, 12(1): 83–98.

Rix, J., Sheehy, K., Fletcher-Campbel, F., Crisp, M. and Harper, A. (2013). Exploring provision for children identified with special educational needs: an international review of policy and practice, *European Journal of Special Needs Education*, 28(4): 375–91.

Robinson, K. (2010). *Changing Paradigms*. RSA Animate. Available at: http://www. thersa.org/events/rsaanimate/animate/rsa-animate-changing-paradigms (accessed September 2014).

Rock, D. 2010. Managing with the brain in mind, *Strategy + Business*, 88–97.

Rolheiser, C., Evans, M. and Gambhir, M. (eds) (2011). *Enquiry into Practice: Reaching Every Student Through Inclusive Curriculum*. Toronto: OISE.

Rose, J. (2006). *Independent Review of the Curriculum*. London: DCFS. Available at: http://webarchive.nationalarchives.gov.uk/20130401151715/http://www.education.gov.uk/publications/eOrderingDownload/Primary_curriculum_Report.pdf (accessed September 2014).

Rousseau, J.-J. (1763). *Émile or on Education*, International Eduation Series Vol. XX. New York and London: Penguin.

Roussou, M. (2004). Learning by doing and learning through play: An exploration of interactivity in virtual environments for children, *Computer in Entertainment*, 2(1): 10.

Russell, M., Bebell, D. and O'Dwyer, L.M. (2005). Tracking the arc of new teachers' technology use, in C. Vrasidas and G.V. Glass (eds), *Preparing Teachers to Teach with Technology*, pp. 45–63. Greenwich, CT: Information Age Publishing.

Rutter, M., Maughan, B., Mortimore, P., Ouston, J. with Smith, A. (1979). *Fifteen Thousand Hours: Secondary Schools and their Effects on Children*. London: Open Books; Cambridge, MA: Harvard University Press. Reprinted 1994, London: Paul Chapman Publishers.

Santer, J., Griffiths, C. and Goodall, D. (2007). *Free Play in Early Childhood: A Literature Review*. London: National Children's Bureau.

Schunk, D.H (2012). *Learning Theories: An Educational Perspective*, 6th edn. Boston: Pearson Education.

Sher, G. (2006) *In Praise of Blame*. Oxford: Oxford University Press.

Shipley, D. (2013). *Empowering Children. Play-based Curriculum for Lifelong Learning*, 5th edn. London, ON: Nelson Education Ltd.

Sigman, A. (2007) Agricultural literacy: giving concrete children food for thought. Available at: www.face-online.org.uk/resources/news/Agricultural%20Literacy.pdf (accessed 25 April 2014).

Simon, B. (1985). *Does Education Matter?* London: Lawrence and Wishart.

Slade, M., Lowery, C. and Bland, K. (2013). Evaluating the impact of Forest Schools: a collaboration between a university and a primary school, *British Journal of Learning Support*, 28(2): 66–72.

Smith, F., Hardman, F. and Higgins, S. (2006). The impact of interactive whiteboards on teacher–pupil interaction in the National Literacy and Numeracy Strategies, *British Educational Research Journal*, 32(3): 443–57.

Smith, M.K. (1997, 2002). Paulo Freire and informal education, the encyclopaedia of informal education. Available at: http://www.infed.org/thinkers/et-freir.htm (accessed 3 January 2013).

Smith, P.K. and Pellegrini, A.D. (2008). *Learning Through Play. Encyclopedia on Early Childhood Development*. London: Goldsmiths, University of London, and University of Minnesota.

Smith, P.K., Cowie, H. and Blades, M. (2003). *Understanding Children's Development*, 2nd edn. Oxford: Blackwell.

Standards and Testing Agency (2012). *Early Years Foundation Stage Profile Handbook*. London: HMSO.

Stangvik, G. (2014). Progressive special education in the neoliberal context, *European Journal of Special Needs Education*, 29(1): 91–104.

Starko, A. (2010). *Creativity in the classroom: Schools of curious delight*, 4th edn. New York: Routledge.

Steinbeck, J. (1945) *Cannery Row*. London: Penguin.

Stenhouse, L. (1975) *An Introduction to Curriculum Research and Development*. London: Heinemann Educational Books.

Sternberg, R. (2006). The nature of creativity, *Creativity Research Journal*, 18(1): 87–98.

Sternberg, R J. and Grigorenko, E.L. eds (2003). *The Psychology of Abilities, Competencies, and Expertise*. Cambridge: Cambridge University Press.

Strong-Wilson, T. and Ellis, J. (2007). Children and place: Reggio Emilia's environment as third teacher, *Theory Into Practice*, 46(1): 40–47.

Sutcliffe, R. (2011). Inquiry-based learning – 21st century pedagogy? Available at: http://www.dialogueworks.co.uk/docs/Inquiry_based_learning.pdf (accessed 18 November 2012).

Sutton-Smith, B. (1997). *The Ambiguity of Play*. Cambridge, MA: Harvard University Press.

Sweller, J. (1988). Cognitive load during problem solving: Effects on learning, *Cognitive Science*, 12: 257–285.

Sylva, K., Melhuish, E., Sammons, P., Siraj-Blatchford, I. and Taggart, B. (2008) *Final Report from the Primary Phase: Pre-school, School, and Family Influences on Children's Development During Key Stage 2 (age 7–11), Effective Pre-School and Primary Education 3–11 project (EPPE 3–11). Research Report DCSF RB061*. London: DCSF.

Tamis-LeMonda, C., Cabrera, C. and Shannon, J.D. (2007): Fathers' Influence on Their Children's Cognitive and Emotional Development: From Toddlers to Pre-K, *Applied Development Science*, 11(4): 208–13.

Tarde, G. (1903). *The Laws of Imitation*, translated by E. Clews Parsons. New York: H. Holt & Co.

Tarr, P. (2004). Consider the walls, *Young Children*, 59(3): 88–92. Available at: http://www.naeyc.org/files/yc/file/200405/ConsidertheWalls.pdf (accessed 23 April 2014).

Thrift, N. (2000) Performing cultures in the new economy, *Annals of the Association of American Geographers*, 90(4): 674–92.

Tickell, C. (2011). *The Early Years: Foundations for Life, Health and Learning. An Independent Report on the Early Years Foundation Stage to Her Majesty's Government*. London: HMSO.

TLRP (2004). *Personalised Learning*. London: ESRC.

Tovani. C. (2000). *I Read It, but I Don't Get It: Comprehension Strategies for Adolescent Readers*. New York: Stenhouse

Tovey, H. (2012). *Early Childhood Practice: Froebel Today*, Ed. T. Bruce. London: Sage Publications Ltd.

Tucker, K. (2010). *Mathematics Through Play in the Early Years*, 2nd edn. London: Sage Publications Ltd.

UNISON (2013). *The evident value of teaching assistants*. London: UNISON.

Van Tartwijk, J., den Brok, P., Veldman, I. and Wubbels, Th. (2009). Teachers' practical knowledge about classroom management in multicultural classrooms, *Teaching and Teacher Education*, 25: 453–60.

Vehar, J. (2008): Creativity and innovation: a call for rigour in language. Available at: http://innovationblogsite.typepad.com/files/c_9-2-08_creativity-vs-innovation-article.pdf (accessed September 2014).

Vrasidas, C., Themistokleous, S. and Zembylas, M. (2010). Cyprus National Strategic Plan for Sustainable Development 2011–2015. An Opportunity for a "social turn". *International Social Watch Report 2010*.

Vygotsky, L. (1978). *Mind in Society: The Development of Higher Psychological Processes*. Cambridge, MA: Harvard University Press.

Wagner, B.J. (1999). *Dorothy Heathcote: Drama as a Learning Medium*. New York: Calendar Islands.

Wang, M. and Peverley, S. (1987). The self-instructive process in classroom learning contexts. *Contemporary Educational Psychology*, 11: 370–404.

Watt, D. (2002). *How Innovation Occurs in High Schools Within the Network of Innovative Schools: The Four Pillars of Innovation Research Project*. Ontario: The Conference Board of Canada. Available at: http://www.schoolnet.ca/nisrei/e/research/pillars/index.asp (accessed 20 March 2002).

Wegerif, R. (2005). Reason and creativity in classroom dialogues, *Language and Education*, 19(3): 223–37.

Wells, G. and Claxton, G. (eds) (2002). *Learning for Life in the 21st Century: Sociocultural Perspectives on the Future of Education*. Oxford: Blackwell.

Wittgenstein, L. (1953). *Philosophical Investigations*. Oxford: Blackwell Publishing.

Wolk, S. (2008). Joy in school, *The Positive Classroom*, 66(1): 8–15.

Wright, H. (2012). *100 Great Innovation Ideas*. London: MCI.

Yeh, H.C. and Lai, P.L. (2012). Implementing online question generation to foster reading comprehension, *Australasian Journal of Educational Technology*, 28(7): 1152–75.

Yilmaz, K. (2011). The cognitive perspective on learning: its theoretical underpinnings and implications for classroom practices, *The Clearing House: A Journal of Educational Strategies, Issues and Ideas*, 84(5): 204–12.

Yonge, C. and Stables, A. (1998). I am 'It the Clown': problematising the distinction between on-task and off-task classroom talk, *Language and Education*, 12(1): 55–70.

Zimmerman, B.J. (1995). Self-efficacy and educational development, in A. Bandura (ed.), *Self-efficacy in changing societies* (pp. 202–31). New York: Cambridge University Press.

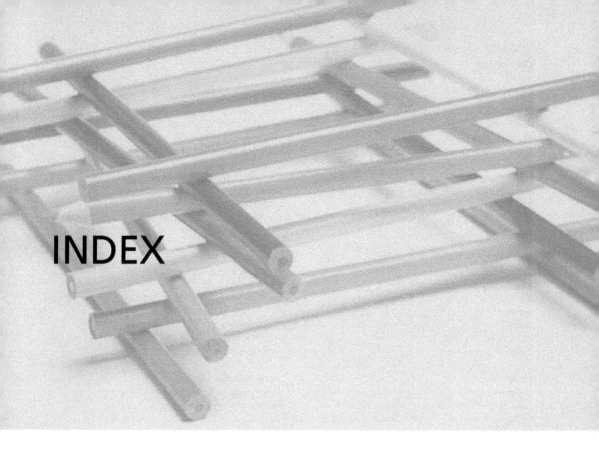

INDEX